ARCHITECTURE & HUMAN RIGHTS

This book is for you,

Nathan,
Theo,
Lilu,
Mitu,
Roby,
Cate,
Nik,
Alino,
Pietro,
and Ugo.

Now it is your turn!

Unregulated urbanization carries a serious risk of disregarding rights of the underprivileged and widening the gap between the rich and the poor in economic, social, cultural, spatial, and political terms. It is time to start looking at human rights as powerful tools to use when we construct cities. By reframing architecture from a people's rights perspective, this book calls for a new approach to urbanization, that could make an important contribution to solving some of the most urgent and globally pervasive problems of our time.

Such right is for all.

— **SALIL SHETTY**
Secretary General of Amnesty International

A BOOK ON human, possible, poetic, poor-friendly, creative, joyful, realistic, fair, food secure, children-friendly, democratic, private, communal, functional, sustainable, citizen centered, just, inclusive, and human rights directed URBAN THINKING

by Tiziana Panizza Kassahun

Any political choice and each single decision at the very local administration has to do with the alteration of space.
So to tell: it has to do with architecture.
Starting from her crude reflection on urban inequity Tiziana Panizza is calling for us as architects to embrace our social responsibility in the process of the city making.
Inequalities split cities and mega cities into two. By giving voice to the city dwellers of Addis (we are all from Addis Ababa) the author is making visible the deep and unfolding links between architecture and human rights reminding us that architecture is never neutral.

Not only because its purpose is to build habitats which make life possible for its inhabitants to live the life they aspire to. The book invites us to reflect on the fact that our projects can give to some advantages or take away opportunities from others. They can move natural resources away from a site and redistribute them geographically. They underpin the power relation between poor and rich cities.

The right to the city is a right to a more civil and community sharing urban life.

— **STEFANO BOERI**
Architect

Architecture   naturally

with   human

Why?

resource

ment   through

We   lack   the

buffer   change,   and

about   the   tough   odds   for

thinks and acts

rights on its core.

Because if so we lack the

to shape the environ-

brute force.

scale to

we constantly thinking

a new place to survive.

A humanist vision looking to the future, seeking alternatives, challenging the institution, turning the architecture in your lab. A critical vision of the social inequalities which is expressed also in the analysis of city design and buildings, and in the ways of city life. The author seeks to counteract the right to the city to the logic of the market, and think of architecture as a tool for social transformation. The exercise of this tool should help shape a new society, a society that has as main concern the welfare of citizens and the stimulus to the collective life, solidarity, to cooperation.

The starting point is human rights. They mobilize the architect, who understands the city not as buildings and blocks, but as a Web of human relationships. How to face the inequalities and segregation between rich and poor? How to offer an alternative based on appreciation of the public space and on solidarity coexistence? The architecture is understood as a possible instrument inspired by a humanist worldview, which should challenge the actual segregated cities and create better and inclusive buildings and cities for their citizens.

— **SILVIO BAVA**
Le Monde Diplomatique Brazil

It can be said that an object is innocent until contrary proven. A knife can cut bread or kill someone, television can entertain and intrigue, even acculturating or without the slightest embarrassment create the most radical bitterness. But what can we say, for example, about a gun, a tank or barbed wire?

Not the same. And it is true for objects of all scales: it can be a square, an architecture, a city. They all can be places of encounters or of separation. Places of peace or of hatred and discrimination.

Both objects and architecture generate behavior and meanings. When a project is human centered, possibly acknowledging his or her conditions, movements, needs, aspirations it is also going to be a human-rights project. The design of such a project will put each part of it into relation with our human-right dimension.

Although there is no shared rule that allows us to eliminate or at least reduce mistakes, unjust, suffering. We do not have a manual of instruction. Rather we should design with intelligence and respect.

A call for common sense which finds room also in the book of Tiziana.

— **LORENZO PALMERI**
Designer

ARCHI- TECTURE & HUMAN RIGHTS

WHO OWNS OUR CITIES —AND WHY THIS URBAN TAKEOVER SHOULD CONCERN US ALL.

by Saskia Sassen

Does the massive foreign and national corporate buying of urban buildings and land that took off after the 2008 crisis signal an emergent new phase in major cities? From mid-2013 to mid-2014, corporate buying of existing properties exceeded $600bn (£395bn) in the top 100 recipient cities, and $1trillion a year later—and this figure includes only major acquisitions (eg. a minimum of $5m in the case of New York City).

I want to examine the details of this large corporate investment surge, and why it matters. Cities are the spaces where those without power get to make a history and a culture, thereby making their powerlessness complex. If the current large-scale buying continues, we will lose this type of making that has given our cities their cosmopolitanism.

Indeed, at the current scale of acquisitions, we are seeing a systemic transformation in the pattern of land ownership in cities: one that alters the historic meaning of the city. Such a transformation has deep and significant implications for equity, democracy, and rights.

A city is a complex but incomplete system: in this mix lies the capacity of cities across histories and geographies to outlive far more powerful, but fully formalised, systems—from large corporations to national governments. London, Beijing, Cairo, New York, Johannesburg, and Bangkok—to name but a few—have all outlived multiple types of rulers and of businesses.

In this mix of complexity and incompleteness lies the possibility for those without power to assert "we are here" and "this is also our city." Or, as the legendary statement by the fighting poor in Latin American cities puts it, *"Estamos presentes"*: we are present, we are not asking for money, we are just letting you know that this is also our city.

It is in cities to a large extent where the powerless have left their imprint—cultural, economic, social: mostly in their own neighborhoods, but eventually these can spread to a vaster urban zone as "ethnic" food, music, therapies, and more.

"If the current buying continues, we will lose the type of making that has given our cities their cosmopolitanism."

All of this cannot happen in a business park, regardless of its density—they are privately controlled spaces where low-wage workers can work, but not "make." Nor can this happen in the world's increasingly militarised plantations and mines. It is only in cities where that possibility of gaining complexity in one's powerlessness can happen—because nothing can fully control such a diversity of people and engagements.

Those with power to some extent do not want to be bothered by the poor, so the model is often to abandon them to their own devices. In some cities (for example, in the U.S. and Brazil) there is extreme violence by police. Yet this can often become a public issue, which is perhaps a first step in the longer trajectories of gaining at least some rights. It is in

cities where so many of the struggles for vindications have taken place, and have, in the long run, partly succeeded.

But it is this possibility—the capacity to make a history, a culture and so much more—that is today threatened by the surge in large-scale corporate re-development of cities.

A NEW PHASE

It is easy to explain the post-2008 urban investment surge as "more of the same." After all, the late 1980s also saw rapid growth of national and foreign buying of office buildings and hotels, especially in New York and London. In The Global City, I wrote about the large share of buildings in the City of London that were foreign-owned at the height of that phase. Financial firms from countries as diverse as Japan and the Netherlands found they needed a strong foothold in London's City to access continental European capital and markets.

But an examination of the current trends shows some significant differences and points to a whole new phase in the character and logics of foreign and national corporate acquisitions. (I do not see much of a difference in terms of the urban impact between national and foreign investment. The key fact here is that both are corporate and large scale.) Four features stand out:

THE SHARP SCALE-UP IN THE BUYING OF BUILDINGS, even in cities that have long been the object of such investments, notably NY and London. For instance, the Chinese have most recently emerged as major buyers in cities such as London and New York. Today there are about 100 cities worldwide that have become significant destinations for such acquisitions—foreign corporate buying of properties from 2013 to 2014 grew by 248% in Amsterdam/Randstadt, 180% in Madrid and 475% in Nanjing. In contrast, the growth rate was relatively lower for the major cities in each region: 68.5% for New York, 37.6% for London, and 160.8% for Beijing.

THE EXTENT OF NEW CONSTRUCTION. The rapid-growth period of the 1980s and 90s was often about acquiring buildings—notably high-end Harrods in London, and Sachs Fifth Avenue and the Rockefeller Center in New York. In the post-2008 period, much buying of buildings is to destroy them and replace them with far taller, far more corporate, and luxurious types of buildings—basically, luxury offices and luxury apartments.

THE SPREAD OF MEGA-PROJECTS WITH VAST FOOT-PRINTS that inevitably kill much urban tissue: little streets and squares, density of street-level shops and modest offices, and so on. These megaprojects raise the density of the city, but they actually de-urbanize it—and thereby bring to the fore the fact, easily overlooked in much commentary about cities, that density is not enough to have a city.

THE FORECLOSING ON MODEST PROPERTIES owned by modest-income households. This has reached catastrophic levels in the U.S., with Federal Reserve data showing that more than 14 million households have

lost their homes from 2006 to 2014. One outcome is a significant amount of empty or under-occupied urban land, at least some of which is likely to be "re-developed."

A further striking feature of this period is the acquisition of whole blocks of underutilised or dead industrial land for site development. Here, the prices paid by buyers can get very high. One example is the acquisition of Atlantic Yards, a vast stretch of land in New York City by one of the largest Chinese building companies for $5bn. Currently, this land is occupied by a mixture of modest factories and industrial services, modest neighbourhoods, and artists' studios and venues that have been pushed out of lower Manhattan by large-scale developments of high-rise apartment buildings.

"Privatisation in the 90s has resulted in a reduction of public buildings and an escalation in large, corporate ownership."

This very urban mix of occupants will be thrown out and replaced by 14 formidable luxury residential towers—a sharp growth of density that actually has the effect of de-urbanizing that space. It will be a sort of *de facto* "gated" space with lots of people; not the dense mix of uses and types of people we think of as "urban." This type of development is taking off in many cities—mostly with virtual walls, but sometimes also with real ones. I would argue that with this type of development, the virtual and the actual walls have similar impacts on de-urbanizing pieces of a city.

The scale and the character of these investments are captured in the vast amounts spent on buying urban properties and land. Those global, corporate investments of $600bn from mid-2013 to mid-2014, and over 1tn from mid-2014 to mid 2015, were just to acquire existing buildings. The figure excludes site development, another major trend.

This proliferating urban gigantism has been strengthened and enabled by the privatisations and deregulations that took off in the 1990s across much of the world, and have continued since then with only a few interruptions. The overall effect has been a reduction in public buildings, and an escalation in large, corporate private ownership.

The result is a thinning in the texture and scale of spaces previously accessible to the public. Where before there was a government office building handling the regulations and oversight of this or that public economic sector, or addressing the complaints from the local neighborhood, now there might be a corporate headquarters, a luxury apartment building, or a guarded mall.

DE-URBANIZATION

Global geographies of extraction have long been key to the western world's economic development. And now these have moved on to urban land, going well beyond the traditional association with plantations and mines, even as these have been extended and made more brutally efficient.

"A large city is a frontier zone where actors from different worlds can have an encounter with no rules of engagement."

The corporatizing of access and control over urban land has extended not only to high-end urban sites, but also to the land beneath the homes of modest households and government offices. We are witnessing an unusually large scale of corporate buying of whole pieces of cities in the last few years. The mechanisms for these extractions are often far more complex than the outcomes, which can be quite elementary in their brutality.

One key transformation is a shift from mostly small private to large corporate modes of ownership, and from public to private. This is a process that takes place in bits and pieces, some big and some small, and to some extent these practices have long been part of the urban land market and urban development. But today's scale-up takes it all to a whole new dimension, one that alters the historic meaning of the city.

This is particularly so because what was small and/or public is becoming large and private. The trend is to move from small properties embedded in city areas that are crisscrossed by streets and small public squares, to projects that erase much of this public tissue of streets and squares via mega-projects with large, sometimes huge, footprints. This privatises and de-urbanizes city space no matter the added density.

Large cities have long been complex and incomplete. This has enabled the incorporation of diverse people, logics, politics. A large, mixed city is a frontier zone where actors from different worlds can have an encounter for which there are no established rules of engagement, and where the powerless and the powerful can actually meet.

This also makes cities spaces of innovations, small and large. And this includes innovations by those without power: even if they do not necessarily become powerful in the process, they produce components of a city, thus leaving a legacy that adds to its cosmopolitanism—something that few other places enable.

Such a mix of complexity and incompleteness ensures a capacity to shape an urban subject and an urban subjectivity. It can partly override the religious subject, the ethnic subject, the racialized subject and, in certain settings, also the differences of class. There are moments in the routines of a city when we all become urban subjects—rush hour is one such mix of time and space.

But today, rather than a space for including people from many diverse backgrounds and cultures, our global cities are expelling people and diversity. Their new owners, often part-time inhabitants, are very international—but that does not mean they represent many diverse cultures and traditions. Instead, they represent the new global culture of the successful—and they are astoundingly homogeneous, no matter how diverse their countries of birth and languages. This is not the urban subject that our large, mixed cities have historically produced. This is, above all, a global "corporate" subject.

Much of urban change is inevitably predicated on expelling what used to be. Since their beginnings, whether 3,000 years old or 100, cities have kept reinventing themselves, which means there are always winners and losers. Urban histories are replete with accounts of those who were once poor and quasi-outsiders, or modest middle classes, that gained ground—because cities have long accommodated extraordinary variety.

But today's large-scale corporate buying of urban space in its diverse instantiations introduces a de-urbanizing dynamic. It is not adding to mixity and diversity. Instead it implants a whole new formation in our cities—in the shape of a tedious multiplication of high-rise luxury buildings.

One way of putting it is that this new set of implants contains within it a logic all of its own—one which cannot be tamed into becoming part of the logics of the traditional city. It keeps its full autonomy and, one might say, gives us all its back. And that does not look pretty.

Saskia Sassen is Robert S. Lynd Professor of Sociology at Columbia University and co-chairs its Committee on Global Thought. Urban Age is a worldwide investigation into the future of cities, organized by LSE Cities and Deutsche Bank's Alfred Herrhausen Society. Its 10-year anniversary debates are held in conjunction with Guardian Cities.

I am not an architect, I am not an activist. So what, you may well ask, gives me the authority to write about architecture and human rights? The answer is in that often overlooked word 'human.'

Most of us humans live in architecture of some sort. But regardless of whether we live in a modern apartment block, a Venetian palazzo, or a hastily assembled tent in a refugee camp, we all have a story to tell. And it is those human stories, rather than any expert authority, that drove me to write this book. I have heard powerful, gripping personal narratives that shed light on what it means to live in a unstoppable and uncontrollable man-made buildings century, the one which is transforming our planet into a city. When such stories strike, we have no choice but to act on them. I simply knew that I must write about them and share them.

As a strategic designer and as a person I consider it my mission, and indeed my duty, to convey the urgency of implementing human rights through design and architecture. I would like to express all my gratitude to the extraordinary people who shared with me the gift of their stories, talent, and support.

This book is yours.

No contribution to this book has been as precious and personally affecting as the one offered by the slum dwellers of Addis Ababa. From their stories we can unfold series of ideas on contemporary urban thinking, and include their very private narratives illustrating how they traverse conflicting territories and experiences. If we don't care about somebody we end up not to think about the way we build that shapes their lives.

This book is about the stories and the people we too often choose to ignore as opposed to the architecture we choose to celebrate. I want to thank these people for enabling us to be both the witnesses and protagonists of their dwellings, and thank them for helping to open up many unexplored paths of architectural knowledge and thinking. All humans have human rights and architecture is at the forefront of these rights. I also want to thank them for challenging us to approach design and architecture in a way that asks whether buildings are serving inhabitants in terms of human rights. Their stories forced us to question the benefits and value of the buildings we design and to see them within the bigger picture of a well-designed environment.

I equally want to thank the architects I met in Durban who promptly took on these challenges and allowed me insight into their thoughts. The people in Addis shared with me their stories of eviction and displacement. That's architecture. The architects in Durban told me about innovative design for communal living that tackled the challenges of housing and land shortages. That's human rights. Thanks to both for initiating an alternative dialogue to the traditional architectural approach that is not design-centered, and that too often stresses architectural intelligence over the myriad human stories at the heart of every city.

You made this book possible.

ALESSANDRO RUGGERA was my host at the Italian Embassy in Addis Ababa for my workshop on Women Rights and Women Wrongs in the Kitchen Design. Thank you!

CHIARA SOMAJNI is the first person I spoke about this project; she is also my first reader. Her sharp thinking, her precision, her critical mind helped me to readdress and reorganize the content several times. Thanks for your support.

EPHRAIM is a medical doctor. Without his help, I could not possibly have recorded the stories of his patients without being harassed by the police. Thank you, Ephraim, for allowing us to meet and speak in your tiny medical care room.

BARBARA CORTI is the friend always ready to share. She shared her Milan house and hosted an event with some of the best designers in town. Our brainstorming on human rights and design brought several valuable contributions to this book. You are an inspiration, Barbara!

ELIAS is an Ethiopian architect and the former Chairman of Housing at the Architecture Faculty of the Addis Ababa University. He opened my eyes to the void, the rich, empty space between buildings, potent with possibility, a ultimate place that inspires imagination in inhabitants.

STEFANO CARDINI, I have to thank him very much for inspiring the students of his design course at Domus Academy in Milan to work creatively on this subject. Thank you for engaging them on the design of a very innovative 'human rights and architecture' app.

JOHANA, the friendly informed and organized assistant every writer wishes to work with.

CRISTINA is my sister. She took on her the task of helping our Mom and Dad in order to let me focus on writing. I appreciate your generosity, Cristina.

PASQUALE ALFERJ is a friend and a sophisticated mind. Without your active encouragement, I would have given up long ago.

YOHANNES is my husband. Because of his love, because of his smile.

BARBARA RACAH is the dynamo who convinced my publisher and who won the generous contribution of Saskia Sassen. I'm so grateful for all you did!

And finally many, many thanks to you for being the reader of this book. I hope it inspires you to work toward an architectural future in which human rights become an integral part of the world we build in the 21st century.

Naming it book design is simply a useful way to avoid confusion. It might borrow from design in terms of process and approach, but it is not. The breathing, talking, and walking pages and the mind-expanding vision of Architecture & Human Rights engage and provoke the audience into action. It is building over the narrative without obliterating the narrators. It follows the course of the narration by entering into the dialogue and at critical junctures compels to take the lead and show a different way forward. It is a way of discussing. It is bringing the horizon of a new architecture practice into view. Thank you, RALF.

The images in the book document the small details of an epochal transformation. They make it visually plausible for us to see behind geography and into a world of neglect. In his short visual essay Stefano calls for us to reconnect with each other and to bridge the distance which separates our individual geopolitical stories. It reveals the threats we face as we confront our struggle to design and build a common future and to embrace a shared destiny.

These beautiful images are an open window into resilience and transformation. Thank you, STEFANO.

Just shortly before this book went to print, at least 65 people were killed in a giant landslide at Ethiopia's largest rubbish dump. Many of the victims were squatters, who scavenged for a living in the 30-hectare (74-acre) dump. Entire families, including many children, were buried alive in the tragedy. The landfill is the country's largest and home to perhaps hundreds of people. Authorities blamed the squatters for digging into the hillside, destabilizing it, and causing it to fall. All the shacks built on the landfill would be demolished and the residents resettled elsewhere.

My deepest wish is to dedicate this book to them, while honoring their choices.

By choosing to live in a landfill they did something remarkable. They took responsibility for their own destinies, and did not allow the wider world to write the story of their lives. It's a hard choice to make, given the limited and equally grim alternatives.

If there's no best option, if the scales don't tip in favor of one alternative over another, then surely the alternatives must be equally good. Indeed, they chose to empower themselves, to become the persons they were, for whom urban living was preferable to living without hope. Even after eviction, forced displacement, and having their previous houses demolished, they chose to write their own narratives. I strongly want to draw on their unique story so that we can reinforce our abilities to empathize with each other and move through the challenges of this century together. No design will be fully human until we also pay attention to the rights of all.

WE ARE ALL FROM ADDIS

Introduction

LACK OF HUMAN RIGHTS WILL WIPE US OUT.

'Human' and 'rights' are two of the words that I most respect and love.

Why? Because, they belong together.

These words also belong to everyone, everywhere. They belong to each of us simply by virtue of the fact that we are human. The beautiful thing is that I am just one of many people who care about human rights. The word architecture comes next: I believe architecture is also revolutionary, because it has the ability to reinvent the way we live and share space together endlessly. Architecture provides us with a physical space, both private and public, that can offer us some sense of relief and connection.

We are told architecture is about constructing buildings. But it is actually more about building relationships. Any building project is a quest for identity, an effort to find the answer to the fundamental question, who are we? Buildings are beacons of identity, and of human connections.

We create places that will either transcend or sharpen our divisions. Social integration is the way we interact with people as we move through our day. This book seeks to explore how universal rights can tap into the deeper threads that bind us together into a community, a city, a neighborhood, a village, a condo, a building, a park, a bedroom, a hospital, a church, a factory, a library, a kitchen, or even a bedroom.

We all need each other; we all are connected. No community is immune to the vulnerabilities that may lead a society to its end and architecture is a means to restore our interconnections to a healthy state. It should not surprise that humanity is currently on an unsustainable path. Some of the early warning signs are there already: We see more and more scrambling over limited space and the rejection of anyone outside our immediate group. In response, we have to make a commitment that we will never let people be depraved of their rights and end up as second-class citizens. Not through our design.

Of course the scale of this problem exceeds the scale of typical architecture. My understanding is that architecture is neither finite nor restricted to mere buildings, but should incorporate a much wider and multivalent field of interaction and forces. The fabric of all reality emerges from the human interactions. The survival of each and everyone of us is tied to the survival of everyone else. Our values will dictate our destiny as a species and what kind of actions we will take in order to get there.

If we do nothing to address urban inequality, if we do nothing to ensure that everyone in our cities gets the same benefits and is equally able to protect themselves from poverty, not only will the poor and vulnerable be exposed to starvation, but universal rights may be crushed before they are ever fully attained. Instead of going back to ideas of justice in the ancient world, let's explore how present-day architecture deals with rights, scarcity, and climate-change issues.

The most exciting characteristic of architecture *for me* is the way it materially and continually reorganizes itself to respond to shifting environmental and human conditions; likewise, the *plasticity* of human rights is the smartest way in which forces of freedom, equality, and opportunity can be molded into a built organization.

Architecture is about helping people build lives of dignity, stability, economic autonomy, and citizenship. For the sake of future generations, for the sake of our planet, for the sake of our future, let's stop constructing for the moment, and start talking about human rights.

ARCHITECTURE AND HUMAN RIGHTS: HOW GLOOMY IS THIS?

The world presents us with challenges and options. Let's take them. Starting with climate change and exploding global population. What are the planetary boundaries within which architecture can safely operate and initiate innovation? Can architecture feed us? Can it prevent genocide and ethnic clashes? Can it secure our survival and the planet's? There are many incredibly important questions we just don't know the answers to. And the thing I realized that really blew my mind is that of all the things that architecture focuses on, the least of these is human rights.

I think we are going to have to change. We inhabit a reality in which humans are fighting not only for resources, but also for self-respect and dignity.

Human rights mean much more than the absence of torture, they signify acknowledgement of equality and fairness in all relationships. Human rights would allow for common ground to be found and it seems obvious that architecture has the power to help establish this common ground.

Why architecture? Because the estimated amount of time that humans spend in the build environment ranges from 80 to 90%. The design thinking that goes into rooms, backyards, streets, sidewalks, subways, buildings, and parks goes beyond the analysis, location, and physical design of architecture; it extends into how to bring rights into the ongoing processes of community-building.

Besides considerations of resources and pollution, ensuring that the man-made environment is one that promotes peaceful living for humans is now starting to be perceived as a crucial architectural challenge. Although protests can be a fine way to show that people want change, on their own, they don't actually create change—at least not change that is fundamental.

There may simply be not enough innovation to deal with any of these problems at a scale using current building models. We have to invest in our transformative capability for moving from crisis into innovation and the ability to rise after a crisis and, of course, to adapt to unavoidable change.

We need to look for best answers from wherever we find them. Human rights provide an evolving framework to guide *problem-solving* efforts, as they are functional to our understanding of issues. They present us with the type of questions which could drive architects to translate the Universal Declaration principles into more detailed guidelines.

Even if the expansion of human rights through binding international laws is declining, there are many other ways to advance the cause of human rights, including the way we build. The real question is not whether architecture and human rights are linked but how difficult a task for architects it would be to link them. Without universal engagement, global rights will continue to exist but only in an increasingly ineffective form. Should human rights be an architecture output beyond what is now legally required?

If we do not want rights to be eternal claims but historical facts, the answer is yes.

CAN STORYTELLING INFORM A NEW KIND OF ARCHITECTURE?

I am a strategic designer trying to incorporate the best of communication, planning, and designing techniques into opportunities for better living.

Let's start with what I thought I knew. We live in a world that is probably freer, less poor, more progressive, and more democratic than it has ever been before. Yet when I volunteered at the Human

Rights High Commission in Addis Aba-ba, I was struck forcefully by the lack of human rights and the widespread discrimination in the man-made environment. I moved to Addis Ababa at the time when more than 4,500 houses throughout the city have been earmarked for demolition. The booming construction industry has contributed to Addis Ababa's rapid expansion and has dispossessed, among others, many poor farmers, while turning them into beggars and day laborers.

The struggle for survival and the largely ignored rights of poor people compelled me to refocus on what really matters in architecture. Communities of brave people that make the city vibrant and connected are the ones from whose properties the developers reap rewards anywhere. They get pushed out in London, in Moscow, in Guangzhou. No one has much incentive to accept an architecture that places their lives under the control of others; that deprives them of meaningful economical and political participation; that deprives their children of the opportunity to qualify for better jobs; and that deprives them of a share of the space of the city they are helping to run.

Stories are what we use to transmit knowledge. They give meaning to our lives. I immersed myself into the stories of these dispossessed people and I quickly came to see that architecture grows out of everyday experiences more often than we realize. What I want to relate here is that architecture offers a critical and ethical arena in which different kinds of knowledge can be generated and exchanged. At its simplest, architecture is about facilitating a range of different voices to articulate the change they want to bring to their neighborhoods and their cities.

However, it's not enough just to tell a story. Though powerful, a story needs to do more than just communicate how its tellers live. It must transform this narrative into an acknowledged right to exist. How would architecture bring our stories to life and affirm our right to exist? Our understanding *begins* with a story but doesn't end there. The information collected and reported are useful and usable to change how we design and how we improve our approaches and outcomes. There is always a better way out that we can try instead.

I FIND AN ADDIS ABABA IN EVERY CITY I GO TO.

If the conversations in this book had not taken place, the silence in their place would have been filled with our indifference. Instead these stories have galvanized many of us working in architecture to bridge the discontented worlds of planning, commerce, culture, politics, and community-building.

These conversations remind us that overcoming the deteriorating conditions in the fabric of our cities is the challenge that will determine the future success of architecture. We are in the midst of a worldwide decline in international human rights. Turbulent and authoritarian urban planning like that of Addis

Ababa force thousands of households into a choice between abiding by the rule of the market or moving elsewhere: I want to drill down again on the premise that Addis Ababa is everywhere and the future of all our cities now depends on how we approach the cities and the citizens of the Global South.

By Addis I mean the vast and invisible world of injustice that surrounds us. Seduced by visions of the future that have no place for the *other*, we have created a world in which the array of human rights violations is bewildering. The intensity of the violence and injustice that results is often appalling. Any story seeking to make sense of human rights must tell the story of suffering and identify those who imposed that suffering. But it should also tell the other side of the story: It should articulate the global aspiration for universal respect and dignity.

And here's the thing: we can meld these very exciting conversations into one in which possible futures are imagined through architecture. Re-imagining new possibilities is the only condition *for* sustainable change and the most ingenious responses will result by focusing on the rights of citizens with intractable problems who inhabit cities.

Architecture can use whatever knowledge it has at its disposal to make the point. Once we understand this, we're in a better position to make sense of architecture when it goes wrong, when it has horrible consequences, and we're in a better position to know what to do when this happens. We have in the past built ways of relating to each other that got us in a city of fracture, xenophobia, resentment, and fear. We can build ways of relating to each other that get us out.

Human-rights-based solutions maximize the participation of all communities—participation itself being a human right, enhancing the impact of development work, as well as its sustainability. To reduce factors such as inequality and the rate at which we deplete natural resources, all perfectly attainable goals, we need to find creative solutions. The link between human righs and architecture is complex, urgent, contemporary, and yet not well understood. But we cannot wait forever. I am convinced now, more than ever, that the real divide is not between beautiful buildings and ugly ones. It is the buildings between us.

UNIVE

DECLA

Prea

O

HU

RIG

ERSAL
RATION

mble

F

I A N
H T S

Proclaimed by the United Nations
General Assembly in Paris on
10 December 1948

WHEREAS recognition of the inherent dignity and of the equal and inalienable rights of all members of the human family is the foundation of freedom, justice and peace in the world,

WHEREAS disregard and contempt for human rights have resulted in barbarous acts which have outraged the conscience of mankind, and

the advent of a world in which human beings shall enjoy freedom of speech and belief and freedom from fear and want has been proclaimed as the highest aspiration of the common people,

WHEREAS it is essential, if man is not to be compelled to have recourse, as a last resort, to rebellion against tyranny and oppression, that human rights should be protected by the rule of law,

WHEREAS it is essential to promote the development of friendly relations between nations,

WHEREAS the peoples of the United Nations have in the Charter reaffirmed their faith in fundamental human rights, in the dignity and worth of the

human person and in the equal rights of men and women and have determined to promote social progress and better standards of life in larger freedom,

WHEREAS Member States have pledged themselves to achieve, in co-operation with the United Nations, the promotion of universal respect for and observance of human rights and fundamental freedoms,

WHEREAS a common understanding of these rights and freedoms is of the greatest importance for the full realization of this pledge,

NOW, therefore, The General Assembly, proclaims this Universal Declaration of Human Rights as a common standard of achievement for all peoples and all nations, to the end that every individual and every organ of society, keeping this Declaration constantly in mind, shall strive by teaching and education to promote respect for these rights and freedoms and by progressive measures, national and international, to secure their universal and effective recognition and observance, both among the peoples of Member States themselves and among the peoples of territories under their jurisdiction.

Article 1
Right to Equality

Article 2
Freedom from Discrimination

Article 3
Right to Life, Liberty, and Personal Security

Article 4
Freedom from Slavery

Article 5
Freedom from Torture and Degrading Treatment

Article 6
Right to Recognition as a Person before the Law

Article 7
Right to Equality before the Law

Article 8
Right to Remedy by Competent Tribunal

Article 9
Freedom from Arbitrary Arrest and Exile

Article 10
Right to Fair Public Hearing

Article 11
Right to be Considered Innocent until Proven Guilty

Article 12
Freedom from Interference with Privacy, Family, Home, and Correspondence

Article 13
Right to Free Movement in and out of the Country

Article 14
Right to Asylum in other Countries from Persecution

Article 15
Right to a Nationality and the Freedom to Change It

Article 16
Right to Marriage and Family

Article 17
Right to Own Property

Article 18
Freedom of Belief and Religion

Article 19
Freedom of Opinion and Information

Article 20
Right of Peaceful Assembly and Association

Article 21
Right to Participate in Government and in Free Elections

Article 22
Right to Social Security

Article 23
Right to Desirable Work and to Join Trade Unions

Article 24
Right to Rest and Leisure

Article 25
Right to Adequate Living Standard

Article 26
Right to Education

Article 27
Right to Participate in the Cultural Life of Community

Article 28
Right to a Social Order that Articulates this Document

Article 29
Community Duties Essential to Free and Full Development

Article 30
Freedom from State or Personal Interference in the above Rights

SAARINEN

For,
in order to be able to live,
one must have space in which to live.

When one of us is enslaved, we are all not free.

—JOHN F. KENNEDY
SPEECH IN BERLIN, 26 JUNE 1963

To protect the people of Addis against military arrest, police harassment, repression, and punishment for speaking about their homes, life, and city, I have given them a voice in these pages but not disclosed their full names or anything that could identify them.

In solidarity with the people of Addis, the architects agreed to use their first names only.

CRITICAL

VERSATIO

ARCHIT

& HUMA

ADDIS

(CITIZEN

VERSA

a.

CON-

ONS ON

ECTURE

RIGHTS

ABABA

CON-

TIONS)

A G O S H

Her beau-
ty is stunning.
It leaves you
breathless and
at the same
time her pres-
ence gives you
a sense of rest
and peace.

THE FIRST EVICTION YOU EXPERIENCED
WAS THREE YEARS AGO.

It was May. It was raining. I was coming
back from work. I knew something was
wrong as soon as I got off the bus. There
was a thin line of smoke line going up.
I took a deep breath. This was not the
time for burning garbage. I felt a shiver
of fear. I had never been so scared before.

Something was very, very wrong. People
stared at me as I walked home as if they
knew something I did not. My home was
not there anymore. I mean it was still
there but it was not the same home as I
had left it in the morning when I went to
work. It no longer had a roof. It had no
door. It had no windows, no inside walls.
It looked like the skeleton of what used

to be my home. I am not sure how long I stood there. I felt a sense of helpless rage.

WHAT ABOUT YOUR POSSESSIONS?

My things were there. There had been no stealing. Nothing had been taken away. Only a few items got broken. Almost everything got wet. It was muddy and dirty.

WHAT DID YOU DO THEN?

I touched nothing. I walked to the ring-road and took a taxi. That night I slept at my uncle's place. I only stayed there one night. The day after I found another house in Goris, went back and collected my things and moved out to the new place.

THIS NEW PLACE IS IN AN ILLEGAL SQUATTERS' AREA AND DUE TO BE DEMOLISHED SOON, RIGHT?

What I fear most is not finding a house inside the city. When I left my home in Bole, I lost my job because there was no transport from Goro to take me to the restaurant. It was a regular job and well-paid, not like now. I sell charcoal on the street. It is not a regular job.

I wish the government could meet us and speak to us. We need advice, guidance. Because we are poor we have to work hard! I know that and I accept it. Working hard is the only way to get out of poverty. I came to Addis when I was 11 years old. I came from Adua by bus. My parents could not feed me. I came with my aunt and things were very clear in my mind: I had to fight and I became rich.

HOW CAN YOU GET RICH?

I am very good at preparing food. My plan is to become a chef. My plan will be impossible to achieve if they push me out of the city where there are no restaurants and no access to water or transport.

I am not asking to be given money or help. I want to get out of poverty by myself and through my own efforts. All I ask is not to be forced into hopeless living conditions. For now, I need to make the best of what I have. I have myself. I have my health. I have my baby. I make a living selling home-made charcoal which I manufacture from a mixture of ash, powdered charcoal, and water. I make an average of 10 ETB (Ethiopian birr) by selling the charcoal at one ETB for three pieces.

BELECHA

Belecha is a slender woman. She accompanies her words with up-and-down movements of her head and shoulders. By contrast her hands are big as if they do not belong to her and she has borrowed someone else's.

WHERE IS YOUR HOUSE?

I live in the big shelter tent. We do not have walls. We do not have doors. Only a sheet divides us from the family next to us.

My boy is my home and I am his home. When we were on the street and he was small we felt the same way. Today it is different. We have been living here five years. He goes to school. He is a good student and a good son.

HOW FAR IS THE SCHOOL FROM THE SHELTER?

Two bus taxi stops away from here. It is close, about 40 minutes' walk. But he would go there on foot even if the school were in another town!

ARE YOU WORRIED ABOUT THE COMING EVICTION?

Living on the street is worse than anything. My son tells me he will build a house for me. One day he will. In the past, I could rent one for 20 ETB, but nowadays it is impossible. There are no cheap houses! We who have no money are going to be evicted: not from the place we live in now but from the city! We will be scattered and dispersed. Where are my friends going to be when I will need them? How will they be able to find me when they want my help? How will we be able to meet one other? How will we be able to cure each other? How will I be able to babysit for their babies?

Being back on the streets means you have no friends anymore, no one who knows who you are. You even lose your name because nobody calls you. And like all nameless things, you stop being a person.

WHY SHOULD IT BE LIKE THAT?

Because there is no solution, or rather no permanent one! Another shelter. Another tent. There is nowhere to go. When we came here, they made us sign to agree we would leave without any form of protest and opposition when they told us to. I'm not afraid of change: I welcome it.

9

4

But the question is where can I find a house that's affordable on my income? I bake injera (Ethiopian sourdough-risen flatbread). I work hard. I could work even harder but I could never ever afford to rent.

WHY IS THIS COUNTRY SO POOR?

Baking injera only pays a few cents. Washing clothes pays peanuts. Cleaning houses pays peanuts. Guarding a villa pays peanuts. Collecting charcoal pays peanuts. Sewing clothes pays peanuts. Shoe-cleaning pays peanuts. Slaughtering sheep pays peanuts.

Bread cost 1.20 ETB. Injera costs 2/3 ETB. Clean water costs a lot. Medicine and doctors cost very, very much. Renting a room is unaffordable. We work very hard and we earn much less than we need to keep us going. We start working at the age of two. The situation has become much worse since they started all the new buildings. Store rents are too high. Sellers have to sell their items for more.
In other places, the residents barricade the roads and burn tires. Living in fear make them feel they have nothing to lose by fighting back. Not us. Not the Ethiopians. You would be mistaken if you think we are weak. Strong-willed individuals do not shout. Instead they go back to their original land, like in the Bible. I'm afraid of where we will be in ten years' time, when more and more of our land is controlled by these foreign investors. Many Chinese and Indian companies operate in the country, flying in their own workers, depriving us Ethiopians of work, land, and history, regardless of our feelings. Selling one hectare for $1. Shame on them!

WOULD IT BE DIFFERENT WITH AN AFFORDABLE RENT POLICY?
Yes. We would all be much better off. The price of our labor goes down and down while the price of food goes up and up.

NIGUSSE

Watching his own hands moving methodically seems to calm his thoughts.

Nigusse and his family have been living in the historic Arat Kilo area for 28 years. They pay rent to the Kebele for a villa with a compound. They are a middle-income family and own a traditional clothes shop in Shero Meda.

HOW DID THE TABULA RASA OF ARAT KILO START?

With a lie! The Government promised that all the inhabitants of Arat Kilo would be moved to condominiums in the neighboring area. The agreement was that we would move out of our house and be cooperative. People did not want to leave Arat Kilo and these were their conditions. Many of them had been settled here for at least four generations.

WHY WASN'T THE PROMISE KEPT AND THE AGREEMENT NOT RESPECTED?

First of all, only people who could afford the down-payment were given a unit in a condominium. Everyone else was put out on the street. Secondly, those of us who paid were scattered all over the outskirts of Addis and not moved into a condominium in the next Kebele as promised. They never actually built the condominiums. It was a lottery: we were sent very far away from our jobs, our children's schools, our friends, our relatives, and our associations. They managed to destroy 100-year-old neighborhood networks.

HOW DID THEY DO THIS?

When the demolition started it did not start with the houses. First, they tore down the walls of the tajalla (the place where tej, Ethiopia's honey wine, is consumed) and other public gathering places. Men used to gather there to drink and chat and discuss what was going on. After that they demolished the Kebeles. They are public meeting places. We use them to hold our assemblies, address our concerns, seek explanations about different issues, find out more about a law, pay our utility bills, and so on.

After that they started demolishing the shops. Residents who could afford it were given a condominium unit and house owners were given compensation payment, but there was nothing for shopkeepers. They lost everything! Their shops; their customers; their goods, which they could not store anywhere because renting is becoming unaffordable. They went out of business. Those people did not deserve such treatment! They invested enormous amounts of money and work in their business and shops. I think this action by the city administration has led thousands of citizens to face extreme hardship and poverty. Even the demolished shops that were built legally were demolished with no compensation. These families are now stranded with no more income.

Still, about 4,352 people in Arat Kilo will be relocated and compensated by the city administration.

Another lie! Many families lived in Arat Kilo for over ten years after receiving plots of land from their families who earned their livings as farmers. Though they did not have any certificate of ownership, several meetings were held with government officials and they were promised that they would become legal owners through the lease administration and that they would receive certificates of ownership.

Their houses were also demolished at short notice during the rainy season. Just because they did not have certificates of ownership and plans, they were labeled 'illegal.' Many families with very low incomes used to rent space in their homes. So all the youngest married couple and families who were renting were suddenly 'illegal' and were evicted with no right to claim accommodation.

WHAT ABOUT YOUR FAMILY?

We could afford the down-payment for a two-room unit and I have already processed the application. What we cannot afford is the transport for me to come to work and for my children to go to their present school. The cost of gasoline needed to drive from the condominium they had assigned to us in Megagne to the shop and to the school is out of question. We are a family of ten people after all.

WHAT DO YOU THINK OF THE FUTURE?

My concern is security and personal safety. There is a lot of robbery and stealing. I was told that people who live in the condominium should gather and walk home together when coming back from work in the evening otherwise they would get robbed or even killed or raped. In Arat Kilo, we had the poorest people in Addis living in terrible shelters without latrines but robbing was unheard of.

WHAT DOES YOUR WIFE SAY?

(Laughing) She is worried about the Iddirs. You know, the funeral associations? They provide financial support to families of the deceased. They provide money for hosting relatives and feeding everyone who goes to the funeral. They pay for flowers, the religious ceremony, the coffin, the crying ladies, the clothing and so on.

All members of the association my wife was part of are scattered in different places and by the time she dies none of them will know and be able to do anything. It takes years of close relationships and trust to build such associations.

HIWOT

She is more afraid of the alien word 'e v i c t i o n' than of moving far away.

YOU STILL CANNOT SAY THAT WORD, 'EVICTION'?

It hurt my heart to tear down my own home and it muddled my thoughts for months. You do not get over it. It creeps up behind you. It started at noon. My dog must have thought it was a game because I could see his tail wagging.

It went on and on and on. No food. No water. No break from work or from crying. It went on until next day. I often wondered if the pain I felt ever bothered the Kebele officers and the policemen attending the demolition. The way they indifferently went about their duty haunted me.

It took me 50 days to find a new place. I stayed with my things at my neighbor's place, then I found the room where I am now. I rent privately and it costs 500 Birr and measures four square meters. I have electricity, I have water.

HOW WAS MOVING IN AND SPENDING YOUR FIRST NIGHT IN THE NEW HOUSE?

My friends from the church came. They brought injera and food. We spent the night praying and singing. They stayed with me two days.

HOW IS YOUR LANDLORD?

He is okay. He did not divide his own house to rent out rooms as many do. Instead, he converted the servants' quarter in the compound into independent rental rooms.
I invited him to our prayers. He did not come. I don't believe he is interested in religion. Apart from that he is very respectful.

HOW IS THE NEW LOCATION?

I like it. It is in Bole close to the Urail Church. It's different from where I was, but not too far away. Piazza has been the real heart of Addis since then. The old town is there. It is the only place you can really say: this is Addis. The same buildings and shops are still there, the families who made the story of Addis. Bole does not feel like Addis at all. It looks like a place built abroad and dumped here by plane by accident. That might be because the airport is so close!

DO YOU FEEL YOU ARE THE SAME PERSON AFTER THE EVICTION?

I used to fear so many things. Losing my house. Losing my neighbors. Losing my means of survival and property. Being alone. Being on the street. Nobody helping me.
Now I fear nothing. My faith in God is much stronger now. Life has its ups and downs.

From where I live now I can see all the new building going on.

It still hurts, but not so much. Digging up my land was the worst thing.
They had to excavate a hole in order to build. It wasn't just any hole, it was the biggest anywhere in Addis and I could feel my heart falling into it continuously.

WHAT ABOUT YOUR DOG?
I take him food once a week. He stays at the construction site. The workers let him stay and are nice to him. At night, he acts as a guard dog. When he sees me he whines. It's difficult to know whether he whines because he wants me to take him to the new place or because he wants me to come back and live with him there.

HEMBET
She smiles like a trapped squirrel. It is so difficult for her to speak and thus so generous of her to let me interview her.

WHERE DO YOU LIVE?
In Bole 0304.

THAT AREA HAS BEEN GIVEN TO INVESTORS?
Our house will be the first on the list to go. I don't have long before I have to tear it down.

TELL ME ABOUT YOUR HOUSE.
My husband and I built it three years ago. We spoke to the Kebele and they told us where to build. They also told us it was illegal and they would not bear any responsibility or give us any form of permission. Oh, it was a big risk we took! What else could we do?

DO YOU REGRET WHAT YOU DID?
It took us a year to build our house. Because it was illegal, we had to work at night. When we made too much

noise, we were afraid somebody would come. It is very difficult to build without making any noise and it was cold in the dark. My husband was afraid of the Kebele officials, but I was afraid of the hyenas.

The most difficult task was the roof. It had to slope slightly so that the rainwater would run off. There was no full moon that night. We kept doing it wrong and having to redo it again and again.

No, I do not regret what we did. I regret that we were not given more life together. It will be very difficult to demolish the house he built without him to help and guide us.

WHY IS A WIDOW WITH A SMALL CHILD LIKE YOU GIVEN NO PLACE TO GO AND NO HELP?

Our house is made of corrugated sheet and plywood boarding. It is plastered with mud and dung. They don't care at all. You see vacant tower blocks and empty buildings all over Addis: signs that the whole city has been put into the hands of the investors. For us, it means an end to conveniently-located, cheap, affordable housing.

WHAT SORT OF DEVELOPMENT STARTS BY FORCING PEOPLE LIKE ME OUT OF THEIR HOMES?

This development is not concerned with us and our future. It does just the opposite: it impoverishes, marginalizes, and affects us. All the energy, work, life, and humanity we put into it. All sunk without trace.

WHAT'S THE RIGHT WAY TO DEVELOP AND BUILD A MODERN CITY?

I do not know about other cities but there are many poor people in a city like Addis. I think if I were an architect I would approach it from the viewpoint of the poor.

We are the majority. I call it selective demolition. Poorer residents being priced out of urban areas into suburbs or more depressed areas of cities. Couldn't they have negotiated a settlement with the community instead of demolishing their homes?

WHAT IS YOUR MESSAGE?

My message is for the Kebele. Before evicting us, demolishing our houses and sending us away, please look for an alternative. Make sure we don't all have to go back to what we are trying to escape from.

YOU WANT THEM TO RELOCATE YOU?

Relocating is almost never an improvement for us. Our livelihood is closely interwoven with the area we live in now. Our survival depends on this place and some of us are going to die for that reason. How is it that real-estate investors and the government continue to steer certain people to certain areas?

DO YOU MEAN ETHNIC MINORITIES?

I mean the poor, and we are considered indiscriminately. The government lets private investors plan and develop new communities in our existing neighborhoods.

WHAT ACTION ARE YOU TAKING?

Me and my neighbors—who are legal and illegal householders—formed a group and we are looking for a place to go. It will probably be in the countryside.

ZEWDE

I am still moved by the sobbing of Zewde. The thin, contagious sobbing of a 17-year-old girl.

YOU ARE NOW EIGHT MONTHS PREGNANT AND STILL WORKING AS FORCED LABOR ON A CONSTRUCTION SITE. WHAT DO YOU DO EXACTLY?

I remove stones.

ISN'T THE WORK TOO HARD FOR YOU IN YOUR CONDITION?

I'll carry on as long as they let me. Actually, I don't think they'll let me work tomorrow. I heard they are replacing me with a new lady.

AREN'T YOU AFRAID OF LOSING THE BABY?

Not now, not when it's inside me. I will lose my baby later, when I give him to the government for adoption.

WHAT MADE YOU TAKE THIS DECISION?

My husband left me not long after he found out I was expecting a baby. He went away. He abandoned me. He left me with all the burdens. When they evict me and the baby, how will I find somewhere to go? It is getting so expensive to rent!

WHERE DO YOU LIVE AND WHO IS THE OWNER OF THE HOUSE?

I live in Gerje. Now I'm alone and before I was with my husband. It is a Kebele house. We moved in as sub-letters. The landlord lives in the same house. He just built a small room to rent out and make some money, so that he could afford a condominium. He didn't tell us they were going to demolish Gerje. A neighbor told us and I went to the Kebele to ask. I didn't get any help from them because I was sub-letting. They only deal with official rentals.

DO YOU HAVE ANY RELATIVES IN TOWN?

Before coming to Addis, I lived in Wollo with my parents. My sister moved here first. She told us life here was much better and much easier. My parents were not happy she went and did not want me to go as well. I took a bus and came. She didn't want to help from the beginning. So I stopped asking. I can't go back to my parents either. They would not understand.

YOU MUST FEEL LONELY.

It's worse at night. Sounds wake me up. I ask, is anybody there? I get no answers.

WHAT SOUNDS?

The sound of cats or rats walking on the tin roof. I believe that if I work hard I will make it, no matter what.

BRAHNU

The matter awoke so many feelings in him: Disappointment, disillusionment, surprise, suspicion, and fear.

WHAT HAPPENED TO YOU?

My children used to go to school. I used to feed my family. We used to have a house. It is over. It is finished. Now, I am alone.

WHERE IS YOUR FAMILY?

My wife, my two sons, and my two daughters are all outside Addis in a rural area. We have no place to live. I do not have a job anymore.

HOW DO YOU COMMUNICATE WITH THEM?

I go to the bus station and ask around. If people are going to the same village I ask them to look for my wife and take a message to her. Sometimes she sends me one back the same way. If possible I send them money. Sometimes I write to them.

WOULD YOU LIKE TO TELL YOUR STORY?

They demolished our house. Without a house, I lost my job. I used to drive heavy-duty machines and excavators. Here is my license. I had a good name. They use to come and seek me out. You have to be presentable, respectable, well-dressed, showered, combed hair, polished shoes. You have to have a place where they can find you and knock at your door. You have to have an address to put on a work contract. You have to have an address for the police.

CAN YOU HELP ME UNDERSTAND WHAT IT IS GOING ON FROM YOUR VIEWPOINT?

Look (pointing at his sunken chest and flat belly): I am hungry, very hungry. Is this development? It's hard to see what's going on during the day. Come after 8 p.m. There are so many of us we are impossible to count! We spend the night here at the market.

Those of us who can afford it pay 3 or 5 ETB to lie on a shop floor with 28 other bodies. And you can bet if that's all the money I have that day, I'd rather spend it like this and not sleep on the street. Sleep one night on the street and it's over. I still think I am going to make it. I am not a beggar. I have a license. I can make it. I can go back to work. I am 55 years old. I am strong. I am young. I want to better myself!

Development is good, but I do not understand what's happening here. Development should be to improve life. To improve people. To improve countries. Nowadays in Ethiopia, the only people who can have a roof over their heads are those who can get into a condominium by paying 50,000 ETB right away and then paying 500 ETB monthly for the next 30 years to become an owner. What about the ones who can't?

WHO ARE THE ONES WHO CAN'T?

Drivers, servants, cotton spinners, recycling workers, small shop-keepers, injera vendors, shoe-cleaners, guardians, old men, old ladies, tailors, street coffee vendors, street vendors, corn collectors, maids, teachers, plumbers, traffic police, church singers, road builders, goat slaughters, cattle watchers, car washers, car mechanics, and grain and coffee bean grainers.

We were paying rent for our homes, sending our children to school, buying books and uniforms for them, opening small shops, starting up new business, caring about old family members, paying doctors' bills, buying medicines, repairing our roads after the rainy season, improving our water supply, and so on.

We were developing! Isn't that the right word to use? Why did they take it away from us? They made us poorer. They made us hungry. They made us dependent on charity.

By transforming the center, they think they can attract business and . . .

Replenished housing stock means improvement for everyone and it will have economic benefits and improve the economic competitiveness of the city center. It increases tourism. Reconstruction comes first. Who pays?

I am not saying I want them to improve my house for free, but they should have worked out a deal with us. Rather than demolish shanty housing, make us pay for the land and work on the reconstruction. They should be finding ways of ensuring that those who are already there pay services and other necessary fees.

You cannot ask the poor for money.

They can make money like anyone else—if you do not close down the market, tear down their shops, and demolish their network.

HOW DO YOU FEEL ABOUT TOMORROW?

As I stand in front of you now, I have no feelings. I am a displaced man and I am directionless.

WHAT DO YOU WISH WOULD HAPPEN?

I can see how things are changing. I can see how people look stressed, afraid, and full of despair. They have lost their sense of confidence in the future. My wish is for them to regain that confidence.

RAHEL

Her look shows defiance of the displacements that have happened to others. Her trembling chin betrays her worry that it will happen to her.

Rahel is renting a studio in a condominium built on a former Eritrean refugee camp in Makenisa, which is now residential quarters for higher military and civil governmental officials.

WHAT DO YOU DO FOR LIVING?

I am a book-keeper. I work for the church part-time and help out some expatriates, who have property here but cannot keep up with all the charges and bills.

HOW DID YOU GET THIS PLACE?

Through brokers known as DeLalla. You can't do anything without them in Addis. If you buy a second-hand car, rent a house, look for a maid or employees, you need them. They con-nect people who have something to of-fer with people who are searching for something. How could it be otherwise? How can you match supply with de-mand in such a big city?

HOW MUCH IS THE RENT?

1,000 ETB.

AND FOR THE DELALLA?

500 from me and 2,000 from the studio's owner.

DO YOU LIKE LIVING HERE?

Being in a modern apartment instead of a traditional house is great. But it is not my house.

WHY DIDN'T YOU BUY IT?

I don't have the money! For a studio condo unit, you have to pay a total of 27,797 ETB, and the down-payment is 6,789 ETB. My friend has spent close to 97,000 ETB to fit ceramic floor tiles and doors as well as for paint and plaster. Besides, the condominiums are not all the same. The ones built for the army are better-quality and in better locations. Otherwise a condominium would not be at the top of your wish list. They have cracks in the walls and a lot of dampness because of the con-dition of the roof. For instance, if you live on the upper floor, you do not get water at all. You need power because the water is pumped upwards against gravity. You keep hearing about burst sewage pipes leaking through all the floors and widespread cracking of plaster on the walls. You also need to buy many expensive items, such as doors and door handles, window glass, and basins.

WHY DID THEY CHECK YOUR BAG AT THE GATE?

Thieves! There is a lot of robbery and stealing going on. We had to get security for the building. Every resident or visitor gets checked on the way out and on the way in.

People often come back from work to find no television, cooking plates, and so on.

I guess it is part of modern life. It happens all the time in big cities.

WHO IS FIT FOR MODERN LIFE IN ADDIS ABABA?

Only people who have a normal job. The ones who work in offices, evangelical churches (as I do), banks, Ethiopian airlines, and private clinics, e.g. nurses and doctors. No one else can use the condominium to set up shops. They are not allowed to sell and they are not happy to leave their traditional houses and small business. Another problem is that condo houses don't have enough space to accommodate family members so relatives cannot visit.

EYABEZ

She is looking at eviction through the eyes of the government. She feels that is the right way. She is doing her best to adapt to the new situation. Her tone is deferential, but another message can be read between the lines.

DO YOU THINK PEACOCK PARK IS A PARK OR A SLUM?

Peacock Park is a wonderful green area inside the city. There are gardens along the river. The park is used by local people for weddings, a children playground, family picnics and gatherings. There is a village where I live.

WHY ARE THEY EVICTING YOU FROM PEACOCK PARK?
They plan to enlarge the existing park and convert it into international zoological gardens.

HOW MANY HOUSES DO THEY PLAN TO DEMOLISH?
About 500. A housing solution will be found for everybody. They will be moved to other houses and a big tent will be put up somewhere else for the homeless.

WHAT DO YOU THINK OF THE IDEA OF A ZOOLOGICAL PARK?
It will attract tourists, who will pay the admission price. It is very good for Ethiopia.

WHY SHOULD TOURISTS VISIT A RELATIVELY SMALL CITY ZOO WHEN THEY COME TO AFRICA RATHER THAN GO INTO THE GAME PARKS AND EXPERIENCE WILDLIFE FIRST-HAND?
Because the zoo will be full of animals they have never seen in their own countries, such as elephants and giraffes.

In few weeks' time, they will transfer the lions that are now in the presidential palace to what used to be a coffee shop inside the park. It is a round building, it already exists. They will build proper fences.

ARE YOU SAD TO LEAVE?
I am happy to leave the place where we live now and I am confident that I can make a better life for myself and my children at the new location.

WHERE ARE YOU MOVING TO?
It will be to Jemo. It was chosen by lottery. The apartment is not finished. It is a long way away. It is much cleaner. None of our neighbors are going to be relocated there. It will be a big change for us. I am very worried about the finance. We pay 1 ETB where we are now and we will pay 600 ETB where we are going. Transport will also be a new expense. We got loans from relatives and neighbors to make the 20 percent down-payment on a condominium house. Our country needs to grow and somehow the price must be paid.

SISSAY

Disorientation and distress is written in his face, in his eyebrows, and his grizzled chin. But when he smiles, the corners of his mouth spread to his ears.

WHAT DID YOUR HOUSE LOOK LIKE?
It was a wonderful villa like many in Addis that were constructed in the 1960s.
Western-style villas tucked into tree-lined gardens, Addis Ababa style.

WHO BUILT THAT HOUSE?
My grandparents. They traded in marble during Selassie's time. They established the first exports. They lost their property when the Derg came. The house was taken away, divided into three apartments and given to army officials.

DID YOU RECEIVE COMPENSATION FOR THE LOSS OF YOUR HOUSE?
Compensation should be based on current market prices and take into account all damages to the owner's livelihood. Any compensation payable to me cannot be less than the current cost of constructing a one-room low-cost house.

WHERE DO YOU LIVE NOW?
I am in interim accommodation and trying to get together the money for a new build on the plot of land assigned to us. It is hard. Expropriation will not be executed until proper compensation has been paid and we are fully settled.

WHEN WILL YOU START BUILDING?
When the price of sand goes down. The sand price rose from 5,300 ETB per 16 cubic meter truckload to 7,000 ETB after the price of diesel rose to 17.73 ETB per liter earlier last month. The price is also affected by the bargaining power of the brokers who earn commission from buyers and sellers. The quality of the sand also impacts on the price; sand containing less mud is worth more. The sand price increase has also led to a hike in the prices of other materials, such as cement, bricks, and metal reinforcement bars. Along with the sand, bricks cost 8.50 ETB apiece, 1 ETB up from two weeks previously. Cement costs 500 ETB per 100 kg if you can find it, while Mugher PPC was selling at 410 ETB per 100 kg prior to the sand price rise; 12 mm metal bars cost 230 ETB apiece, up from 210 ETB. In addition to paying skilled daily laborers up to 120 ETB per day, building the foundation cost 10,000 ETB per day.

WHY IS IT SO DIFFICULT TO GET ENOUGH CEMENT TO BUILD YOUR NEW HOUSE?

One million tons of cement and iron bars are being brought in from as far away as Turkey and the Ukraine to deal with the surge in demand for materials for condominium projects. By the time my house is not far beyond the foundation stage, I will have already spent more than the compensation I got, making it impossible to finish my house.

WHAT HAVE YOU DECIDED TO DO?

I will build a small structure instead. In order not to lose the plot, I must start developing within two months of being assigned to it.

SELEM

She has a nose for a bargain and the eyes of a market dweller, who knows that everything on earth has its price.

HOW DID YOU END UP IN THE SHELTER?

I was a housemaid. I worked in that house for many years. I was practically a child when I started. It was a good job. I liked it because I had a place to stay, food, and a family I liked. The problems came when I got sick. They forced me out and I ended up on the street. I did not go to school. I am illiterate. It's not easy for me to get a job.

I was on the street until they offered to move me into the shelter. I have been living there with my cats for five years. They have been trying to take them away from me. They blackmailed me and reported me to the Kebele authorities for keeping cats in the shelter. I was called in and questioned about it. I explained: I have no children, I have no husband, I have no sisters, I have no brothers. I have my cats and I should be able to live with them.

The cat chose me first. It followed me all the way home. Then I decided, okay we will live together. Now there are five of them. Let me tell you their names: Embuto, Melk, Hunbet, Omsew, and Chalochew.

You should not think we are not aware what's going on . . . we talk and talk about the coming eviction but we cannot see solutions.

HOW DO YOU SUPPORT YOURSELF?

I wash clothes and I have many clients here in Peacock Park, though I will lose them as soon as they are forced out of their houses. Many wealthy people who work for the government live in Peacock Park.

WHAT ABOUT RENTING A ROOM IN A KEBELE HOUSE?

The money I make with my work is barely enough to buy some food. Renting is unaffordable for people like me. And even if I could find an affordable room, which is becoming impossible, all the houses in Peacock Park must go: the ones made out of mud, the ones made out of tin, the villas, and the stone-built ones. Even the ones with the compounds and the wire fences. A lot of protesting went on the day the Kebele officials gathered all the village in the big hall, particularly among families with children. They have to take them out of school and this is bad for them. Protesting didn't make any difference and will not stop the development.

SO YOU WILL ALL HAVE TO LEAVE IN THREE MONTHS?

They can't stop talking about it. I can't bear to think such thoughts personally.

Sure, it's hard in the tent. It is too cold at night. It is too hot in the day. Some people won't stop listening to music. There's quarreling and shouting. It is too loud!

The shelter is jam-packed. There are too many of us and we are packed in too close to one another. No doors, no privacy, but it's still safe. No stealing, no rape. We and the Peacock Park people are just one village.

Well, we are stigmatized. For example, children have to put up with insults and bad words, sometimes stones, on their way to school. But the area is nice! I like it here.

A B A Y

Abay is the Amharic name for Nile. She is sinuous, secretive, self-contained, lonely as a river.

WHAT IMPACT HAS THE DISINTEGRATION OF YOUR NEIGHBORHOOD TIES HAD ON YOUR DAILY LIFE AFTER YOUR EVICTION FROM BOLE?

In Unireka Sefera, Bole, some days there was no injera at my house so my children ate in our neighbors' house. Some days there was no food in our neighbors' house so their children shared food with mine. There were ups and downs for all of us. Some of us got sick and could not work. My neighbor's husband passed away and she was alone with her baby. She could count on us, always. Even if living conditions got tough, you were not left alone. Community is the real loss, not houses. When we left Sefera village we lost all our friends. We were dispersed. Displaced.

WHERE DID YOU GO YOURSELF?

We came to Urael because here we could still find affordable houses to rent.

HOW COME—KASANCHY IS DOWNTOWN, A VERY BUSY COMMERCIAL AREA?

People avoid places like that because of the evictions. Look! The houses are earmarked for redevelopment by the city government. Can you see the red painted mark on the front? This is a historical part of the city. In the beginning, everyone was very poor. Not now. It is different. It is better. I like my children to be here and learn.

HOW OLD ARE THEY?

They are nine and seven years old, both boys. They cried when we were forced out of Sefera. It was wearing me down. They are good sons. They are also a great help to the family! They sell prayer mats to Muslims. They were eyewitnesses the day the police stormed the place where Muslims pray at Arat Kilo to demolish it.

HOW OLD WERE YOU WHEN YOU CAME TO ADDIS?

I was 13. I was working as a shepherdess, looking after sheep and cattle.

WHICH IS YOUR STRATEGY?

Today I work doing forced labor at the Beleruanda building construction site. After work, I walk in all directions and look for a place.

HOW DO THINGS LOOK?

I feel like dying, because when the time comes I will have to send my boys to their grandparents' house in Wollo. Shelter is more important than food, drinking, clothing, or being together.

HAVE YOU EVER WORKED AS A DEMOLISHER?

Yes. I did. I was employed by the government. It was work. It was sad. The people were just watching and crying. I was sad. Everybody was sad.

TIZITA

She seemed perfectly willing to speak to me and confident with her short modern haircut and smart look.

WHERE DO YOU LIVE?

We live in one room, my sister and me. It's a very narrow room with no windows. It is a private rental room. We have to look for another place because they are soon going to demolish. We have been living there for one year. Before we were in another house not far from where we are now but the rent got too high and we had to leave. They increased it from 250 ETB to 400 ETB. In the house that we live in now, we have water and electricity.

WHAT DO YOU LIKE BEST?

I like the area. It is very well served with transport. It is safe for two girls to live on their own.

HOW DO YOU FIND LIVING WITH YOUR SISTER?

We love each other and we understand each other very well. My sister is younger.

She works as a cashier and she is regularly employed in a shop. I work on a daily basis myself, in construction, in private houses, or as a maid. We have fun listening to music, laughing, making friends, eating good food, and being together.

WHY ARE THEY DEMOLISHING THE HOUSE WHERE YOU ARE STAYING?

It is illegally built. In that area, more than 200 families have been evicted and displaced. There is no hope of finding a house available for an affordable price. We are looking for another illegal place. We know that sooner or later they will kick us out. We are looking for a small place and are not interested in a bigger house. It's very important for us is to stay in the city.

Life in Addis: this is how and where we like to live.

WHAT MAKES LIFE IN ADDIS SO SPECIAL FOR YOU AND YOUR SISTER?

People in Addis help each other. This may be because most of them come from outside and go through a lot of difficulties. It could be because that is the way in the city. We live so close to one another and so tightly-packed that it makes us closer. In the rural area where I come from, Showa, life is more individual, for example. People are isolated and dispersed. The houses are separated from one another by plots of land. The separation is both physical and mental.

The family is also internally separated. Land plots gets divided up and the more brothers and sisters there are, the less land there is. Land brings many quarrels and fights. My sister and I never quarrel in Addis.

AND WHAT DO YOU THINK ABOUT THE DEVELOPMENTS GOING ON?

When I see one of these new tall glass buildings, I am amazed. But in the end, it boils down to separation again. They separate the poor from the rich and the less poor from the very poor. The ones who can afford a down-payment get a condominium unit. The one who cannot afford it do not. They separate the community. They separate the old people from their houses, from their memories and from their neighbors. They separate friends. They separate families.

GETACHE

She was standing against the wall propped up on her elbows wishing she could sleep in her bed forever.

ARE YOU OKAY—SHOULD WE CANCEL THE INTERVIEW?

They knocked down the wall protecting my house today, and they say they will come back tomorrow to destroy it all.

THIS IS THE FINAL WARNING: ARE YOU READY TO LEAVE?

No. I like it here.
Demolition is scheduled in three days. The ferengi (the word for foreigners; in this case it refers to Chinese workers) are already working on the road construction.
I pray to God to spare this house. If He allows me to stay longer, the rainy season will come. When it starts raining they will stop working on the road construction. I do not need electricity or gas. I can use fire. I will not buy charcoal; I will collect wood myself. For

water, I will use the construction pipes. I will wash myself there and take some home for cooking.

HOW DO YOU SUPPORT YOURSELF AND YOUR DAUGHTER?
I go to Entoto with other women. We collect eucalyptus leaves. I also serve coffee to the construction workers.

WHAT DO YOU LIKE MOST HERE?
The door! (pointing to the entrance door, made of corrugated iron sheet) I like to be indoors.

There are no locks on this door.
It's closed, isn't it? There is no need to lock it.

WHAT ARE YOU AFRAID OF?
Nothing! Hyenas (she laughs)

WHERE WILL YOU GO?
I do not want to go back to working as a servant. Where I used to work, they never let me wash myself and they wouldn't give me food. Because I was not able to wash, I had sores. I didn't have anywhere to shut myself away and be alone and I used to starve. Most of the time, the son (who was thirteen, two years older than me) beat me for no reason. When I asked him why he was doing it, he beat me again.
I will go to Sheromeda (the cotton district, where children from rural areas are sent to work). Please tell me that they will stop the demolition.

EPHRAIM
The day he decided to change thingsheletouta timid shout and tears fell from both his eyes.

CAN YOU TAKE ME TO SEE YOUR HOUSE?
I live in a single room measuring about 10 square meters on the ground floor. The same room on the upper floor is occupied by another family. It houses children, grandchildren, and extended family members. Before moving to this house, I was living in a house that was demolished by the upgrading project and replaced by new houses.

WHO DID YOU TELL ABOUT WHAT WAS DONE TO YOUR HOUSE?
No one is listening. Who could I talk to? No one wants to hear about it. No one can or wants to stop it.

They took your property. They said it was for road construction but no road will actually be built on the area where your house stood.
You build relations for 20 years and then they break down in 20 days because of relocation and because of blackmail. If you blackmail someone, you will be

promoted. People can damage each other very effectively, especially people who are close to you.

We spent years together in happiness and sadness, sharing ups and downs but they turned into traitors overnight. I felt an overwhelming sense of shock and hopelessness at the sight of my once good neighbors turned into betrayers at the side of our expellers. People I trusted. People who shared so many good and bad times with me. I do not blame them. I blame the system. You have to be a member of the party to get a job or house or to keep your house.

ARE YOU ONE?

No, I am not. This is why I have been trying to get a license to open an internet café for six years. I doubt I will get one. I should leave the country but I do not want to. They can take everything away from me but not the fact that I am Ethiopian.

WHY DO YOU CARE ABOUT LOSING THIS HOUSE? WHAT WILL YOU REALLY MISS?

I don't think it will be possible to start again. We have to build the houses ourselves.

There aren't anymore plots we can build on. We used to buy land directly from farmers or build where there was empty land that no one had any claim on.

DID YOU BUILD THIS HOUSE AS WELL?

This time it was different. We got help from an NGO and the work was done under their guidance. You can tell by the structure of the house. The two rooms, which are connected by an internal staircase, were originally designed for a single family. The housing unit originally had one outside entrance door leading to both the ground room and the upper floor. Later, for privacy and keep us separate, we added an extra door made of corrugated iron. We formed a self-help association. We rebuilt destroyed latrines and so on. We also paid rent to the association until we had covered the cost of our homes under a rent-to-own scheme—then ownership of the houses was transferred to us.

WHAT DOES IT MEAN TO YOU TO BE ETHIOPIAN?

I was born in Ethiopia and so were my father and mother, my father's father and mother and my mother's father and mother.

WHY DID YOU INVEST ALL YOUR MONEY IN A HOUSE THAT WAS NOT YOURS?

They promised that they would give us a legal certificate of ownership and my certificate of legal ownership number was to have been YEKA 10/2497.

SO WHY DID THEY EVICT YOU WITHOUT COMPENSATION?

They said our houses did not fit into the city's master plan and so they were illegal.

WHICH IS THE GREATEST LOST YOU SUFFERED?

My children had to drop out of school and the fact that we spent all our money, work, and time to improve a house that does not exist anymore.

WHAT DO YOU HAVE TO LOOK FORWARD TO IN THE FUTURE?

Competition for space, for the outdoor kitchen and for garbage disposal. Offenses against my children by grown-up members of the neighboring household. Conflict.

AYALENSHE

She is a fighter. Not the aggressive kind, ready to jump into battle, but quite m i l d - m a n - nered and patient. A person who most people would p a t r o n i z e .

WHY ARE YOU HERE?

I came from Wollo to Addis to work as a housemaid. I was a little girl in the big city. And now that I am not a girl any longer, I still feel like that. This is a difficult, complicated, tough place to live.

My first job was with a family living on the outskirt of Addis. The payment was 15 ETB per month. I didn't have enough money to go to school, buy food or buy shoes. All I did was work and live for them. I carried so much water on my back that I used to fall over.

I am married now. I live with my husband in Bole. It is a privately-rented slum house. I had a child with another man before my wedding and he doesn't live with us.

WHY NOT?

We had to agree to many restrictions to live here and I am allowed to get two bowls of water a day. If I need more I can't have it. Children are not allowed. Sharing a social life with our neighbor is not allowed because he is renting illegally and we have to be as invisible as possible. We are not allowed to have guests. Even if relatives visit us, they are not allowed to use the toilet. Washing and drying clothes in the compound is forbidden.

IS IT ACCEPTABLE?

Yes, it is. Out of fear of being evicted. Out of fear of not being given a place. Out of fear of not being able to afford much higher rents. It is very difficult to find a place to rent that doesn't cost more than 300 ETB inside the city and it is even more difficult to find a good landlord. It's better to follow the rules and please him. The gate is locked at 8 o'clock in the evening for example. This is a problem because when my husband works late he gets locked out.

WHAT ABOUT LOOKING FOR A BETTER LANDLORD?

I pay rent and I also work for him for free out of my good will, not out of duty. He never says thank you. I am told stories of much bigger abuses and worse conditions.

I myself have had worse experiences. Whether I fear him or not, we are going to be evicted. Not because of him but because of the government.

Addis still offers what the huge mass of Ethiopians in rural areas cannot have: opportunity to work at something. And for a reasonable wage. Get out of Addis and it is over. All our sacrifices, our victory over poverty, our struggle for better life conditions. All cancelled out, all in vain.

No, I don't mind having a mean landlord. Actually, I want one. I need one, I am looking for one who's even worse, even meaner. Unfortunately, I know I'm not going to find one. Not in Bole, not now, not anymore. Not in Addis.

For those at the bottom of the economic pile the city has ceased to be a friendly place.

Walking around Edna Building feels like being a ferengi in your own country. The Bole area has been turned into beautiful malls and high-rises, but to us that means eviction, impoverishment, sickness, tears. We will never buy the expensive items or eat in the expensive restaurants you can see there. This is why we will never be able to rent another little room without a latrine and electricity like this one. I look at them with fondness but also a sense of loss.

ABEBECH

She is sure that if she finds something better to think about, everything will improve.

YOU SEEM SURPRISED.

I first heard the news about the demolition in 2005. Back then, almost ten years ago, I did not believe that it would happen. However, it seems all too real now that my house and those of the other residents in the area are on the list of houses to be demolished this week.

TELL US YOUR STORY.

I came to Addis looking for a job. Life in Barda was difficult. I wanted to be on my own. I started out as a housemaid. I married and gave birth to my son, then we separated, and here I am.

YOU ARE A WOMAN OF FEW WORDS.

Ethiopians do not like storytelling. We stick with the facts. All the rest is private. It is embarrassing to talk about. It is embarrassing to listen to. We do not like to let out what we keep inside.

WHERE DO YOU LIVE?

I am renting from a private individual. It is illegal. In three weeks, we have to go. I rent one room and it's very small. There is electricity, but no water. I fetch water myself. The area has already been partly demolished. Now they are going to finish the demolition and start building.

HAVE YOU FOUND A NEW PLACE TO GO?

No, I haven't.

MOST OF THE HOUSES DON'T MEET HEALTH STANDARDS. THEY HAVE NO TOILETS OR WINDOWS. DON'T YOU THINK THAT THE GOVERNMENT ACTION TO DEMOLISH THEM IS SOMEHOW JUSTIFIED?

Why not build the missing infrastructure instead? Why not bring the water and sewers to us? We are poor and because of that we can work harder. We can dig, we can clear stones, we can build, we can paint, we can work for free. Men, women, children, families, and individuals. We could make Addis the most beautiful city, if someone just asked us and gave us some guidance.

WHAT ABOUT THE CONDOMINIUM THE GOVERNMENT IS BUILDING TO TAKE MANY OF YOU OUT OF THE SLUM?

You call it a slum. We call it a village. Condominiums are not for all of us, but only for the few who can afford a down-payment plus the mortgage. Even if there are a lot of them, there are even more of us who can't afford it!

WHAT IS YOUR MESSAGE TO ETHIOPIAN WOMEN LIKE YOU?

Do not leave the original place you came from. Stay close to your original family and build your future there.

THAT'S EXACTLY THE OPPOSITE OF WHAT YOU DID.

Because it is hard. Very hard. And it is going to get harder. Very soon I will not clean my client's houses because their houses are going to be demolished just like mine.

WHAT IS YOUR GREATEST WISH?

That my boy will go to school and he will teach me what I did not learn myself.

AKELU

A woman whose image cannot be reflected by any mirror and to her astonishment nobody can see.

HAVE YOU FOUND SOMEWHERE TO GO?
I want to be happy here until the last day! I will enjoy it up to the last moment.

WHAT ABOUT PLANNING WHERE TO GO?
Why should I anticipate a problem before it happens? So far, they have not burned the house down. I am enjoying being inside it. I am happy to have this house.

AND THEN?
Before coming here, I was living with my aunt. I was a servant in the house.

In the future, I will continue to be independent. Luckily enough, my baby will be a boy.
Males suffer less than females and as a mother I will suffer less for him.

WHAT WILL BE BUILT ON THIS SITE?
Hotels.

HOW DO YOU FEEL ABOUT THAT?
I have no anger or bad feelings like most of the old people here have.

WHY ARE THE OLD PEOPLE ANGRY?
They have been living here so many years! They are old. They do not have any income. They are dependent on support from the village. They cannot survive eviction or resettlement to a place where nobody knows them. Who is going to support them? They do not have the strength or resources to survive.

HOW DO YOU EARN YOUR LIVING?
I am part of a women's association that prepares food for public places, such as health centers.

CAN YOU AFFORD THE CONDOMINIUM DOWN-PAYMENT?
I asked to be given the choice of another Kebele housing scheme, as I cannot afford to pay the down-payment required for the condominium. I have tried to voice this concern to the district officials many times.

WILL THEY HOUSE YOU?
No. There will be no Kebele houses in the future. This is an inevitability, sooner or later around 140,000 Kebele houses from all around the city will be demolished under the city development plan. I have been living in this house for 20 years and paying 3 ETB rent. I can't afford to rent any other kind of house. Most days, I go without eating. Food is also becoming unaffordable.

WHY?
Because our food is being exported to foreign markets. For instance, all oil-

seeds produced in Ethiopia are sent abroad to Arab countries. Actually, oil-seeds are the second biggest export item in the country after coffee. The same applies to sugar and teff (the edible seeds of Ethiopia's native Williams' lovegrass). This is the real reason for the price hike. We have to buy palm oil imported from Middle Eastern countries, which is very expensive, does not taste good, and is very unhealthy.

HOW CAN YOU GO ON WITHOUT A PLAN?
I am a hard-working woman. God, wherever you are, help me! I only need 3,000 ETB to pay for and start a small business. People like coffee. I will sell it to my customers and sit with them and chat. We will live like that. I will work from 4:30 am until 10 at night. My son will study. We will make ends meet. Some days we go to sleep without eating. I don't know how we'll manage to sleep when we have no bed!

WHAT WOULD YOUR DREAM HOUSE BE LIKE?
A stone house with small garden, toilet, and washing machine.

WHAT IS YOUR PRESENT HOUSE LIKE?
A mud house with a small garden and separate kitchen.

ASKAYE
After a time, she showed signs of knowing she had much to learn, and secretly had much more to teach.

DO YOU PAY RENT AT YOUR PRESENT HOUSE?
No, I pay tax on that property. It is our own home. We have been given a legal permit to build. My husband built the house. We farmers have an informal association and we help each other with the building work. The government gave us a deed and because of that they cannot send us away without compensation.

SO HOW DOES IT WORK? CAN THEY EVICT YOU FROM THE HOUSE AND THE PLOT OF LAND YOU ARE FARMING?
They make the laws. They dispose of us and of the land. The area is for development. Where there are farmers' settlements now, there will be condominiums in the future.

WOULD YOU LIKE TO BE IN ONE?
No space, no privacy, no freedom. There are so many stories about what it's like

to live there. For example, if you leave your shoes out, someone will wear them. If you have to slaughter a goat, you have to carry the goat all the way up to the fourth floor, if you live there, and slaughter it on your bedroom because they don't allow you to do it outside. Some people can't get back into their apartments because the corridor and staircase are covered with berbere (a spice blend used in many Ethiopian dishes).

We are farmers and always will be. They will give us a new plot of land somewhere else.

WILL IT BE THE SAME FOR YOU?

Not at all. This land we have is very fertile. It is all we need. We harvest wheat, teff, onions, and cabbages. We have water. We have kettles. We have sheep. We have chickens. We are very close to the town and there are markets every day. Our children go to very good schools. They are close by. There is wood and plenty of grass for the cattle.

I like my house. I like every part of it. The entrance faces east and I enjoy the sunrise every morning.

WHAT WORRIES YOU MOST?

The size of the new plot. There is a land shortage. It will not be as big as the one we have now. I don't think we will be able to keep all the animals. In that case we already know how and where to sell. It's unfair but like or not, it will happen, and we have to be ready.

HOW DID THIS LAND SHORTAGE COME ABOUT?

An Indian investor gets as much land as he wants for free for 90 years.

HOW ARE YOU GETTING READY FOR THE CHANGE?

I am ready! All the cereal is in jars. We spoke to the children and told them we are going to a better place. There will be water in the house and electricity. We don't want them to have to go through an eviction and we asked them to help us demolish our own house when the time comes. That's how it must be. We built it and we will destroy it.

We planted eucalyptus trees and have not cut them down yet. We will use them to build the new house. It will take three to four days by donkey and seven hours by car to transport them.

It will be difficult to sell the things we are not taking with us because everybody is going to be evacuated like us. We help each other and make sure that all of us can start a new farming life under the best circumstances.

HOW DO YOU FEEL ABOUT THE CHANGE?

I am in favor of development. Development is good and this is the way it should be. If we cannot support ourselves by selling our land and dairy products in the new place, we will change our business. We will stop being farmers and open a shop. I'd like to sell oil, sugar, and vegetables.

ESHETWA

She pats her slightly rounded belly and sucks it in as much as she can, before she is forced to let it bulge out again.

WHEN IS IT GOING TO HAPPEN?

In September, all the houses must go. It was originally planned for July, but because of the schools we persuaded the authorities to postpone it until the school year ends and not interrupt it, which would have negative repercussions.

YOU HAVE A FEW MONTHS TO FIND A NEW HOUSE. HOW DOES IT WORK?

At the moment, we don't have a new place to go to. It looks unlikely that we'll find one, but we are doing our best. I work at the health center and I see many people. I ask all of them to help me find a place.

We really want to live in Bole. Our children love their teachers and their school. I work in this area and so does my husband. This is the place we want to be.

DO THE TEACHERS TALK TO THE CHILDREN ABOUT IT?

Yes, they do. They say it is better to leave. It is for a good reason. Development will bring benefits to all. They advise us not to resist and to help the transformation that is going on.

WHAT ARE YOUR CHANCES OF STAYING IN THIS AREA?

Well, we certainly can't afford a condominium and we are looking for houses without facilities like a toilet, water, or even electricity.

CAN YOU STILL FIND SUCH HOUSES?

Yes, they are very much in demand so there is a long waiting list. If you know people, it's easier.

HOW OLD IS YOUR DAUGHTER?

She is 12.

WHAT WAS THE HOUSE LIKE THAT YOU LIVED IN WHEN YOU WERE 12 YEARS OLD YOURSELF?

It was not in Addis. It was in Nazareth. It was dirty! The roof was made out of grass.

WASN'T THAT BETTER THAN A TIN ROOF: NOT SO HOT DURING THE DAY AND NOT SO COLD OR NOISY DURING THE RAINY SEASON?

Yes, you are right. But a tin roof is cleaner!

I had to walk a very long way to school. It was a long way to walk every day, especially in the rainy season, and it was muddy.
My children have their own room, but all ten of us of used to sleep in the only room in the house. We used to eat and prepare food there and sleep with our domestic animals. All in one room! There

was no privacy. My children have their own clothes. We used to wear anything in the house that fitted us. There was no private property. We had no mattresses. Sunshine did not enter the house. When my children eat they have their own plates. We used to eat food from the same plate. But what I like most is the cleanliness. We have a separate kitchen and there are no animals in the house.

FEYDA

There is nothing provocative about her. Nothing out of place. Nothing western. At the same time, she does not show any signs of the tradition that marks so many.

HOW DID YOU END UP IN GERJI?

They notified us several times and also gave us a document. Since none of us had a place to go, we carried on living there. You never know how long it is going to take before work starts. You wait until then.

One day we came back from work and we found our houses sealed by the police. If this happens, you are not allowed to break the seal and have to wait for the police to come and do it. At two o'clock they came. We were all standing outside our house doors and waiting. They came with some workers recruited by the

Kebele. They went into our houses and threw all our things out.

We collected our things, took a taxi, and left for Gerji.

WHY GERJI?

It was not the new, clean Gerji where they built the condominium. It was still a slum area called Roha Bread because it was around the bakery. I was sure that because that area is almost on the outskirts of Addis and not downtown, no investors would be interested in it. How wrong could I have been!

HOW DID ROHA BREAD'S PEOPLE REACT WHEN SO MANY OF YOU CAME TO LIVE IN THE SAME AREA?

They welcomed us. I suspect the reasons were both business-related and humanitarian.

WHAT DID YOU DO ONCE YOU GOT OUT OF THE TAXI?

I spotted a place and set up a plastic shelter to give us a roof for the coming night.

In the morning, our neighbor came to us. When we told him our story he blessed our coming and offered us a deal. The deal was: he would build a house for us and we would pay him rent. The amount of rent was set at 152 ETB per month. We agreed and both parties were satisfied.

HOW IS LIFE IN GERJI?

It's the last place on earth you would want to raise your child. It is a very dirty, overcrowded, unhealthy area. Garbage and waste collection is only once a month. There is no mains water and the water is delivered once a week.

NEVERTHELESS, IT SEEMS YOU ARE VERY CONCERNED ABOUT THE UPCOMING EVICTION AND YOU WOULD DEFINITELY RATHER STAY.

If the investors come even here then there is no hope for millions of people like me, whose incomes are low. I earn my living by recycling and the work pays hardly anything, but my life is in Addis. Ask me today whether I still like Addis Ababa and I would answer you 'No.' Ask me today where I want to live and I would answer 'Addis'. If they push us out of the city we will be forced to enter the rural areas and the farmers won't let us. They will stop us and push us off their land.

HOW DO YOU SPEND YOUR DAY WHILE WAITING FOR THE LATEST EVICTION?

I go every day to the Kebele office and I ask where they are going to send us. Where are we going to live? Where are my children going to sleep and where are they going to school?

Their answer is: we cannot tell you where you will go. We cannot tell you if we will provide you with a place. They will only tell me the exact day the shelter will be demolished weeks in advance. That does not interest me.

WHY DO YOU THINK THEY WON'T TELL YOU WHERE THEY WILL PUT YOU?

I will ask and ask and ask until they answer me.

WHY DOES A DETERMINED LADY LIKE YOU WISH TO LIVE IN ROHA, WHICH IS A WASTE DUMP AND WASTE SITE?

Because of freedom. My freedom. My children's freedom.

Yes. Our health is greatly at risk. There are too many sick people there. We are too packed in and constrained. If anything happens there is no emergency exit. During the day it is too hot. It stinks, but still . . . I am independent! Nobody orders me about. Nobody tells me what to do or what not to do. Nobody orders my children about. Anyone who comes to visit us can stay. I can raise my children the way I want. They are free to learn. They are free to tell me if they have a wish, a problem or a need.

It is my own house. In my parent's house or in somebody else's house I would be a parasite. I would be ordered around. I would not be respected. I would have to wait on everybody. In rural areas children work and do not have time to learn.

HOW OLD ARE YOUR CHILDREN?

Fourteen, eleven, and nine years old! It is hard in such a small place for them to do their school homework or play. If they grow up in Addis and go to a good school, once they are adult, it will be easier for them to find a good job. Displaced children have a hard life and have no future.

IS THE NEXT SHELTER GOING TO BE TEMPORARY AS WELL?

Isn't everything in a person's life temporary? Look at my last boy: soon he will be a big man.

HOW DID YOU COME TO ADDIS?

I was a child. I think I was 12/13 years old. I got on a bus and came.

When I arrived in Addis I got off the bus. I did not know anybody. I just knew that in Addis you can get a job and people help you and you can build a new life.

A NEW LIFE AT 12 YEARS OLD?

In Wollo, there was no food. A new life meant a life with food and a future.

DID IT HAPPEN?

A person, a man, did show interest in me as soon as I got off the bus. He was so kind and invited me for lunch.

He introduced me to the owner of a bar who offered me a job. I have been working there for 12 years.

WHY DID THEY SACK YOU?

Because of the child. There is a rule: if you get pregnant you have to go!

WHERE IS THE FATHER OF YOUR OTHER TWO KIDS?

He left. He went back to the countryside.

DID YOU BREAK UP?

He was not happy to become a father, that's all. He still calls me. We were okay. We got along pretty well before. He asked me to have an abortion. I could not do it because I was already 12 weeks pregnant. Now I need to help myself.

MELKAM

When she finally broke her silence to speak, her eyes were open wide, anxious and brave.

TELL ME ABOUT YOUR HOUSE?

We built the house by ourselves. We mainly used plastic. There are some shops where you can buy it. We found some parts amongst the garbage waiting for collection. It is all recycled and second-hand material. It happened after they evicted us from our previous house. It was seven years ago. There was no alternative. Building an illegal house was better than living on the street. Now it is time for another change.

DID THEY TELL YOU ABOUT THE COMING DEMOLITION?

They came from house to house. Door to door. They just told us we were illegal and so there was nothing they could do for us and we should go. There was no blame, no show of force, no judgment, no fright tactics. They were friendly this time.

We knew from the beginning. We knew it was going to happen. We knew it was not forever. Any house built during the 2005 elections or during the post-election period had to be pulled down.

YOU DO NOT SEEM WORRIED ABOUT WHERE TO GO.

God has been very kind to me. My husband and I understand each other very well. We love each other. We spoke about what to do next and decided not to go back to Gonder. To catch the bus as a family and go back is not good. It was easy for me to leave. There were too many quarrels going on between my parents and their relatives. Everybody was at war. I was happy to leave.

HOW DID YOU MEET YOUR HUSBAND?

He was the guard; I was the housemaid.

TELL ME ABOUT YOUR COMMUNITY AND NEIGHBORS.

We have a very strong bond and we cooperate easily. We do a lot together. For instance, we built our individual houses and even the street you took to come here together. I belong to a group. We have coffee ceremonies and enjoy life. We laugh and make fun of many issues. We even can laugh about our eviction and displacement and the development. We have a lot of fun together! I save 2 ETB for the ceremony every 15 days. Actually, I am not afraid of being parted from my girlfriends because we will all go and move together. My best friend is older than me. She has had a tough time. She is so strong.

THE QUESTION IS WHETHER YOU WILL FIND A HOUSE YOU CAN RENT?

Help does not come from humans. It comes from God. He is always helping me. And He will this time too.

HOW MUCH WILL IT COST TO REBUILD AN ILLEGAL HOUSE?
Even birds have nests. So, there is no point crying over spilt milk: we'll just have to roll up our sleeves. What I mean to say is, we have to strive for a better life, all of us have to support each other in order to live properly in Ethiopia. Otherwise there will be no improvement, everyone will stay hopeless and poor.

MARTHA
She knows in-stinctively what she wants; and she usually gets a sign to tell her what to do.

TELL ME ABOUT YOURSELF?
I am Martha. I spent 34 years of my life in a beautiful house in Bole until the government earmarked it and then demolished it. I am the firstborn of six children. I have three sisters and two brothers. They are all unmarried. I myself am divorced. We all live with our mother. My dad passed away four years ago. We are all educated and from a wealthy family.

HOW DID YOU LOSE THE HOUSE?
Because of the urban development plan. They planned to build two skyscrapers called the Sky Towers on the spot where our house stood. They gave us five months to leave before starting the demolition work.

DID YOUR PARENTS OWN THE HOUSE?
No. During the Red Terror, properties were taken away from people and the government rented them out or gave them to eligible people. My father was

employed by the oil company and he was eligible to rent the house from the Kebele. It was a beautiful building. We moved in when I was three years old. My brothers and sisters were born there. We have all been living there together ever since.

WHAT DID YOU AND YOUR FAMILY DO DURING THE FIVE MONTHS YOU HAD LEFT?

Twenty days after we were told about the house demolition, my mother was asked to go to a certain office at a certain day. She went and another 14 people went on exactly the same day. They went to the same place at the same time for the same reason: the lottery. It works like that. The urban development officer cut 15 strips of paper from a page listing available houses. She folded them carefully and put them into a pencil case. She shook them around and asked everyone to take one.

The paper my mother picked showed our future house: the location, the number of bedrooms, the floor, the building number and the house number, the subscription and the subsidy area. My mum was not the luckiest: we got a 63.51 square-meter apartment in a condominium 30 kilometers away from our present place!

HOW MUCH IS THE NEW RENT?

There is no such thing as renting! You have to buy. You must. It is obligatory. The unit my mother 'won' has a cost: 150,000 ETB. So, she was required to make a down-payment of 46,000 ETB out of her savings to secure the unit and had to sign 'Form 03' at the branch housing transfer and administration office as a form of contract with the office for the first stage of the transfer. Then she entered into a contractual loan agreement with the Commercial Bank of Ethiopia on the basis of monthly repayments including the principal and interest at 8.5 per cent. Once paid, the bank issued my mother with a receipt which she had to deliver to the HDPO along with Form 03 to initiate the signing of the title deed.

WHAT HAPPENS IF YOU DO NOT PAY?

If you have not paid by the time the five months are up, you will be on the street! They don't wait for you to find a place. It happened to our neighbor.

A 70 year-old couple decided not to leave. The federal police and the demolition people came and took all their things then, threw them out on the street. Most of the old people who lived in our compound cannot afford to pay. They used to be teachers and employees and now that they have retired their pension is around 400 ETB. Since they spent all their money raising children and getting them an education or sending them abroad they saved very little if anything. My mother gets 1,200 ETB pension after 42 years working for Ethiopian Airlines. She wouldn't have enough to live on without us. There are six of us children, all educated and with jobs. We have no children or new families and were able to put together the money. If you do not start a new family, you stay with your original family no matter how old you are.

WHAT WAS THE HARDEST MOMENT?

When we went to see our future house. We went by car. As we left the main asphalt street we found ourselves in the middle of nowhere. No sign, no lights, no city life.

We drove for 20 minutes along a muddy road before we got to our destination. There was no water or electricity. The house was not finished. How could the eight of us—my mother, myself, my brothers, my sisters, and our maid—live in 63 square meters? What do we do with the beds? Where do we put the mattress during the day? Where do we put them at night? What do we do with all the furniture we have? The sofas, dining table, chairs, fridge, blankets, stove, injera maker, cupboard, patio chairs, flowers, plants, books, clothes, shoes, pots and pans, and so on?

MASKARAM

Her smile celebrated the little continuities that are important when everything else seems to be changing.

WHERE ARE YOUR CHILDREN RIGHT NOW?

The little one is with my husband. The other two are at school.

WHERE DID YOU MEET YOUR HUSBAND?

When he gave me a lift! He is a taxi driver. After we married, we came to Lideta because it was cheap to rent and possible for us to start a family, but we do not like it here.

HOW CHEAP?

We pay 15–30 ETB per month for electricity, 80 ETB per month for rent, 2 ETB per month for Idr, and 10 cents for a bucket for water.

WHAT DON'T YOU LIKE ABOUT LIVING IN LIDETA?

So many families using a single toilet! In these conditions, it is impossible to stay healthy and clean. I do not like the filth.

Neither do I like the mud in the rainy season or the stink and the heat in the dry season.

SO, WHAT DO YOU THINK ABOUT THE RESETTLEMENT PLAN AND THE EVACUATION?

It is good! It is an improvement! We do not have money for the studio, but we will have in two years.

HOW?

By saving and working more. No meat. No clothes. I am looking for a second job. For a third one if necessary.

My husband and I agreed about it. We decided to go for it! It is for our children. We should do the best for them. They have to grow up in a condominium and not in a slum like this. We agreed that only by taking them out of the slum they will have a better future. This is our strength: the children.

DO THEY ALSO AGREE WITH YOU?

They like it here because of their friends. They are attached to the place and their neighbors. But they also like the idea of living in a house with a flush toilet. They do not talk about it but they are ashamed to use a common latrine while other school children have at toilet at home.

DID YOU EVER CONSIDER IMPROVING THE HOUSE YOU LIVE IN?

My husband wanted to do that, essentially by building another room. Many others did. At the time, NGOs provided financial support with microcredit for what was known as self-improvement housing and we were told that negotiations were going on with the government to give us property deeds. We were planning to do it when I got pregnant, but luckily we didn't go ahead. The families who improved their houses are now going to be evicted and they won't get compensation for what now the government calls "unauthorized extensions."

ELIAS

He looks like a child. A tired child with pointed eyebrows, grey stubble, and fingers that seem too short for his hands.

TELL ME ABOUT THE CHANGES IN ADDIS?

New roads and new buildings are reshaping the skyline of Addis. They prefer to push plans that are heavily dependent on engineering.

I will never forget what one little girl said when she came back from school and saw the house had been pulled down. She cried, 'what kind of human being can do that?'

DO YOU MISS YOUR HOUSE?

I miss the life I had there.

DO YOU VISIT THE DEMOLITION SITE?

When I cannot bear it any longer, I go there. I stand and look at the hole left by the demolition work. I am never alone. One or the other of us is always standing or sitting and looking. We start asking each other, where was the bed, where was the kitchen, where was the masop? Whose window was that one there? Where was the entrance? We point. We look. We know. We remember. We argue. The crater, the stones, the sand . . . it makes it so difficult to remember the space we used to occupy.

Did you see the little girl again?

Many children gather at that site. They have powerful memories and even more powerful minds.

THE SPACE IS STILL THERE, WHAT WAS LOST?

What is lost is the future. Which kind of future can bulldozers and destruction bring? Roads should unite towns, not dismantle relationships between people and the natural world and the close interpersonal connections that build our legacy. Land holds memories. Our houses will still be there even when we stop existing.

WHAT DOES THE RESETTLEMENT AREA LOOK LIKE?

They transfer people to places where there is no graveyard. Do they think we are immortal?

WHY SHOULD A BURIAL PLACE BE SO IMPORTANT?

Did you hear about the St. Joseph Cemetery?

The land is needed for development and families have to remove the remains of their relatives. Addis Ababa can expand in several directions and there is no shortage of land. So, it is not clear why the ruling junta is forcing hundreds of thousands, maybe millions, of families to go through the process of exhuming graves and reburying them in some plot of land on the road to Jimma.

Displacement, eviction, resettlement of the dead . . .
The St. Joseph Cemetery is about as old as the city of Addis Ababa and almost every resident of the city has some relative buried there.
We have been warned that bodies that are not moved by a certain date will be dumped in a mass grave. This is much worse than displacement!

HOW WOULD IT BE WORSE?
You can count back the generations. I can tell you who my relatives were up to my great-great-grandfathers and on. My daughter's children cannot. Family disintegration is what I fear most of all. We call displaced people tefenakkai— the uprooted. I am also seriously concerned about my funeral and whether it will take place at all.

HOW WOULD YOU LIKE YOUR FUNERAL TO BE?
Like a wedding party, but even bigger with people coming from all over the place. Good food. Excellent home-made honey drinks. A big tent to accommodate relatives, friends, travelers, neighbors, authorities, and children.
I would like them to get the best of me when I go. A farewell blessing for everybody.

HOW COULD YOU AFFORD SUCH A FUNERAL?
We have burial societies called Idrs that help when there is a death. Society members pay in money monthly.

WHERE ARE THE MEMBERS OF YOUR IDR NOW?
Dispersed.

ABRAHAM AND SAMIRA

Abraham 'won' a studio unit in the resettlement lottery. He needs 20,000 ETB. This is not happening without stress and great concern in his family.

HOW ARE YOU GOING TO GET 20,000 ETB ?
The children will come out of school for a year and help. They can make 200 ETB each as shoe cleaners.

HOW OLD ARE THEY?
A: The two going to school, who are six and eight, and the little imp in front of you who's four.
S: Tell her about Nuredin as well.
A: He left a month ago. His mother is

making a big deal out of that and telling me it's my fault. I am not worried. I did the same at his age, 12 years old. In Ethiopia, you are grown up at that age. When we get into the condominium he will come back.

WHY DID HE LEAVE THE FAMILY?

S: Food!
A: We take turns. The ones who have breakfast don't have lunch and dinner. If we have dinner, we do not have breakfast and lunch.
She is a great cook and we sell the food she makes to the construction workers. We started with coffee and it sold well. Now coffee beans have got too expensive and difficult to get. Our coffee is for export, not for Ethiopians!
S: We are borrowing too much money and it is starving us.

ARE YOU BORROWING FROM THE BANK?

A: The bank won't give us money. There are private lenders whose interest rates are very high, three or four times higher than the bank's. If you are poor, money is very expensive. If you are rich, money is cheap and everybody wants to lend to you. On the other hand, the private lenders are kind of flexible with time. You can extend the term with no problem. Also, there is no foreclosure if you fail to pay as happens with the bank.

There are associations too. I am a member of an iquib, but they won't lend you much money: no more than 300 ETB.

LET ME GET THIS RIGHT. BANKS ARE NOT PROVIDING YOU WITH FINANCIAL SERVICES. AT THE SAME TIME, THE GOVERNMENT CLAIMS YOU HAVE A RIGHT TO A LOW-INCOME HOUSING

UNITS. THE PROGRAM WAS ACTUALLY INTRODUCED FOR LOW-INCOME HOUSEHOLDS LIKE YOU, WHO LIVE IN PRECARIOUS HOUSING SITUATIONS.

A: What they say and what they do are two different things.
In Kebele, you pay very little rent and electricity for houses like this one. You can extend a small house by building yourself an additional room, for example to store goods for local shop-keepers, and you can get rent for that. You can burn wood at night to make charcoal and sell it.
S: You can convert a house window into a little kiosk. Women can roast corn and sell it to the neighbors without fear of being robbed and without having to go too far. They can keep their babies with them.

IN ADDIS, MORE THAN 80 PERCENT OF THE 1,150,000 GOVERNMENT HOUSES WERE CONSTRUCTED WITH MUD AND STRAW LIKE YOURS AND ARE OLDER THAN THEIR ESTIMATED LIFE SPAN OF 30 YEARS.

Yes . . . but look . . . we are living in it and we are getting better and better off. We are organized and we have associations for funerals, for saving money and for mending roofs. We have jobs, we have shops, we have churches, we have mosques, we have schools, and we have water. Why not improve the existing area and houses? Why not work together? Where will they find a new place for these people to stay? Where is the government going to settle all of them? They do not have enough money for the condominium and nobody is giving them that money. So where should they go? Where should they live? How should they live? Many have been pushed out of Addis to rural areas around the city.

They are sick. They have no food. They are dying. One, two, ten, . . . how many thousands of them? What is going on is slum clearance. Mass eviction. The difference between this and other slums in India, Kenyam, and Mexico is that Addis does not just have one slum to clear. Addis is one big slum!

YOU HAVE A BIG FAMILY, FOUR CHILDREN, A WIFE AND A MOTHER-IN-LAW. HOW CAN YOU FIT ALL OF YOU INTO A STUDIO?

A: We lie on the floor and it accommodates all of us.

WHAT DO YOU THINK ABOUT THE NEW BUILDINGS IN ADDIS?

A: It is good for the government. They get money for leasing our land. They get money for building permits. They get money from the banks. They get money from investors. They get money from foreign countries.

They say the Ethiopian government is at war against poverty. I say the Ethiopian government is at war against the poor.
S: Don't talk like that. The government will issue them with better shelters after they have demolished those houses. Then people will start living better, clean, and healthy lives.

LUBABA
A lady with a fresh outlook; but she is old, with a long way to go.

WHAT WOULD YOUR DREAM HOUSE BE LIKE?

Four square meters with water and electricity. A separate kitchen shelter for cooking traditional food.

LIKE THE HOUSE THAT YOU ARE BEING FORCED TO LEAVE?

I really do not ask for more. This is good enough for us. Especially the kitchen shelter. It is a space I use for working. I cook traditional food and sell it. The kitchen should be separate from the living area because of the smoke. If it is indoors the smoke causes serious health problems, such as eye, respiratory, and skin problems.

HOW DO YOU PREPARE FOOD FOR YOUR CUSTOMERS?

I start working at 3 a.m. I begin by simmered or sautéing a large amount of chopped red onion in a pot. Once the onions have softened I add Ethiopian butter, which is infused with ginger, garlic, and several spices.

WHAT IS THE MOST DIFFICULT TASK?

Keeping the food preparation and storage area clean and tidy. Cracks in the walls or floor can harbor insects and rodents. Leftover foods and dirt should be removed properly. Waste has to be burned or buried.

COULD YOU COOK TRADITIONAL FOOD IN A CONDOMINIUM KITCHEN?

For one thing, they won't allow me to work from home. Secondly, I have to use a smokeless stove and not charcoal. I cannot use electricity for injera baking, because it needs a much higher voltage. I mustn't make noise at night and wouldn't be able to prepare food on time for my customers. Lastly, I won't have enough room for food storage and food preparation.

COULD YOU AFFORD THE CONDOMINIUM?

I cannot afford the condominium and can also not afford to rent it.

HOW SHOULD A MODERN CITY ACCOMMODATE PEOPLE LIKE YOU?

Why be concerned with a modern future, when traditional Ethiopia is more compelling and unique?

WHAT DO YOU LIKE MOST?

People! Helping each other. Coming back home after church. Praying.

WHAT DON'T YOU LIKE?

Sitting and staying home during the day. I was working as waitress before, but I lost my job because I am old.

TAMRE

For a moment Tamre's smart and smiling face makes me forget about the suffering I am witnessing. As soon as he speaks, this nagging reality comes back.

DO YOU HAVE A DEED OR A TITLE?

Only a few people have full title deeds. Many more have customary land ownership, an informal rental arrangement. Even then any house that is not in line with the city's master plan and those living in it are illegal. The association tried to lease the same plot but in vain. With no property deeds, it is impossible to get compensation.

I have never stolen, offended a public official, or cut down a tree. I have never done anything against the law. Why do they say I am illegal?

IS THE DEMOLITION BECAUSE OF THE POOR QUALITY OF THE HOUSES?

This has something to do with the election; we are being punished for voting one way or another.

WHAT HAPPENED TO YOUR NEIGHBORS?

They had to move to a temporary place because the house in Bole Garage we owned is to undergo reconstruction. In other words, they have to add two extra floors to it by law.

WHAT IF THEY DON'T?

They will lose their rights as owners and the house will be given to someone else who is willing to build the two extra floors or even higher.

WHY DON'T YOU MOVE INTO THE CONDOMINIUM THAT YOU WON?

We cannot live there until our debts are paid off. We had to rent it out.

HOW LONG WILL IT TAKE FOR YOU TO PAY OFF THE CONDOMINIUM DOWN-PAYMENT?

Two years. Owning a house is our first priority. Then we won't pay rent and we'll save money.

CAN YOU AND YOUR FAMILY ADJUST TO LIVING IN A PLASTIC HOUSE FOR SO LONG?

Like many others, I once attempted to migrate to Saudi Arabia and I was held to ransom by traffickers twice. I managed to escape. I didn't think I was going to make it home. After my escape, I decided there was no place like home.

E L S A

There is nothing not to like on her calm face, which isassoftandpleasant as a cushion.

WHAT IS YOUR REACTION TO YOUR EVICTION?

I am so scared. I cannot sleep. I cannot eat. I cannot hug my children. They keep asking me about our house—I have to tell them that now it is in God's hands.

WHAT DO YOUR BOYS KNOW ABOUT THE EVICTION?

I did not tell them. I do not want them to worry.

THEY WILL DISCOVER SOON, WON'T THEY?

The later the better. They should focus on their studies. If they start thinking about it, they will lose their minds and concentration.

HAVE YOU LOST YOUR MIND?

They want 5,000 ETB. I can make 1,000 ETB at most. Which means no studio in the condominium for us. I guess my mind is working overtime.

WHO CAN YOU OPEN UP TO AND TALK ABOUT THIS?

What for? Which good does it do to make me to speak about it? Nobody is going to help me or listen to me anyway. If you start describing your problems to other people, they will tell you about their own.

If I say to them "I cannot pay and I do not know where to take my children, but I am a nurse and I have a job," another will say "I cannot pay either and I do not know where to take my children, but I have no job." Then another will say "I cannot pay and do not know where to take my children; I have no job and my children are sick." The poor have to help themselves!

IT IS A BIG BURDEN FOR YOU TO BEAR.

How long do I have left? Not long. I do not want to spoil it.

Coming home from work, that's what is great! Cooking food in my kitchen and having meals sitting at this table with my boys. Buying groceries in the Gherkose market, the best in Addis. Asking my friend Titzu to bake injera for us, because our injera stove is broken. Being woken by the song of the Deacons and praying before the sun rises. I love our church, Kidane Mhiret, so much! It is my church! It is where my husband and I got married. It is where I spend the night of Saint Gabriel.

There are plenty of reasons why I like it here. The location and the transport. From here I can jump on any taxi bus and go anywhere.

When I lost my husband, things got very hard. Tared is going to university now. There are rumors that demolition will start soon. All this could end at any moment. I cannot fool myself that it will not happen because I've seen it happening to other houses just two blocks from here. I saw everything. The people did not want to leave their houses. One night the police came and said there was a fire. For safety reasons, everybody had to run out of their houses and stay in the open: men, women, old people, children, and babies. They called it a fire emergency. It was an evacuation.

HOW BIG WAS THE FIRE?

There was smoke, but no fire. The smoke was white and coming out of a truck. Some people said it was an army truck. The houses were occupied by people who may not support the present government. I have the feeling that there is much more going on.

There are whispers of racially and politically motivated moves to rid the neighborhood of the influx of Eritreans.

SO, WHAT WILL YOU DO?

I will ask friends to store some of our things. I will sell what we cannot take with us. I will give away what we cannot sell. I will clean the house, close the windows, and leave.

WHAT DO YOU THINK ABOUT THE CITY DEVELOPMENT?

When I see the new constructions, my heart starts beating very fast and my mind races. I also like the city being crowded with so many new cars.

AREN'T YOU AFRAID TO BE ON THE STREET?

People can be separated from their places. People should not be separated from their people. I will stay with the people who are displaced like me and do what they do.

SAMSON

Salomon is thoughtful as he tells us his story, humming a happy tune.

WHAT'S LIKE MOVING INTO THE CONDOMINIUM?
I like it. I like it very much.

BETTER THAN YOUR FORMER HOUSE?
No, not better, but I like it here. Now we have only two rooms. In the old house, I had a bedroom all for myself.
I miss some other things. Mostly I miss my friends. And the crashing coffee noise is annoying.

WHAT IS BEST THEN?
It is modern! It feels modern. Moving here actually closed the gap that separated me from all the other young people in the world. It is about belonging and recognizing each other as one family.
I used to watch movies. The characters were the same age as me. They had the same problems and the same dreams, but somehow, I still could not be one of them. You know, I wouldn't have been able to tell them what I do, how I think, what I like, what I want to change. I guess it was still living in the past that made me feel they were so far away.

Now we have something in common and one day we could even meet. Why not?

HOW OLD ARE YOU?
I am sixteen. It's just two years before I go to University to study medicine.

For one thing, we will not celebrate my graduation here because there is no room for family and friends. Also, you aren't allowed to slaughter goats in the bathroom or in the kitchen even if people here still do it! I see them walking up the staircases with a live goat tied up and bleating.

WHAT IS LIFE LIKE IN THE CONDOMINIUM?
Kids shout as they play and it can be difficult to concentrate when studying. Children also enter apartments freely without knocking or asking. On the other hand, doors are kept open mostly for the heat and ventilation, but also for cultural reasons. In Kebele housing compounds, indoors and outdoors are the same thing during daylight hours.

HOW DID IT FEEL TO WIN THE LOTTERY?
When my parents applied for the lottery, we were not really hoping to win. It was just a trial and we did not even go to check if our name was on the winning list. It was a friend of my father who told us. He did not win himself, but he saw our name and called right away. That was a surprise. I think we were really happy: happy to win the lottery, happy to become owners of a studio in a condominium, happy to be so lucky. At the same time, we are sad for all the other people who did not win and have been evicted: our former neighbors and friends.

DO YOU THINK THE LOTTERY IS A GOOD SYSTEM FOR ASSIGNING PLACES IN THE CONDOMINIUM? IT IS RANDOM, HOW CAN IT BE?

A lottery is not a good system because, as I told you, our community got dispersed like many other in Addis. It's very unlikely for two people from same neighborhood to win a unit in the same condominium.

People like to be resettled in the area where they originally lived or, in the worst case, to move into a new area as a group. In this case, people can take their organization, their customs, their associations, their business, and their rules along with their furniture. Then they can continue to live the same life in the new place. Men, not lotteries, can provide places for those who've lost their homes. We are actually compelled to live an isolated existence now that we have lost our former communities. Lotteries are also not good because they are based on luck and are unfair to the losers.

CRITICAL

VERSATIO

ARCHIT

& HUMA

DURBAN

CHITECT

VERSA

b. CON-

ONS ON

ECTURE

N RIGHTS

(AR-

S' CON-

TIONS)

EDGAR

He wears eye-glasses with thick, yellow plastic frames. He could only be an architect.

IN THE FINAL ANALYSIS, WHY DO WE NEED MORE ARCHITECTURE?

The realm of design is not in the hands of architects, but in the hands of controlling authorities and economic powers. We should find ourselves fighting to provide better living conditions for the inhabitants of our cities, better services, homes, infrastructures, and economic development; fighting to provide present and future sustainability for the different population groups and communities.

Without restoring the discipline of design to a significant role and without empowering the participants of urban activity in the creation of the physical form of the city, we have what I described.

WE ARE SURROUNDED BY BEAUTIFUL ARCHITECTURE WHICH MAKES US AND THE GLOBE VULNERABLE.

To have a leading stance as an architect does not therefore mean to adhere solely to the wishes of the client, but to acknowledge and work with the desires and needs of these 'others.'

Civic infrastructure—like buildings and the spaces between them—are investments against risks and failure. In crises, buildings can perform to reduce vulnerability, but they should also be designed to strengthen the social capital of the community. There are the spatial instruments, such as architectural thinking, to orient or inspire dwellers toward each other. Because actually people don't want to live in a beautiful building. They want to live in a beautiful city.

ARCHITECTS MIGHT FIND THEMSELVES IN SITUATIONS IN WHICH GOVERNMENTAL BODIES ABUSE PLANS AND MASTER PLANS TO PROMOTE IDEOLOGICAL AGENDAS, THROUGH WHICH HUMAN RIGHTS ARE VIOLATED.
Urban residents feel the strains of a lost personal connection to the city; their cultural roots having been dismissed and their physical space transformed. As the physical environment is recreated in ways that ordinary citizens have no influence over, the spaces they occupy begin to lose their personal meaning.

OTHER THAN ABSTRACT, TECHNICAL DESIGN STANDARDS, LITTLE TO NO REFERENCE IS MADE TO QUALITY OF LIFE OR THE IMPORTANCE OF HUMAN RIGHTS IN THE BUILD SPACES.
Architects can facilitate a discussion and help a range of different voices articulate what they want to achieve.

As architects and planners making plans, master plans, spaces, buildings, and giving shape to people's living en-vironments, we find ourselves as major players, or master puppets of political planning, in this territorial conflict.

SHOULD WE BE MOVING TOWARDS A BROADER DEFINITION OF WHAT AN ARCHITECT'S OBLIGATION IS, SO THAT THOSE PEOPLE WHO COME INTO THE PROFESSION IN THE BROADEST SENSE, THROUGH SCHOOLS OF ARCHITECTURE, HAVE THE WIDEST OPPORTUNITY, AND THE WIDEST RANGE OF INFLUENCE?
The architecture practice is evolving in an exchange of ideas across disciplines and human experience and social strata.

I'll finish off now. In the post-globalized city, residences can essentially become engines in the movement of social and economic changes taking place through the physical environments they produce. Buildings express what a community is: its history, ambitions, issues, hopes, and constraints.

WE ARE EXPERIENCING A COMPLETE UPHEAVAL OF THE HUMAN CONDITION: THE GAP BETWEEN INFORMAL COMMUNITY, PRIVATE INVESTORS, AND GOVERNMENT; TOO MANY CONFLICTING INTERESTS AMONG CITY STAKEHOLDERS. CAN ARCHITECTURE FILL THESE GAPS?
Cities are not designed for people. They are not really designed at all. The cities are constructed to serve the needs of business. Citizens are a secondary concern. Architects often find that an obligation to a client's needs is at odds with the needs of the general public and need to take the courageous stand of challenging unreasonable client demands.

This is why we need more architecture and less power concentration in the hands of business and economic interests. Actually, we should be really energized by what is going on: The enormous diversity of people, all coming to in the same metropolis. Architecture means not simply buildings and public spaces, but also "the way people are in them."

SHOULD ARCHITECTS WHO TAKE THE COURAGEOUS STAND OF CHALLENGING UNREASONABLE CLIENT DEMANDS, BE GIVEN MORE AUTHORITY?

I always used to see the architect of the past as, you know, the leader, the absolute ship commander. But I think he's no longer driving; now he/she's become just a ship passenger. They're just one of the persons on board and you need to get back to being the captain again. Because no one else brings all this training, all these wider influences that we encounter all the time, their professional ethic, to the task. And no one else is better equipped to put that team together and to focus on everything, from the district to the door knob, from the micro to the macro, no one else is better equipped to do that. I think architects should just take the lead and recover that ground. Architects are best placed to pay attention to the site, its population, its history, and its resources. To give people the necessary skill sets that they will need to bring to the job and do whatever needs to be done.

Today the resolution of conflicts does not require an aesthetic decision, it requires action and negotiation to resolve situations in which competing principles and interests are at the core of the construction projects. I think this is the point at which we should add more architecture. We definitely need more architecture to generate social change—much more than the arrangement and design of buildings, public spaces, transport systems, services, and amenities. It concerns more than the arrangement, appearance and functionality of towns and cities, and the shaping and uses of urban public space.

MONICA

Her iPod earbuds are firmly in place even when she is speaking.

IN WHAT WAYS CAN ARCHITECTURE EMPOWER WOMEN RIGHTS?

I can tell you how you can violate women rights with architecture. That is more common.

I am terrible concerned with the Board of Health of the State of Virginia. They approved new laws deploying building codes and architectural regulations sanctioning that clinics offering first trimester abortions meet the same building specifications as newly-constructed, full-service surgical hospitals. I'm just amazed by their unrealistic and draconian views of how we're going to transition from a doctor's office that provides abortions to a surgical center.

SO STRINGENT RULES COULD FORCE MOST OR ALL 22 OF THE STATE'S ABORTION PROVIDERS TO CLOSE?

If the additional architecture was really about 'protecting women,' these building codes would extend to dermatologists and cosmetic surgeons' clinics, the largest consumers of cosmetic surgery.

Thousands of Virginia women, particularly low-income women, will lose affordable access not only to abortion care but to the comprehensive services like family planning and well-woman care that these centers provide. These excessive building regulations have nothing to do with the health, safety, and welfare of patients and everything to do with the politics of space. These are arbitrary and capricious building codes. The requirements include, for example, five-foot-wide public hallways, large janitor's closets and at least four parking spaces for each surgical room and an ambulance awning to shelter the entry doors.

HEALTHCARE ARCHITECTURE IS POSITIONED UNEASILY BETWEEN CORPORATE AND PUBLIC INTERESTS, SCIENCE AND CULTURE, AND POLITICS AND WOMEN'S RIGHTS. WOMEN SHOULD INQUIRE ABOUT ARCHITECTS AND ARCHITECTURE.

They will be surprised to identify the political implications of design and planning. It is incumbent upon architects as professionals to put the community's interests ahead of their own.

PATRIARCHAL REGULATION OF WOMEN'S BODIES AND FEMALE SEXUALITY HAS A TROUBLED HISTORY BUT DOCTORS HAVE AN ETHICAL DUTY TO PROTECT HUMAN RIGHTS AND HUMAN DIGNITY SINCE 1948 WITH THE DECLARATION OF GENEVA (PHYSICIAN'S OATH) WHEN THE WORLD MEDICAL ASSOCIATION TOOK THE RESPONSIBILITY FOR SETTING ETHICAL GUIDELINES FOR THE WORLD'S PHYSICIANS.

In Richmond, almost 200 physicians took a public stand, denouncing the politicians and urging the State of Virginia to reject the architectural alterations.

WHY NOT THE ARCHITECTS?

I do not know.

NOOLEN

Her eyes smil-
ing, she talks
rapidly, so fast
that you can
be caught up
in the motion
of her com-
ing thoughts.

Freedom of expression and public libraries! The design of a library is an
assignment par excellence, which is primarily not focused on the creation of an
exterior composition, a compilation of
facades, but which is especially focused
on designing the inner world. After projects such as the Bishan Library of Sin-
gapore, designed by LOOK Architects,
libraries around the world are heading
into the future, creating a more dynamic, multi-level environment for learning
and pleasure. For an architect, this is a
once-in-a-lifetime project.

**DO YOU KNOW THAT THE LIBRARY'S
MOST LOYAL BUT UNDERSERVED PATRONS
ARE THE HOMELESS?**

I guess it is easy to assume that homeless
populations use libraries as a safe place
to avoid the elements or to sleep.

They may take up space by sleeping in
the comfortable chairs, or they might
use the public restrooms to wash their
clothes or themselves. The conceptu-
alization needed would in this case go
toward the metaphor of libraries as a
refuge.

**WHAT ABOUT EMPOWERMENT? HOMELESS PEO-
PLE USE LIBRARIES PEACEFULLY AND APPROPRI-
ATELY. THEIR READING FOR ENTERTAINMENT AND
WEB ACCESS MAY BE CRUCIAL, IF THEY HAVE NO
PERMANENT ADDRESS AND NO CELL PHONE. IN
ADDITION TO E-MAIL, HOMELESS PEOPLE ARE US-
ING THE INTERNET FOR NEWS, SOCIAL NETWORK-
ING, AND TO STORE PERSONAL FILES.**

In situations where they might otherwise lose dignity, trust, self-esteem, safety, and hope, empowerment processes
should definitely be factored into design.

**AND WHAT ABOUT THE SMELL OF FOUL ODORS?
NO, I AM NOT TRYING TO BE RUDE; I JUST WANT
TO EMPHASIZE THE IMPORTANCE THAT ARCHI-
TECTURAL DESIGN AND ITS COMPONENTS CAN
FORM DIFFERENT TYPES OF VENTILATION BASED
ON THE ARCHITECTURAL SYNTHESIS OF EACH
BUILDING.**

The effect of natural ventilation on architectural design produces a new approach to the architectural design process and leads to an innovative kind of
architecture called 'breathing architecture.' Consider the aspects of space design that offer comfort and encourage
learning, such as access to daylight, the
use of natural materials, comfortable
seating, and places that provide shelter,
e.g., booths or nooks, and are composed

of environmentally healthy finishes. The perception of the materials used, the details, the scale, the contrast between light and dark, open versus closed, are all heightened by movements within the structure you design. Exploiting the space potential of noise segregation. Also, the contemplative is an important aspect in the design of the interior of the library. Libraries are our heritage. They contain all knowledge that humankind has acquired. Libraries are the avant-garde of civilization. They have to evolve, and look accommodate people, not only books.

PUBLIC LIBRARIES AND HUMAN RIGHTS ARE IN-EXTRICABLY BOUND. TAKE FREEDOM OF EXPRESSION. SUCH FREEDOM IS EXTENDED TO THE RIGHT EVERY OF US HAS OF ACCESSING INFORMATION AND A DIVERSITY OF OPINIONS.

The crucial importance of inclusive architectural design in challenging inequalities and making spaces accessible to all is about discovering new perspectives and features on the structure of the design! Building new libraries, additions, and even remodeling can be a daunting task. Why not also install some storage areas, locker rooms, and showers in the basements of the libraries? That way homeless people can clean up a bit and store their belongings before sitting down to read. They are members of the public and are entitled to use the libraries just like everyone else.

THE CORE TASK IS THE REMOVAL OF ALL BARRIERS TO LIBRARY AND INFORMATION SERVICES FOR EVERYBODY?

I first have in mind a space that can address the needs of all the patrons. For example, children need places where they can regroup to rest their eyes, their bodies, and their minds, and a space where it is okay to do so. So, let's set out fixtures that encourage movement and activity, while fostering imagination.

ARTICLE NUMBER 19 SAYS: EVERYONE HAS THE RIGHT TO FREEDOM OF OPINION AND EXPRESSION; THIS RIGHT INCLUDES FREEDOM TO HOLD OPINIONS WITHOUT INTERFERENCE AND TO SEEK, RECEIVE, AND IMPART INFORMATION, AND IDEAS THROUGH ANY MEDIA AND REGARDLESS OF FRONTIERS.

In short, the aim is to go beyond a library that is merely transactional—a place where you go simply to check out a book—and to create a library that truly transforms lives.

VICTOR

Legs crossed and eyes opened, his back upright; he is the stray waiting for the coming challenge.

WHY DID THE AMERICAN INSTITUTE OF ARCHITECTS INITIALLY REJECT A PROPOSED AMENDMENT TO ITS EXISTING ETHICS CODES ON HUMAN RIGHTS?

The assumption that all AIA members would refrain from designing spaces involving human rights violations is not clear. When do such violations occur?

IT WAS IN THE PETITION. ARCHITECTS CAN FACILITATE THE SUFFERING AND THE DEATHS OR THEY CAN PREVENT THE MISTREATMENT OF THOSE HELD IN SUCH PLACES BY THEIR REFUSAL TO DESIGN THEM.

How do you enforce it? There is not a clear answer to that. That's the reason why it has been rejected. The code of ethics must provide members and the public with strong and clearly stated guidance concerning the lawful and ethical practice of architecture.

Let's take, for instance, the architectural design specifically intended for execution or for torture or other cruel, inhuman, or degrading treatment or punishment, including prolonged solitary confinement. Although architecture used for purposes in violation of human rights is obvious in cases such as execution chambers, it is more difficult to recognize in other situations, such as defining what constitutes prolonged solitary confinement.

WHY DID THE AMERICAN INSTITUTE OF ARCHITECTS RECONSIDER ITS PREVIOUS REJECTION?

Enforceability at the end has not dissuaded the institution from pursuing more clearly defined rules, as the mistreatment of those held in such places could be prevented by architects' refusal to design them. The AIA has highlighted suicides brought on by the psychological distress of solitary confinement, remarking that architecture facilitates this suffering and could expedite these deaths.

MY FUNDAMENTAL QUESTION IS: SHOULD ARCHITECTS REFRAIN FROM DESIGNING SPACES INVOLVING HUMAN-RIGHTS VIOLATIONS OR NOT?

If you refer to the design of execution chambers, interrogation rooms intended for torture, and 'supermax' security prisons in which prolonged solitary confinements take place, they are now amended into the ethics codes.

On closer inspection, the right to live is linked to all the others. The loss of one's life deprives one of all the freedom, experiences, activities, projects, and enjoyments which would otherwise have constituted his/her future.

In the past architecture has provided technical support and spaces for colonization, apartheid planning, encampment, and other forms of violence. Yes, I agree with you. But it cannot happen all in once.

GERHARD

His eyes click while the mind scans the list of options that appear for a n s w e r i n g.

TALK TO ME ABOUT URBANIZATION AND CHILD MIGRATION.

Urbanization starts with the journey of rural girls and boys that go into town. It sounds promising and romantic.

Child migration is a strategy for moving out of poverty. It is often a risky investment, it has low short-term returns, has the potential to end in disaster, exposes children to exploitation and trafficking, hard labor, and abuse. And it is the engine of urbanization. This does not involve ideas such as family or professional migrations, or multiple breadwinners, the way we think of them. This is not about working adults. It involves youths under 18 years old and they will make up 60 per cent of urban populations by 2030.

Now focus on this number and tell me what you think. Where do they go? Where do they sleep? What do they eat? What do they drink? Where do they play? Where do they learn? How do they sustain themselves?

They are invisible and vulnerable. They come to improve their schooling and work opportunities, enabling them to build more secure futures for themselves and their families. They often end up with an illegal broker and working an average of 64 hours per week and earn an average of $5 monthly. Many who make the trip are minors left stranded far from home.

I am thinking of the need for temporary housing for young migrants. Because of its simple structure and minimal material pallet, we will be able to put up a structure in just 25 days using an unskilled volunteer workforce. And it can also be quickly dismantled and removed. I am also thinking about safety public spaces and recreation sports facilities.

Inadequate living conditions are among the most pervasive violations of children's rights. The lack of decent and secure housing, and such infrastructure as water and sanitation systems, makes it so much more difficult for children to survive and thrive. Hidden inside cities are millions of children struggling to survive. The urban crises we are facing is not demographic; it is an architectural crisis.

In terms of the key drivers of Africa's urbanization, child migration is one of the most important, together with fertility, and life-expectancy. Despite the hardship and deprivation, migrant children are our future.

Street infrastructure is becoming not just a place of people and vehicles, of trade and collective, but also the space of child survival. It is a new urban world reversing our perception that residential architecture should house families, professionals, and the working class.

Children whose needs are greatest are also those who face the greatest violations of their rights. The rights of every child include survival; development to the fullest; protection from abuse, exploitation, and discrimination; and full participation in family, cultural, and social life.

Why has this extraordinary, vast reverse in the demography of our cities not changed our way of building yet?

MANY ARE PREYED UPON BY HUMAN TRAFFICKERS WHO OFTEN LEAVE THEM STRANDED, OR WORSE HOLD THEM FOR RANSOM. CHILDREN ARE VULNERABLE TO EXPLOITATION OF ALL KINDS, FROM RECRUITMENT BY ARMED GROUPS TO BEING FORCED INTO CHILD MARRIAGE OR HAZARDOUS WORK.
IF CHILDREN'S HUMAN RIGHTS ARE DENIED, WHAT SORT OF OPPORTUNITIES WOULD BE DENIED TO THEM?

There is no effective right to play without a safe place to play, no enjoyment of health within a contaminated environment, no right for shelter without a roof.

No city can fulfill every hope and desire, let alone every human right, of its inhabitants, so it helps to know which matter most to the majority. So, it's vital to speak to the youth and the children coming from rural villages into the urban settlement. Investing in the capital of children will create a self-sustaining cycle of urban improvement. Children's rights could be an umbrella and we could find our own 'architecting' within it: starting with temporary housing for them that is safe, affordable, and an asset to the surrounding community. The opportunity to actually shape the new city paradigm is, I think, a big responsibility.

CAN CHILDREN'S HUMAN RIGHTS PUSH ARCHITECTURE PERFORMANCE INTO NEW TERRITORY?
Building children's communities that work, that are sustainable and are socially cohesive is vital. They must be built on the bond that unite these children rather than on what separates them. This is an absolutely new challenge. Survival is much more than accessible food and shelter. For these migrant children, it must include a sense of belonging and cohesion where resources are scarce and where myths and stereotypes are promoted about newcomers, which fuel a sense of mistrust.

ALVAR

You can tell his critical mind from the n o n - s t e r e o - typed, non-urban, chic architect's look on his intelligent and bitter face.

IS THERE A BLIND SPOT FOR HUMAN RIGHTS AT THE LEVEL OF YOUR PROFESSION? IS THIS ANOTHER TRIAL TO MODERNIZE AND REINVENT THE PROFESSION BY MAKING USE OF OUR EXPERTISE IN THE UNBUILT?
I have in mind the sphere of influence that an architect has for example in the physical/spatial dimensions of urban areas, and the role of cultural diversity in terms of ethnicity, language, gender, sexuality, etc. in either bridging or reinforcing the urban divide. There is no such thing as racial or sexist architecture. There are racial and sexist people.

There is a substantial body of research devoted to understanding the relationship between urbanization and human-rights performance. Architecture is a solution not simply in terms of needs, but in terms of society's obligation to respond to the rights of individuals.

Each profession seeks the social good in a different form, according to its particular expertise: doctors seek it in the form of health; lawyers seek it in the form of justice; and architects in the form of safe, efficient buildings.

While it is hard to find an architect who would express objections to the concepts of sustainability, we certainly find architects, engineers, and planners—development decision-makers—who, through their actions, actually do subvert these concepts, partly by setting other priorities and partly by a lack of knowledge of the relationship between their actions and these concepts.

Buildings should be shaped according to rules that can be justified on a logical and scientific basis, and not by philosophy or dogma, or even humanity. I must think about a building's style, safety, and sustainability to ensure it meets all the requirements of state regulators. As a licensed professional, I am also responsible for public safety.

Your obligation can be interpreted more widely. I think. It can involve more than the requirement to save people from disaster. It implies a radically egalitarian obligation.
After all, if architecture would allow us to protect all human rights of all people all of the time, how come we're not there yet?

ALBERT SPEER WAS AN ARCHITECT MUCH TO THE SHAME OF THE PROFESSION FOR HIS DESIGN OF ABHORRENT NAZI SLAVE LABOR CAMPS.

You are using the general concept of human rights to add weight to your inconsistent arguments. Albert Speer was a Nazi! He was an architect, but he could have been as well a medical doctor, a writer, a soldier. Human rights refer to binding international human-rights laws; and it is up to states to respond to the violation of these laws.

Contrary to human rights violations, there is no legal standard prohibiting an unjust and grossly unequal urban planning. What's next? Shall architects be banned from designing buildings that sell guns? Buildings that perform domestic violence? The building is not the issue. Their uses are.

Architecture is not a sufficient condition, although probably a necessary one, at least in terms of urbanization, for the implementation of the full set of human rights, and for the equal enjoyment of all rights by all people.

I cannot do anything about it, because I have no power to do anything about it.

WELL-DEVELOPED AND INCLUSIVE PLANS DO BETTER AND PROVIDE A WIDE RANGE OF OPPORTUNITIES FOR URBANIZATION, DON'T THEY?

These consist of political goals and policies. Not architecture.

Economic, social, and cultural human rights involve immediate obligations in three ways regardless of resources: non-discrimination; obligation 'to take steps' and to ensure the core minimum of rights. But do I have a social obligation that extends beyond my practice?

It lies in part in believing that architecture can create better places, that architecture can affect society, and that it can even have a role in making a place civilized by making a community more livable.

Modernism was a political ideology, combining philosophical ideas. It is perhaps the only style in history that ignores the human use of buildings.

ALINA

She has long dyed-black hair twisted over one shoulder and huge brown eyes that blink inquiringly at the crowd.

HOW CAN DESIGN AND ARCHITECTURE PROMOTE EQUALITY?

Promoting equality for all is a vast subject matter and concerns various issues such as race, ethnicity, nationality, class, disability, age, sexuality, and gender. Often these issues cross lines and create complex intersections of discrimination.

Ideology and culture form the basis for how things are designed. The ideas about gender roles are a part of that ideology and therefore a part of our designed world. Bathrooms are explicitly gendered, alienating those who don't conform.

WHO GIVES INSIGHT INTO THE TOILETTE SPATIAL CONTEXT OF HUMAN GENDER IDENTITY?

Individuals who don't conform to stereotypical notions of gender often struggle when faced with two restroom doors, one marked male, one marked female.

It's a form of exclusion that's written into state building code, presenting an obstacle for gender-neutral bathroom advocates. Yet the need to pick and conform to a particular gender identity is embedded in the way we design buildings around segregated restroom facilities.

TRANSGENDER PEOPLE ARE AT RISK OF HARASSMENT AND VIOLENCE WHEN THEY NEED TO USE PUBLIC FACILITIES.

They are still often met with ridicule from a society that does not understand them. This stigma plays out in a variety of contexts leaving them vulnerable.

MORE INCLUSIVE ARCHITECTURE—RETROFITTING OR ADDING GENDER NEUTRAL BATHROOMS THAT ARE DELIBERATELY MADE ACCESSIBLE TO EVERYONE, WHETHER OR NOT THEY IDENTIFY AS MALE OR FEMALE—WOULD HELP.

Building design has long been used to spatially enforce gender stereotypes. Despite modern attitudes about the sharing of parental duties, men's rooms still frequently lack changing tables.

WHAT ABOUT A BATHROOM EQUIPPED FOR EVERYONE'S NEEDS, REGARDLESS OF GENDER, AGE, OR PHYSICAL ABILITY? FOR THE MOST PART, THIS MEANS SINGLE STALL, LOCKING RESTROOMS—WHICH ALSO BENEFIT PEOPLE WITH DISABILITIES, PARENTS ASSISTING CHILDREN, AND OTHERS.

Gendered toilette is a form of exclusion that's written into state building codes. Transgender people come from all walks of life. They are dads and moms, brothers and sisters, sons and daughters. They are your coworkers and your neighbors. While visibility is increasing, they still face discrimination, stigma, and inequality.

People experience the built environment differently according to who they are.

SO, A BATHROOM IS NOT JUST A BATHROOM, WHETHER THE LITTLE FIGURE ON THE DOOR WEARS A DRESS OR PANTS?

The transgender community still faces considerable stigma based on over a century of being characterized as mentally ill, socially deviant, and sexually predatory. They represent all racial and ethnic backgrounds, as well as faith backgrounds. The full diversity of this experience needs to be considered if all of us are to be comfortable and feel that a public bathroom or place is a place that I can use. That all can say "it is for me."

RODNEY

He has the long, sculpted fingers of a thinker, and he has left them abandoned and still on the cover surface of the UIA program.

CAN ARCHITECTURE PREVENT GENOCIDE?

Conditions in African cities are now the most unequal in the world. They are already inundated with slums and a tripling of urban populations could spell disaster. Clearly cities can be place of huge pain and conflicts. Globalization, standardization, and high-speed innovations are transforming urban centers such as Jimma, Mbabane, Addis Ababa, Lagos, Juba, and many others.

The array of conflicts driven by these transformations is bewildering. The intensity of the violence often stunning. Armed confrontations have erupted throughout Africa over such issues as: diversity of identities and values, in particular with reference to ethnicity and religion; displacement of communities; tensions between traditional and modern practices; police-related violence; land; environmental damage; political power and offices; economic power and opportunities; renewable natural resources, including livestock forage, wood stocks, and fisheries; 'slums' and the boom of construction. Real estate development and luxury urban living are integrally related: both are products of the social relations and dynamics of neoliberal transformation in Africa.

What is not so clear, perhaps to any of us, is the extent to which architects and urban planners have been complicit in this misfortune. They may be complicit by privileging spaces of luxury over spaces of necessity; or by privileging individual expression over the cultural roots of the residents.

DOES THE RESPONSIBILITY TO PROTECT GIVE THE PROFESSIONAL A DUTY FOR THEIR DESIGN TO PROTECT CITIZENS FROM MASS ATROCITY?

The relegation of design to luxury status, the construction of tourist heritage, the use of African forms to proclaim national and nationalist identities is indicative of the utter disregard the design profession has shown towards its potential role in society, shrugging off the opportunity to generate better, more appropriate designs in the developing city.

Urban residents feel the strains of a lost personal connection to their cultural roots, having been dismissed and their physical space transformed. Attaining Africa's aspirations in the creation of a global, urbanized context will require bold new ethics in building.

The surest way to prevent genocide would be to see it coming. Legally, genocide is oddly defined—why is it worse to seek to eliminate an ethnic group than a socio-economic one? It is also hard to prove. In the next ten to fifteen years the population of Nairobi could double, while Addis Ababa is expected to grow by over 60 percent. Lagos will become the largest city on the continent, surpassing Cairo. The message these statistics convey is clear: African architects cannot afford to ignore the rapid urban transition taking place across the continent. They should not only address physical urban inequalities, but seek to counter individual and group-based feelings of historic grievance, marginality, disempowerment, and discrimination. The biggest threat to sustainable development in Africa is rapid and chaotic urbanization, because it is a recipe for disaster in terms of increased tensions and pressure. Architecture should be part of the solution!

OUTSIDERS OFTEN ASSUME THAT IN RWANDA THE GENOCIDE SPRANG SPONTANEOUSLY FROM PRIMEVAL, ETHNIC ANTAGONISM.

We often assume that the genocide springs spontaneously from primeval, ethnic antagonism. On the contrary, it was planned over many months. Militias have to be organized, machetes bought and distributed, and Hutu peasants persuaded, through skillful propaganda, that all Tutsis were their enemies.

The residential settlement can offer a framework for the smaller family network, provided that social ties reach beyond the walls of the dwelling, integrat-

ing poor and rich into society. In such a way, neighborhoods can start to fulfill social as well as practical needs.

Social cohesion matters for our survival. Social cohesion can be an important tool in the arsenal of genocide prevention. If architects value prevention instead of permanence, buildings could reduce vulnerability rather than increasing risks. Such a reorientation of values could radically improve our cities and our lives. There are the spatial instruments, such as design where dwellings are orientated toward each other. Social cohesion can be measured using three item clusters: how well people know their neighbors (Integration); whether they undertake activities together (Together); and to what extent they rely on each other in time of need (Help).

As I said, social cohesion can be an important tool in the arsenal of genocide prevention because social cohesion matters for our survival. Buildings can perform to reduce vulnerability, but they should be designed to strengthen the social capital of the community. In contrast, consolidation of ethnic territoriality and identity should be the guiding criterion wherever there exist 'hard' interfaces of strict definition, lingering violence, and the presence of ethnic militia guardians.

WHERE DOES THE PROCESS OF RECONCILIATION BEGIN, WITH WHOM, AND WHEN? THESE QUESTIONS CAN BE PUT INTO A DISCUSSION ON ARCHITECTURE?

Reconciliation is part of architecture! In order for the seed of urban stability and co-existence to grow, the public sphere should be developed physically. We are faced with a challenging dilemma—to respond to group wishes and to sharpen territorial identity or to focus on the commonalities of the city and lessen divisions. In the long term, will simply living together eliminate former enmity? I do not think so! It is crucial for us to explore architecture's role in addressing oppression and conflict and to consider how spaces for reconciliation can be created. While many factors are at play, and a multi-pronged approach is needed to reduce conflict, physical space provides opportunities to focus on the commonalities between groups and to work toward coexistence.

This ability to accommodate a diverse range of social and political structures makes architecture and landscape an extremely significant factor in achieving reconciliation. Space sharing, for instance, can bring opposing factions together in a neutral and inclusive environment. It is a place that offers freedom without 'assimilation.' In cities of increasingly circumscribed social, racial, or economic enclaves, space sharing has come to both symbolize and provide neutral territory, a ground where people can gather on a common plane.

HOW DO SUCH PLACES LOOK LIKE?
In spaces constructed to encourage interaction, there should be an absence of undesirable, intimidating, and single-group-identifying artifacts. Instead, there should be functional and aesthetically equal treatment for different ethnic users of such facilities, so that they become multicultural community centers. In terms of specific project or building design, there should be dual entry/exit ways for antagonistic communities so that a facility is perceived by all as located in shared space, but is nonetheless functionally connected to ethnic space on either side. These should be places free of aggression, conflicts, and tensions. They are spaces for meeting and dialogue, designed with respect for all people's identity, for their dissimilarity and diversity, with a sense of tolerance and love for one another.

Architects are faced with a challenging dilemma—to respond to group wishes and sharpen territorial identity or to focus on the commonalities of the city and lessen divisions. Reconciliation through architecture and landscape design can take many forms. In some urban districts, connectivity across the ethnic divide is a suitable goal; in others, consolidation of ethnic neighborhoods should be the preeminent concern.

In post-conflict situations, reconstruction must not solely be physical, but also address the social and psychological scars that remain after the active conflict period ends. Instead of focusing on the inflammatory choice between segregation versus integration of residential areas, concentration on improving public spaces offers a third, less politically difficult approach. Many immediate and existential foundations of inter-group conflict frequently lie in daily urban life and across local ethnic divides and, importantly, it is at this micro level that antagonisms can be most directly influenced by architecture interventions aimed at their amelioration.

...IF ARCHITECTS VALUE PREVENTION INSTEAD OF PERMANENCE?

As I said, social cohesion matters for our survival and social cohesion can be an important tool in the arsenal of genocide prevention. We often assume that genocide springs spontaneously from primeval ethnic antagonism. On the contrary, it is planned over many months. The small gang of Hutus who organized the genocide were rational men in pursuit of a rational—albeit evil—objective. They wanted to stay in power, and they harnessed ethnic hatred as a means to that end. So, once again, the question is: Why is it worse to seek to eliminate an ethnic group than a socio-economic one?

PHILA
Her passion and empathy are shown in the flaring of her nostrils with each breath.

WHAT DOES ARCHITECTURE DO TO FIGHT HUNGER?

Farming can start in some of the most unusual places. Existing urban buildings and structures can be adaptively reused for incorporating agricultural technologies to produce food for urban populations.

Let's keep in mind that in 2050 nine billion people will live in cities. Architects may be one of the first to look at how to use design to maximize food production and incorporate agriculture into cities.

Architecture doesn't have any obligation to deliver food, but it can create an environment that enables people to exercise their right to adequate food without any discrimination and to use all available resources.

EVERYBODY SHOULD CONSTANTLY HAVE PHYSICAL AND ECONOMIC ACCESS TO ADEQUATE FOOD OR THE MEANS FOR ITS PROCUREMENT.

If every household had a garden space either on their property or in a community-owned space growing local wild and semi-wild greens along with a few fruit trees and bushes, they would indeed be well fed, and able to take on even more global problems, with their exceptionally nourished bodies and minds.

Rising food prices hinder poor people's ability to feed themselves at an acceptable cost.
A new paradigm is emerging for eco-system based, territorial food-system planning. This new paradigm seeks to build diverse supplies of food geographically close to population centers: that's urban agriculture. But I like to call it agro-architecture. And so far, we've not had to ask anybody for permission to do this.

ULTIMATELY, HUNGER IS A HUMAN-RIGHTS VIOLATION.

Hunger is imposed on people as an active act of discrimination and marginalization. We need a vision for the future that goes beyond short-term fixes. As you said, hunger is also an architecture question, not just an economic problem. Take, for example, the agro-architecture solutions proposed by Brooklyn Grange, the group of urban farmers determined to run a commercially viable farm in New York City.

Hundreds of families living in 'slums' produce their own vegetables right inside their homes in micro gardens using a curious array of containers including recycled water bottles, old tires, and trays. Unfortunately, many residents, authorities, architects viewed these agricultural activities as a nuisance.

The feeding of humanity, the majority of which now lives in cities worldwide, involves a complex system of ecological, social, and structural thinking. Cities suffer from floods, dust encroachment, water shortage, soil erosion, and landslides associated with significant costs in terms of lost infrastructure and human deaths. The sustainability of agriculture in and around cities depends of the watershed and landscape management.

The world is shaped by food. We need a reconceptualization of the city that is shaped by food security. But it does demand that we think things differently. Agriculture and cities need each other! They have to come together. We need open-to-air structures that are purely focused on farming activities and sustainable functions, such as generating renewable energy and performing air, and water filtration. We must integrate organic, hydroponic, aeroponics or aquaponic farming technologies into buildings of all types: single-family home, multi-family housing, mixed-use buildings, schools, restaurants, institutional buildings, as well as vertical farms, hoop houses, and greenhouses that are designed for urban conditions. Instead of tacking greenery onto roofs and balconies, we can also incorporate agriculture into cities by dedicating entire buildings to the cause and bringing acres of crops into the dwelling habitat.

CAN WE FIND AN ARCHITECTURE THAT CUTS ACROSS POVERTY AND CITY DWELLING THAT WILL HELP PEOPLE TO FEED THEMSELVES AND FIND A NEW WAY OF LIVING?

If we can use space around buildings differently, can we think about the resources they use differently, can we learn, through architecture, to interact and access food differently?

If we can start a community that encourages farming and spinning, and promotes the growing of fruits and trees through community involvement, we can really start to feed people in need. This would be food self-reliance, with which we could really challenge the enormous inequities that exist in the food systems of both poor and rich countries by the empowering of people and their rights.

AND WHAT ABOUT FISH FARMING?

Urban livestock keeping has been in existence for many years, and despite perceptions to the contrary, it may even make a comeback thanks to its various roles such as effective utilization of empty plots, cleaning up of waste, and the provision of both fresh food and income.

JEAN JACQUES

His spoken words seemed hushed and were oblivious to my ears.

IS DISPLACEMENT AN ARCHITECTURE ISSUE?

And the answer would appear to be yes, and the reason would appear to be city renewal. Most of European capitals were once ringed with large shack settlements. We tend forgetting people will adapt and overcome.

DON'T YOU FIND THAT IT IS ESPECIALLY CONTROVERSIAL TO BELIEVE THAT 'EVICTION,' INTIMIDATION, LAND CONFISCATION, CAN PRODUCE BEST SAFE EFFICIENT BUILDINGS? OR THAT GOOD ARCHITECTURE CAN BE DESIGNED WITHOUT ANY PARTICULAR CONCERN FOR HUMAN RIGHTS?

Don't get me wrong I care a lot and anytime I have an opportunity I support organizations such as Amnesty International and the like. I just do not see how realistic and viable are your claim on architecture as such.

NOT THAT RENEWALS AREN'T NECESSARY, BUT THEIR CURRENT IMPLEMENTATION INTENDS TO

OCCUPY AND INTIMIDATE. EVICTION AND FORCED DISPLACEMENT CREATE MORE SUFFERING AND DEATH THAN MALARIA AND WAR.

Is any specific human right to protection against forced displacement as such?

IT IS INHERENT IN A NUMBER OF HUMAN RIGHTS, INCLUDING THE RIGHT TO RESPECT FOR THE HOME AND FOR PRIVACY, THE RIGHT TO AN ADEQUATE STANDARD OF LIVING, INCLUDING FOOD AND HOUSING, AND THE RIGHT TO RESPECT FOR THE FAMILY. EVICTION IS ALWAYS CARRIED OUT IN A MANNER THAT VIOLATES THE RIGHTS TO LIFE, DIGNITY, LIBERTY, AND SECURITY OF THOSE AFFECTED.

Frankly: my work is about fulfilling a contract to encompass the design, construction, respecting zoning requirements and operation of buildings.

FORCED DISPLACEMENT IS NOT JUST A PASSING EVENT IN PEOPLE'S LIVES. IT IS A DEVASTATING TRANSFORMATION. IT MEANS THAT FROM ONE DAY TO THE NEXT FAMILIES LOSE THEIR HOMES AND LIVELIHOODS AND ARE FORCED TO LEAVE BEHIND ALL THEY HAD CHERISHED.

Do I have the mandate, the capacity, or the resources to physically protect displaced individuals and communities as architect?

THE DESIGN PROCESS COULD ACTUALLY HELP YOU TO ANTICIPATE POSSIBLE RISKS DURING THE DESIGN AND DETAILING OF A PROJECT. BECAUSE OF EVICTION THESE RISKS MAY INCLUDE: HYENA'S ATTACK; ABUSE WHILE IN SEARCH OF SHELTER; FAMILY SEPARATION, INCLUDING AN INCREASE IN THE NUMBER OF SEPARATED AND UNACCOMPANIED CHILDREN; HEIGHTENED RISK OF SEXUAL AND GENDER-BASED VIOLENCE; ARBITRARY DEPRIVATION OF LAND, HOMES, AND OTHER PROPERTY; AND DISPLACEMENT INTO

INHOSPITABLE ENVIRONMENTS, WHERE THEY SUFFER STIGMAS, MARGINALIZATION, DISCRIMINATION, OR HARASSMENT.

Architecture can fix a problem. Architecture can worsen a problem.

AN ABSOLUTE EVICTION IS THE WORST FAILURE OF ARCHITECTURE.

When it comes to visuality, buildings are indeed something to look at; the first thought to come to mind when you think of a city is its skyline.

Now you tell me I should seize opportunities rather than remaining passive. I could even resolve human-rights dilemmas.

And in order to do that I should find the right approach, identifying intervention, being creative, and making decisions that are in the best interests of people. An inventive process, especially one that recognizes and develops local narratives, can facilitate or even inspire design outcomes.

That makes architecture pretty much a perfect field to prove our humanity, intellectual abilities and worldliness.

PETER

When he says yes, you see the street. When he says no, you see the horizon.

AFTER THE 'AGE OF DISCOVERY,' WHICH HAS BROUGHT WITH IT ALSO A DISRUPTION OF THE ENVIRONMENT, ARE ARCHITECTS NOW FACING THE 'AGE OF URBAN RESPONSIBILITY'?

New York became the greenest community in the United States, and one of the greenest cities in the world. The key to New York's relative environmental success is its extreme compactness. Manhattan's population density is more than 800 times that of the nation as a whole. Placing one and a half million people on a twenty-three-square-mile island sharply reduces their opportunities to be wasteful. The city is the most environmentally benign form of human settlement and it is not hard to think that it can also be the most sustainable socially benign form of habitat. Not just ecologically. In other words, let's pay more attention to the role of communities in creating and enhancing sustainability. Failure to do this is increasingly being recognized as a critical stumbling block to the sustainable growth and prosperity of cities; this brings to the fore the pivotal role of architecture in delivering 21st-century cities of sustainable communities.

DO WE REALLY NEED HUGE, BRAND NEW CITIES, BUILT FROM SCRATCH, FOR EXPANSION OF A CONSUMER LIFESTYLE? WHAT CAN THIS KIND OF DEVELOPMENT POSSIBLY DO TO NURTURE COMMUNITY AND PRODUCTIVITY?

Yes, we do! Cities are so much more successful in promoting new forms of income generation, and it is so much cheaper to provide services in urban areas, that the only realistic poverty-reduction strategy is to get as many people as possible to move to the city. The goal is to eliminate poverty? That is possible. The task is to minimize the consequences of architecture on poverty and to remove obstacles in places that disadvantage the poor and marginalize them. We are still strongly influenced by urban 'developmentalism,' which emphasizes 'the city as growth machine' and de-emphasizes redistribution.

HOW ABOUT HUMAN RIGHTS THROUGH ARCHITECTURE?

I think that's one thing that's really up in the air and we struggle to define really what the services should provide. Slum upgrading, slum prevention; formal and informal housing markets; Gender equality and shelter; participatory urban management; cultural pluralism and tolerance; empowerment and participatory planning.

I don't think of myself as an architect, I think of myself as a creative problem solver. Good architecture is intentioned. It somehow touches the people who use it and live in it . . . it somehow touches the human soul. I realize these phrases sound somewhat exaggerated, but truly good architecture has the ability to relate to individuals in a very profound way. There is an interaction, an overlapping between environmental sustainability and social equity, as well as social and environmental sustainability. There might be the link between architecture and human rights.

The future depends less on building and more on how we manage scarcity and conflict.

We do not live on this planet.
We live with this planet.

SINDILE
Her eyes express the joy in her heart which reaches all the way to the ceiling of the conference hall.

YOU HAVE SAID THAT SLUMS AND SHANTYTOWNS ARE PLACES OF SURPRISING INNOVATION?
The magic of squatter cities is that they are improved steadily and gradually by their residents. To a planner's eye, these cities look chaotic. To my eye, they look organic: A spontaneous growth of eclectic design and regionalism, mixed use, walkability, mass transit. Yes, there are plenty of alternative ideas and architecture to be discovered in the squatter cities of the developing world. In the developed world, people leverage their wealth to get mortgages that enable them to buy materials, hire contractors and build their homes all at once. Squatters do not have that luxury.

HOW DOES AN ARCHITECT ASSIST A COMMUNITY IN EVALUATING ALTERNATIVE DESIGNS?
Instead of just compiling numbers and filtering them through theory, we hung out in the slums and talked to people.

All the residents know each other's faces and voices and doro (chickens). It is a community. The real question should be: what can I add to the system to create value?

Working with slum communities is not just a possibility that they can use their powers of analysis and criticism to transform a problem into a solution. Here in Durban, we are making progress on that.

Most cities are built on a consumption model. The consumption model is strongly polarizing between mega-wealth areas surrounded by poverty and its spatial practices has led to a deepening of the problem by furthering segregation.

The Human Rights Commission in South Africa for instance found that the use of road closures / boom gates has the potential to, and does indeed in practice, violate a number of rights. They also pointed out that these measures cause social division and dysfunctional cities, and that they lead to further polarization within the city.

The informal economy of Warwick Junction is a significant force within the city. Approximately two-thirds of all informal traders in the city, some 7,000-8,000 people, are located in the area. The real concern is one of imbalance. One in seven people on the planet live in squatter communities or in shantytowns' informal economies. These markets and neighborhoods provide housing and jobs that government and formal private sector fail to deliver. From trade to transport to shelter, the impact of the informal sector is pervasive in the lives of many. The informal sector presently contributes significantly to the GDP of numerous developing countries. In Africa alone, an estimated 75 per cent of the basic needs in the majority of African cities are provided informally. Just as squatters have been building the neighborhoods of the future, street vendors are creating the jobs of the future.

THE WARWICK JUNCTION URBAN RENEWAL PROJECT GOAL CREATED A MORE PARTICIPATIVE ENVIRONMENT THAT WORKED WITH, NOT AGAINST, THE STREET TRADERS' INTERESTS.
The informal sector has clear and profound spatial properties. Its spatial network cuts across the city, consisting of multiple relationships and deliberate choices and actions not prescribed by any 'formal' institution or plan. Micro-urbanism in urban leftovers, third spaces, queer-spaces, reclamation of landfills, and ephemeral architecture particularly allow the street traders to coexist along with retail shops and along with large malls.

All peoples have the right to self-determination. By virtue of that right, they freely determine their political status and freely pursue their economic, social, and cultural development.

ECONOMIC AND SOCIAL RIGHTS GUARANTEE THAT EVERY PERSON BE AFFORDED CONDITIONS UNDER WHICH THEY ARE ABLE TO MEET THEIR NEEDS.
This isn't about giant interventions that bring in hundreds of volunteers from out of town to 'transform' a neighborhood. This is about daily pride at living

this life, and how our engagement in our surroundings might influence our neighbors and those around us.

And yet all we're doing is providing a platform for the skill, talent, love, and genius of those who are already there. Now street traders are able to sell higher valued goods and offer greater quantities. Having a secure space to conduct business also helps to forge cooperation between them.

SO THIS PROMOTES ENGAGEMENT INSTEAD OF CRIMINALIZATION AND GIVES BUSINESS LICENSES TO STREET VENDORS?

There are thousands of informal settlements and their mainly young populations test out new ideas unfettered by law or tradition. These places have, out of necessity, become hives of inventiveness, industry, and self-made enterprise. Street infrastructure is not just a place of people and vehicles, but of trade and collective, opportunistic exchange based on fluid identities. These activities often are mechanisms of survival: a persistent cycle of poverty means that the movement and activities that came to define squatter areas are for most part linked to the most basic level of subsistence. Despite the hardship and deprivation, such illegal communities are the crucibles of the global future.

WITH THIS PROJECT, YOUR ARCHITECTURE AND DESIGN ARE PROTECTING A FUNDAMENTAL ECONOMICAL HUMAN RIGHT, THE RIGHT TO DIGNITY AND A DECENT LIFE.

There is a pervasive problem keeping poverty alive: space. If we work on that, we can make progress in poverty reduction on a larger scale. Poverty is man-made. Overcoming poverty is not a gesture of charity. It is an act of justice.

How could we seriously talk about democracy and sustainable urbanization without involving the poor? Human rights are about making sure people are protected from poverty.

E L I A S

Many thoughts and worries had furrowed his once brown eyebrows.

DILAPIDATED, CRAMPED, BADLY INSULATED, UNHEALTHY, AND NOT INCLUSIVE: DOES IT ALL MAKE HOUSING MORE AFFORDABLE?

We tend to house poor people in the least healthy environments, with the greatest likelihood of environmental hazards such as flooding and pollution. They are, consequently, less safe and less healthy. With very high life costs on them and at a very high price both moral and money on us.

Moving into squalid and alienating condo units had often decreased the quality of people's lives. Rather than re-conceiving the space of the street to accommodate them, the informal dwellers are evicted, putting the livelihood of an entire segment of the city's population in jeopardy. Building right in the first place, however, is typically more cost-effective than retro-fitting existing settlements. But relocation entails a social cost that needs to be factored in, and there is limited land available and little enthusiasm for the expenditures required for entirely new communities.

So, some combination of upgrades and selective, nearby relocations may represent a solution.

Economic and social inequalities are the backdrop to the neglect of human rights; for example, we all have a right to a standard of living that is good enough to meet our physical and mental needs.

The poor are always more likely to get a disproportionate share of economic opportunities and so have more to gain from interventions to promote economic equity and rights. Design can address inequality, and drive and shape change by providing practical solutions. Good design costs much less than bad design, which increases problems and inequality; in the long term, it also costs less than no design at all, which ignores problems and kills opportunities. It's important to understand that low-cost housing has to be just that—low-cost, both to the inhabitants and to the government organizing the construction.

But the design of the building, both in terms of architecture and materials used, will have an impact on the health of an already at-risk group. If the impact on health and community is negative, it will have a negative impact economically—sick people can't work, and poor people will use publicly funded resources if they can't afford private health care.

More than this, badly designed public housing causes problems that can potentially extend across economic barriers. What we need are open spaces and housing designed purposely to be pleasant, and less like the depressing concrete towers we know.

Of all the architect's responsibilities, welfare remains less well defined. Not to be confused with the system of governmental support for unemployed people, the welfare obligations of architects do share with those governmental programs the goal of helping people thrive and prosper.

Our responsibility is to address problems. Well-designed environments enhance a sense of well-being, enable healthy lifestyles, and contribute to a more equal, inclusive, and cohesive society. The focus should shift to converting the dilapidated, overcrowded, and unhealthy buildings into vibrant, affordable housing. These can feature green and traditional design elements, including low-toxicity materials, use of bamboo and local materials to protect indoor air quality, increased natural light, energy-efficient heating and lighting systems, and green roofs. They could also include high-performance boilers, ventilation, and lighting systems that maximize natural light and solar heat, as well as water-saving fixtures, and sun-filled pepper storage areas for preparing the traditional barberee (Ethiopian curry).

Well-designed environments should also include areas for community markets, made available for use by the neighborhood residents and organizations; and fruit gardens in an attempt to foster a supportive environment focused on connectedness by transforming individuals, buildings, and neighborhoods. This restoration can help catalyze the revitalization of the Addis inner center neighborhood and introduce a new, results-oriented approach to addressing housing. Housing the poor, not in condominiums on the outskirts of cities, but with dignity and access to economic opportunities, is a less intractable challenge than it seems. Commitment to adequate housing can be animated through the provision of supportive architecture that the poor owns and manages.

DO WE NEED MORE OR BETTER CONDOS?

We need many more houses and many more players in the house-building sector.

Architecture has too often been rated highest for its individual originality. As a result, the most relevant questions—those of why a building is made, and for whom—have been forgotten. Slum communities can develop their own cooperative institution and mutual construction societies that share labor and allow them to build their homes together. This is where the involvement of occupant groups—not usually included in the design and planning and construction process—can really make a difference in terms of affordable quality. If so, the location and design of a place, its facilities and equipment may fail less to take into account cultural requirements such as ethnicities, minorities, faith, traditional cooking, washing facilities, ceremonies, and room sizes. Architecture should be an inclusive and participative process, and a constructive integration of diverse actors, aimed at empowering people. Therefore, let's turn these once barren expanses of concrete into friendlier 'people places.'

LUCIANO
His voice is bound up with a thong.

It really hurts. And also, I don't think it's so bad to want to integrate them into our cities, I don't know, I'm an architect but I'm also an activist and I do like protests, and that we are for and not against these changes. I mean we build really, really big things and we have loads of influence, and surely, I'm not so sure that migration is a bad thing.

The group includes people fleeing war-torn countries such as Syria, who are likely to be granted refugee status, as well as people seeking for jobs and better lives, who are economic migrants whose governments are likely to rule over.

Cities are often the first port of call for migrants, due to the level and quality of services and infrastructure that they provide.

FOSTERING INTEGRATION AND MUTUAL TRUST IS MUCH HARDER THAN SETTING A SHELTER.

Since their origins, cities have had to deal with interactions between the dominant hosts and immigrant communities, for migration is much older than cities.

migration is fundamentally the story of the human race.

Integrating the migrants into public space is a less intractable challenge than it seems. We can focus on fostering migrants' integration by redesigning much of the urban public space in a way that it addresses the challenge of increasing immigrant involvement immigrant integration, public space access, and space use. How do they use the local park? What changes might make them use it differently or more often? While also keeping up with the changes in a temporary urban environment, numerous small projects allow the city to meet the needs of current migrants on a micro-scale and allow communities to initiate these strategies themselves. Streets, sidewalks, subways, parks, and street markets bring together immigrants and non-immigrants in shared public spaces daily. This makes broad, inclusive involvement in those places all the more crucial. This will enrich social diversity and promote innovation. Still, if this integration into the urban fabric is poorly managed, it can result in multiple problems and ineffective solutions.

The common perception is that the concentration of immigrants and the influx of foreigners drives up disorder and crime, because of the assumed propensities of these groups to commit crimes and settle in poor, presumably disorganized communities.

The immigration debate has many aspects. Whatever one's position on it may be, there is little that can stop global migration. An integration system is a conversion of the existing public space to respond to the requirements of the immigrant communities that live there, and includes creating spaces and services for arriving asylum-seekers. By making public processes and established civic structures accessible, architects can encourage immigrant participation that in turn helps create parks and public spaces that reflect the unique character of our neighborhoods. An imaginative new approach to design in these cases would weigh up the interplay between the traditional aims of spatial planning and the quality of a new urban life experience.

STATES HAVE AN OBLIGATION TO RESPECT, PROTECT, AND FULFILL THE HUMAN RIGHTS OF ALL INDIVIDUALS UNDER THEIR JURISDICTION, REGARDLESS OF THEIR NATIONALITY OR ORIGIN AND REGARDLESS OF THEIR IMMIGRATION STATUS.
Linking immigrants to civic life has real effects in public space; when people see each other face to face in parks, distant 'immigrants' become the neighbor settling next to you.

Architects can finally transform the architectural design process from a local narration of spatial living scenarios into collective, diverse, interactive, and constantly reiterated spatial stories. Integration is a process that establishes and develops connections between one's past experiences and those of others. I think that, we sometimes call it 'architecting solutions,' because it's actually a process of 'architecting' things. But it isn't architecture. This is why urban design is one of the most powerful forces for change in the world.

HASSAN
He seemed perfectly ready to hold his speech and confident of his persuasion.

THE RIGHT TO ASSEMBLE PEACEFULLY, TOGETHER WITH FREEDOM OF EXPRESSION AND FREEDOM OF ASSOCIATION, RESTS AT THE CORE OF ANY FUNCTIONING DEMOCRATIC SYSTEM. WHERE AND HOW CAN PEOPLE CONGREGATE TODAY?
Public space should serve not only as a place for social gathering and recreation but also as a space for active political expressions and dialogues. Public space is the city's commons, where dissident views find a voice.

Freedom of peaceful assembly is a fundamental human right. Assemblies may serve many purposes, including the expression of diverse, unpopular, or minority opinions. The right can be an important strand in the maintenance and development of culture, such as in the preservation of minority identities.

HOW DOES THIS ENGAGE YOU AS ARCHITECT?
The implications are in the political quality of public space: public space should be open and inviting from the sidewalk, easily seen, and read as open to the public, and convey openness through low

design elements and generous paths leading into the plaza, which is visually interesting and contains seating.

OUR DEMOCRACY DEPENDS ON OUR WILLINGNESS TO ENGAGE.

Let us make sure public places exist that allow ideas to be nurtured, discussed, refined, and animated. In order for an assembly to be possible the space should be accessible and enhance pedestrian circulation, located at the same elevation as the sidewalk; it should provide a sense of safety and security, contain easily accessible paths for ingress and egress, be oriented and visually connected to the street; be well-lit; and it should provide places to sit—it should accommodate a variety of well-designed, comfortable seating for small groups and individuals.

Privatization limits human rights more subtly than direct prohibition, but just as effectively. Commercial redevelopment is not considered a human-rights issue, but it is often a background for official actions against freedom of assembly. Business trumps human rights.

ASSEMBLIES ARE AS LEGITIMATE A USE OF PUBLIC SPACE AS COMMERCIAL ACTIVITY OR THE MOVEMENT OF VEHICULAR AND PEDESTRIAN TRAFFIC.

This must be acknowledged when considering the necessity of any restrictions.

As architects, designers, and planners we have the ethical responsibility to protect not only public health, our safety, and welfare but also to protect social equality and the rights of citizens and communities to public space.

This is a struggle that architects, landscapers, designers, and planners must participate in; they must link human rights to their design and their aspirations to protect and promote public space.

As the Occupy movement spread around the globe and as other privately-owned public spaces were similarly taken over by protesters, a growing sense of awareness spread in many other countries and continents that similar hybrid spaces worldwide exist at the nexus between public and private spheres.

Design such spaces with human rights in mind and, in the process, architects can prove they have the ability to educate, organize, and inspire citizens' rights to free and informed speech.

ZAINAB

There is nothing out of place in her calm soft friendly voice.

WHAT HAS BEEN A REAL REVOLUTION FOR ARCHITECTURE?

My guess is the invention of the arch, or concrete, or the elevator. My answer is: design.

Design is a Renaissance notion of organizing spatial ideas via drawings and models.

WHY DO YOU CONSIDER DESIGN SO REVOLUTIONARY?

Because it is about processes. Less obviously, the key attribute of design is that it is human centered.

In science and technology, 'design' implies the re-arrangement of materials and ideas for innovative purposes.

There are countless definitions of design. 'Design' has become a key concept across a multitude of disciplinary domains and social spheres. One can even think of societies and social arrangements being 'designed.' The idea is that design is a process, a way of approaching challenges which designers and non-designers alike can learn to use to create positive change in the world.

Sustainable design and ecological building are the most significant global challenges for the design profession. To meet new building regulations and national targets for carbon emissions, all future buildings will be judged on their 'green' merits.

Design is important to every aspect of human lives. It forms the places in which we live, work, learn, heal, and gather. While social outcomes are not dependent solely upon design, it is difficult for a street, condo, or school to be successful if it is poorly designed. Design can promote and/or hinder economic, environmental, and social processes. It works best when it is done with respect to social equity, economic stability, and the protection and enhancement of environmental accessibility.

The design of the built environment involves architects, planners, and engineers in activities that have a profound effect on people, their actions, their rights, and their environment.

Making abstract thoughts and inspirations concrete has more value when they concretely impact on real life for the better.

A responsible design approach in architecture fundamentally shifts the dialogue away from a reactive posture of "how much value does design give to the building?" to an expansive notion of "how much value does design give to the people living in the building?" as well as "how might we maximize the odds of that potential value improving life and society?" Such an approach goes beyond architecture's definition of "making buildings" and reaches out for global views on architecture and design, broader attitudes to social structures, with a view to creating sustainable environments to live in.

The right to directly and indirectly participate in political and public life is important in empowering individuals and groups, and is one of the core elements of human-rights-based approaches aimed at eliminating marginalization and discrimination.

PARTICIPATION RIGHTS ARE INEXTRICABLY LINKED TO OTHER HUMAN RIGHTS SUCH AS THE RIGHT TO PEACEFUL ASSEMBLY AND ASSOCIATION, FREEDOM OF EXPRESSION AND OPINION, AND THE RIGHT TO EDUCATION AND TO INFORMATION.

For example, bottom-up approaches towards improving urban space have paved the way for citizens to become active agents involved in the decision-making processes associated with the making and remaking of their cities. It is based on the architect's extensive dialogue with communities and this exchange takes the form of encounters, shared time, questions, and extensive research to lend substance to shared projects and visions.

COULD YOU IMAGINE HUMAN RIGHTS BY ARCHITECTURE DESIGN?

Good architectural outcomes—especially when the goal is to create new sources of value in the world—are most often achieved through a well-structured design process that is more holistic and inclusive than the notion of good design. This focus on humans inspires great ide-

as and ensures that solutions meet real needs and really embrace rights. Design is in essence good thinking. Good design thinking can create things of enormous value to humanity.

THABO

He speaks as if words are chasing him.

IF I SAY VILLAGES RAZED BY FLOODING, BY A HURRICANE OR TORNADO; FAMILIES WHO HAVE LOST EVERYTHING, PEOPLE RUNNING TO SAVE THEIR OWN LIVES AND FLEEING WAR, FAMILIES LEAVING THEIR HOMES IN SEARCH OF SAFE PLACES TO CONTINUE THEIR LIVES—WHAT COMES INTO YOUR MIND?

Ikea!

These people in the path of these natural disasters suffer; as refugees; as returnees, as members of economically disadvantaged groups and as members of ethnic and/or religious minorities.

I like the Ikea proposal of a new type of shelter which will replace the outdated tents currently in use in refugee camps worldwide. In an enormous refugee camp, refugees find it difficult even to source the barest essentials for life. Providing a sense of normal life in the refugee camps is absolutely essential to helping them, and their families, to recover and cope with life as refugees.

The combination of natural disasters and armed conflict has displaced nearly 50 million people. The Zaatari Refugee Camp on the border of Syria hosts 80,000 people.

The design challenge is huge. The structure has to be easily disassembled, transported, and either reassembled or repurposed; it has to provide a sense of normality and, importantly, should create a space that they feel safe in. The design of Ikea is innovative and carries a number of advantages, such as increased space and privacy, better temperature control, and enough solar energy to power a light in the evening. The design is currently being tested in Ethiopia before being deployed worldwide.

BUT IF I SAY THOUSANDS PEOPLE OF ALL AGES AND PROFESSIONS HOUSED ON THE SAME TERRITORY AND THE ORGANIZATION OF SUCH A PLACE WITH ITS NETS AND INFRASTRUCTURE, WHAT COMES INTO YOUR MIND?

That is architecture. That is urban planning. That is a town.

WHICH IS THE DIFFERENCE BETWEEN A REFUGEE CAMP AND A TOWN?

Since hosts can't accommodate refugees indefinitely, a camp that could be moved into and out of an area with relative ease could be attractive to all parties involved. The consideration of mobility in design proposals, for example, could provide a solution to the 'impermanent permanence' of refugee camps. Refugee camps are provisory towns whose inhabitants are not citizens and their houses are not houses. It is a stand-by town where architecture is banned. These three issues: scale, community forming, and the temporary nature of dwellings, indicate some of the largest concerns any city or city dweller faces.

UNBELIEVABLE HUMAN RIGHTS ABUSES MAKE DISPLACED REFUGEES AND WOMEN UNABLE TO MAKE DECISIONS ABOUT THEIR LIVES AND THEIR COMMUNITIES.

A refugee camp needs more than countless handbooks, manuals, and papers on the formation and maintenance of these camps. The information in these handbooks lays out a system that is filled with contradictory instructions, vague references, and strict limitations. It's rigid and quick to lay out structure, and this creates military-like camps that decrease cultural connection among occupants. The stresses upon displaced people lead them to isolation.

STILL THIS IS NOT YET ARCHITECTURE NOR URBAN PLANNING: SO WHY HAVE THE ARCHITECTS NOT BEEN THOSE CHARGED WITH DESIGNING THE REFUGEE TOWNS?

The issue of temporality is one of the most important factors and one of the most ignored. While local governments want to limit the time during which displaced people will consume their resources, occupants will naturally seek a sense of permanence in their life. The absence of designs fails to function both permanently or temporarily.

SPACIAL CONFIGURATION IS A KEY COMPONENT IN FORMING COMMUNAL SPACES.

The integration of these spaces on every scale is core to achieving success. Issues of permanence can be addressed though alternative building methodologies. By including local people in the design process and looking at local building typologies, camps can become more relevant to the populations that live there. I would focus on communal connections in order to encourage people to take ownership of their surroundings. Cluster, neighborhood, and planning give occupants more freedom and responsibility when it comes to their individual shelter.

ARCHITECTURE CAN HELP, AND IT SHOULD—SO THAT WE CAN CEASE TO CALL THEM 'REFUGEE CAMPS' AND CAN START CALLING THEM 'LIVING TOWNS.'

Camps are a breeding ground for virulent disease and violent crime—and as camps grow larger and older, reports of violence against women increase disproportionately.

We must be pragmatic, daring, and optimistic, and learn from forms of emergence that are outside the scope of architectural practice, and draw inspiration from them.

SAMANTHA
A fresh mind grew out of life, not out of books.

DOES ARTICLE #10 OF THE HUMAN RIGHTS DECLARATION IMPACT ON THE COURTHOUSE BUILDING'S ARCHITECTURE?

What does Article #10 say?

EVERYONE IS ENTITLED IN FULL EQUALITY TO A FAIR AND PUBLIC HEARING BY AN INDEPENDENT AND IMPARTIAL TRIBUNAL, IN THE DETERMINATION OF HIS RIGHTS AND OBLIGATIONS AND OF ANY CRIMINAL CHARGE AGAINST HIM.

The new Courthouse building is in the realm of iconic architecture incorporating a variety of courthouse iconography in a very contemporary fashion. This is a 690,000-square-foot structure featuring extensive gardens and courtyards. However, the Courthouse architecture doesn't come without constraints and deference. And by the way, courtroom trials have been eclipsed by alternative dispute resolution in private settings; many litigated cases are rendered private by unpublished dispositions.

WHAT ARE THE DEFINING FEATURES OF THE NEW SPACES FOR THE ADMINISTRATION OF JUSTICE?

Recommendations issued by enclosure comes in this way: glass walls and sound systems might be used to separate the adversarial space from the public observation space. Visual accessibility, audibility, movement, and document flow should be among courtroom principals. Points of access among subordinate participants and principals and press and public areas should be positioned just outside these triangles of communication. Closed-circuit television to centralize public observation space on the lower floors of a multilevel building is also highly advised.

Once court days drew all levels of society and all manner of social engagement. Today secrecy, control, efficiency, and the coldest of bureaucratic rationalities reach their apotheoses on court days.

The contemporary architecture of justice facilities is more about enclosure and providing an efficient layout, creating a quality environment, and improving the job performance of staff.

INDEED, IT SUGGESTS THAT THE LOCATION, DESIGN, AND USE OF COURTHOUSES HAVE NOT BEEN SIGNIFICANT TO THE ARTICLE 10?

Both the separation of the public from the action area of the courtroom and the separation of jurors from witnesses and attorneys through edited video recording stand in no small degree of tension with Article 10. Meanwhile, trial has remained the governing metaphor for due process, notwithstanding the fact that actual courtroom trials are vanishing.

WHAT ARE THE CONSEQUENCES OF DISAGGREGATING THE SITES IN WHICH JUSTICE IS ACTUALLY ADMINISTERED FROM THE SPACE THAT GIVES SHAPE TO OUR HUMAN RIGHTS ENTITLEMENT OF PUBLIC HEARING?

The gradual process of enclosure in the design and operation of courthouses to ensure meaningful participation and accuracy in administrative decisions have been strained to breaking point. The displacement and private enclosure of adjudicative space alters the very epistemology of justice. Finally, inside the courtroom, the right to a meaningful hearing is more honored in the breach.

CARLOS
He weighs the central tensions of our urbanized world carefully.

DOES URBAN SECURITY MEAN MORE MILITARIZATION, METAL DETECTORS, PRIVATIZATION OF PUBLIC SPACE?

In cities across the world 'security' has become an increasingly central concern. The militarization of urban space can be defined as the visible integration of security elements into the built environment.

The measures associated with these trends often involve a trade-off between security and human rights, including the rights to privacy, freedom of movement, and equal treatment before the law. The militarization of urban security involves a move towards more aggressive and intrusive forms of urban planning, which tend to intensify socioeconomic and ethnic divisions.

THE TENSION IS BETWEEN THE RIGHT TO SAFETY AND THE RIGHT TO PRIVACY?

In Africa, many poor neighborhoods, where residents are tightly interconnected through network ties, do produce collective results such as the social control of disorderly behavior, keeping violence and homicides at the lowest rate. Slum dwellers, for example, refer to the slum as the village and they mean it is a place organized by norms and trust that facilitate coordination and cooperation for mutual benefits. Neighbors also engage in informal surveillance of one another's property. Architecture does not create neighborhoods. Neighborhoods are interdependent and characterized by a functional relationship between what happens at one point in space and what happens elsewhere. Meanwhile zones, districts, and sectors are boundaries imposed by census geography and ecological properties neighborhoods are shaped by social interaction.

Planning has been surprisingly slow to adapt tools of spatial analysis, especially in a framework that accounts for a competing explanation of clustering—selection effects based on community ties, key structural and social characteristics of life within the boundaries of focal neighborhoods.

Urban militarization and seclusion are dismantling that organization.

SOCIAL DISORGANIZATION IS THE INABILITY OF A COMMUNITY STRUCTURE TO REALIZE THE COMMON VALUES OF ITS RESIDENTS AND MAINTAIN EFFECTIVE SOCIAL CONTROLS OF DELINQUENT SUBCULTURES.

Such trends are clearly deeply troubling from the point of view of human rights. Residentially unstable and poor neighborhoods display less social control, and they, in turn, suffer higher delinquency rates. That spatial embeddedness, internal structural characteristics, and social organizational processes are each important for understanding neighborhood-level variations in rates of violence. Low economic status, ethnic heterogeneity, and residential networking and stability lead to community organization; but when these conditions are missing in the urban environment, or when they fail to take hold, delinquent subcultures and high rates of delinquency can fill the void.

URBAN MILITARIZATION IS BASED ON PRE-EMPTIVE SURVEILLANCE, THE CRIMINALIZATION OF DISSENT, THE EVISCERATION OF CIVIL RIGHTS, AND THE OBSESSIVE SECURITIZATION OF EVERYDAY LIFE TO SUPPORT INCREASINGLY UNEQUAL SOCIETIES.

Hope calls it 'moral minimalism,' the achievement of social control through weak ties among neighbors by emphasizing privacy over communalism and denying strangers access to the community and its resources. The ultimate vision of architecture should be to build society. Cities should be planned for people who live there, not just for visitors. Citizen participation in planning is important as it helps create invested engagement.

WHANG

Had he lived two hundred years ago, he would have had the continent of Africa to explore.

SHOULDN'T WE FINALLY START MAKING ARCHITECTURE RACIST-FREE?

Twenty years on into democracy, South Africa is moving away from both the geographical and human rights violations of apartheid, which separated people in many ways, including by its divisive urban planning.

MOST AFRICAN CITIES SEPARATE FAIRLY NEATLY INTO POOR AND RICH AREAS 'LIKE A SUNNY-SIDE-UP EGG,' WITH SLUMS SPREADING OUT FROM THE RIM.

Space is and remains the primordial basis of architecture and a basic prerequisite for occupying the city. Our urban lives are literally embedded in space. We are constantly surrounded, affected, and shaped by it. Our spaces both reflect the values and power relationships in our societies. It can both bring together or separate and discriminate.

DOES CONTEMPORARY ARCHITECTURE ORGANIZE OR RATHER DISORGANIZE SPACE?

TRANSFORMING THE BUILT ENVIRONMENT USES THE MYTHS OF DEMOLITION VERSUS NEW CONSTRUCTION.

This is leading to a system of belief in which human values like dignity and moral character come into sharp focus through the application of intimidation, land confiscation, the cutting of all social services, forced eviction, and displacement. In this case, one should honestly raise the question of whether architecture and planning are being used to organize or disorganize space. But can I react to an imposed master plan that can turn off a neighborhood overnight?

RACISM IS NOT ONLY A POLITICAL, SOCIAL, AND ECONOMIC CONSTRUCT. IT IS A SYSTEM THAT IS FUNDAMENTALLY SPATIAL.

Places and spaces are sometimes deliberately designed and managed to exclude people, and the implications of this needs careful thought. Architecture and urbanism can be considered as spatial dimensions of an ideological war of different interest groups in cities.

MY GOAL IS TO PROMOTE HUMAN RIGHTS AS A POSITIVE CATALYST FOR ARCHITECTURE, A POWERFUL AND INSPIRATIONAL DESIGN TOOL.

Architecture, in the building sense, is certainly based on ethics, and that's the reason for my interest in the field—to make people's lives better. Whether it's ethic, in the human-rights sense, is still somewhat debatable. What does a "Human Rights by Architecture" manifesto really mean? Does it mean that architects should ensure their design complies with the Convention of Human Rights whenever they deal with governments, with future occupiers, with communities, with investors, with contractors? Does this apply from the design stage to the implementation stage, at one end of the spectrum, to termination and eviction at the other? Again, does this really involve learning about standards, norms, mechanisms, international bodies, etc.?

Your understanding is that architecture is primarily concerned with the conceiving and implementing of spaces for serving not just the many activities of human beings, but also for meeting their human rights in a meaningful, inclusive, socially connected environment. This demands both access to knowledge and a clear direction in the way in which professionals choose to use their skills. You see human rights as a tool for understanding and designing. It is also a tool to be used toward the achievement of equality, tolerance, fairness, and many other features essential to just and peaceful societies. My rationale is this: work, play, consumption, relaxation, eating, entertainment—all these actions have driven design in most western architecture; so why shouldn't other factors drive architecture elsewhere: factors such as food, security, an informal economy, cultural heritage, gender equality, urban farming, traditional cooking, economic opportunity, as well as traditional customs, such as goat slaughtering, the coffee ceremony, common prayer, community mourning, and so on?

TO BRING THE PIECES TOGETHER, DESIGN CAN USE MANY STRATEGIES: BONDING, CONNECTING, LINKING, ADHERING, FIXING, OR SOLIDIFYING.

Buildings are prototypes of how we arrange our lives in both functional and social ways.

MELVIN
Everything about him has a bracing air of real 'nowhere architecture.'

WOULD CITIES BE SAFER FOR ALL IF THEY WERE DESIGNED WITH WOMEN ON MIND?

The answer is yes! It will improve the quality of life in the city as a whole. Yes, we all know it's the right thing to do. It's not a zero-sum game, but a win-win that will result in more opportunity and more happiness for everybody. Design can break down barriers and stigmas, if we just could change how the space is organized and focus on different types of architecture. Considering women's concerns doesn't hurt men or other groups.

So long as women continue to be victims of sexual harassment, domestic violence and rape, they will have a radically different experience of what constitutes safety in homes, towns, and public spaces. This reflects the fact that women and men have very different experiences—and the fact that women and girls often face gender-based discrimination because of architecture design. Violence happens on streets, in and around public transportation, schools, and workplaces, in public sanitation facilities, water and food distribution sites and parks. This fact often reduces women's and girls' freedom of movement, their ability to participate in school, work, and public life. It limits their access to essential services and their enjoyment of cultural and recreational opportunities. It also negatively impacts their health and well-being.

LIVING FREE FROM VIOLENCE IS A HUMAN RIGHT.

Yet millions dof women and girls around the world encounter rape, domestic abuse, mutilation, and other forms of gender-based violence.

Women's need for safety is paramount. Planning and designing safe public spaces for women and girls requires constant attention to physical and social characteristics of space. It also requires constant evaluation of the social and physical implications of planning and design processes.

There are both human-rights and pragmatic arguments for acting on gender equality and inclusion in the built environment.

Design is so fundamental in dealing with changes in everyday life and situations. In order to create spaces that improve women's lives, we need to disarticulate the architecture from the gender issue. The things and objects around us, the technology we use, the clothes we wear, the images we encounter every day, the buildings we live in, the public spaces, the offices we work in, the schools our children go to, they all are impregnated by the cultural construction of masculinities and femininities and ideologies. The spatial organization of the home and of the city also expresses attitudes about how the activities of daily life should be ordered. Gender can no longer be considered an optional add-on to design. Residential architecture, among other features, reflects ideals and realities about relationships between women and men within the family and society.

DOMESTIC SPACES ARE CODIFIED AND REPRODUCE THE ROLE OF WOMEN IN THE FAMILY, HOUSEHOLD, AND IN SOCIETY.

Sexism takes many forms in architecture. In the oldest known book on architecture, the ancient Roman Vitruvius described Caryatids—the female-figure columns of the Acropolis in Athens—as prototypical images of servitude, the architecture of bondage. So where women go to work, earn less, do most of the housework and shopping, and care for elders and children, there is a whole range of issues related to architecture, which will impact differently on the sexes.

THE RATIONALE IS THAT OUR WORLD IS MAN-MADE, MAN-OWNED, MAN-CONSTRUCTED, MAN-LEGISLATED, MAN-DESIGNED?

It is rather a way of constructing without having women and their rights in mind. Women experience the built environment differently. The premise of change is to put women at the core. Jane invited us to feel the experience of being smaller, of being pregnant or needing to breastfeed a baby, of feeling unsafe after dark or walking in a desert street, relaxing in a park. We should add also the experience of being a woman in the south, of being poor and in need of sharing spaces, experience and services, or of working and having children, and so on.

IT SEEMS TO ME THAT THERE HAS ALSO BEEN SOME SORT OF BREAK BETWEEN WOMEN RIGHTS AND ARCHITECTURE.

Paying attention to women's needs is, of course, essential. But gender is a broader concept. It looks at how society works, who has the power and how roles between members of the society differ. It helps us to understand the profoundly different ways in which women and men experience the same events, and to identify the different responses needed to keep them alive and healthy and to ensure their dignity.

Equality has two different sides: equality in law and equality in fact. Many laws recognize that women and men are equal before the law. However, in practice, women and men rarely experience this equality.

NADIA

When she speaks she reveals an exuberant spirit and a definite personality.

WHO SUFFERS MOST FROM DISEASE?

Each year infectious diseases kill 3.5 million people—mostly the poor and young children, who live in low and middle-income countries.

The relationship between architecture and health has historically received little attention, beyond the design requirements of healthy buildings. Recent work has changed this and has established a more holistic awareness of the role of architecture in health. The intersection of public health and the built environment presents an extraordinary opportunity for architects.

HEALTH IS NO LONGER SIMPLY A QUESTION OF ACCESS TO MEDICAL TREATMENT BUT IT IS DETERMINED BY A RANGE OF FACTORS RELATED TO THE QUALITY OF OUR BUILT ENVIRONMENT.

The emphasis is on ill health as a result of the effects of environmental characteristics such as overcrowding, noise, water, air quality, and light.

The human right to health means that everyone has the right to the highest attainable standard of physical and mental health, which includes access to all medical services, sanitation, adequate food, decent housing, healthy working conditions, and a clean environment. To effectually enhance human health, building design needs to move to more holistic approaches that take their cues from health-supporting human behaviors.

HOW CAN WE USE DESIGN CONCEPTS TO PREVENT THE TRANSMISSION OF AIRBORNE DISEASE?

Design can make better choices easier or constrain behaviors by making certain actions more difficult. In poverty, actions linked to washing, nutrition, crowding, animals, clothes, and waste are made critically negative by faulty construction design. There can be no doubt that many negative physical health outcomes result from poor housing and a poor built environment; for example from bad water quality; or a lack of electricity, ventilation, or sewage systems, which, in turn, all have negative implications for physiological health.

THE INTERSECTION OF PUBLIC HEALTH AND THE BUILT ENVIRONMENT PRESENTS AN EXTRAORDINARY OPPORTUNITY FOR HUMAN RIGHTS.

If we see health and well-being as interdependent, we will hold prevention as important as cure, and look for long-term solutions rather than more immediately attainable treatments. These solutions, in turn, increase the importance of the spatially relevant definitions of well-being and their relationships to health. They are about enhancing the physical environment and thus the mental well-being of the people who live work, play, or struggle to survive within that built environment. Good design can influence health outcomes. And it means thinking way beyond medicine.

GIOVANNI

He pats his slightly bulging forehead and presses his finger on the curved arc of his temporal line.

people who are designing systems. In the future, architecture will be something else entirely.

DO YOU SUGGEST HUMAN RIGHTS WILL BE THE THEORY THAT BINDS OUR TEACHING TOGETHER AND EQUIPS STUDENTS TO SOLVE PROBLEMS AT MANY DIFFERENT LEVELS?

In the final analysis, the full realization of human rights in architecture depends on the extent of attitudes, skills, awareness, and action taken by architects to ensure its enjoyment and to explore the potential of space as a platform for social, economic, and environmentally inclusive development. Human-rights-based approaches to architecture are as much about how architecture is approached as what is actually designed and built.

DO YOU TEACH HUMAN RIGHTS IN YOUR ARCHITECTURE BUILDING COURSES?

Human rights has been a buzzword for years in many contexts except for architecture.

IS IT JUST ONE OF THOSE BUZZ WORDS THAT APPEARS ONLY TO VANISH AGAIN WHEN A NEW CRAZE HITS THE SCENE?

I do not think so; however, human rights and architecture still needs to be nurtured by practical experiences in order to sharpen its edge. There are many pressures on the curriculum of architecture schools; they all compete to meet future expectations.

YET 50 YEARS AGO THERE WERE FEW, IF ANY, ARCHITECTURE CURRICULA WITH COURSES DEALING WITH ENVIRONMENTAL ISSUES.

Architects are now thinking about an expanded field of architecture, they see themselves as spatial agents. They're

IT WOULD BE REALLY VALUABLE TO SUM UP A LIST OF CRITERIA WHICH HAVE PROFOUND IMPLICATIONS ON THE PRACTICE OF ARCHITECTURE AS IT RELATES TO HUMAN RIGHTS VIOLATIONS.

Human-rights enforcement through architecture requires not just knowledge about standards and norms, but the right attitudes and skills. Many of these are not inherent in the curricula and current professional requirements; however, they can be developed and refined over time, at both the individual and professional levels.

COULD YOU LIST SOME FOR ME?

I can reduce all to three main principles: participation, non-discrimination, and empowerment.

IT WOULD BE ALSO REALLY USEFUL TO SEE A 'SOLUTION' TO A HUMAN RIGHTS ISSUE THAT USED THE SAME METHOD TO COME UP WITH TWO DIFFERENT ANSWERS.

This is not really difficult: look at people in wheelchairs struggling to navigate over coir mats—those rough doormats outside hotels and public buildings that are impossible to wheel over in a straight line—or even worse, steps leading to an accessible toilet. The physical and technical access to a place and its usability remain vital design issues against discrimination. A human right that architects has overlooked for years.

SO AN ARCHITECTURAL EDUCATION SHOULD FACILITATE THE DEVELOPMENT OF CRITICAL THINKING ABILITIES, WHICH CAN BE APPLIED TO SOLVING PROBLEMS AND ADDRESSING SITUATIONS BEYOND DESIGN CONDUITS FOR YOUR OWN COMMUNITY SERVICES: WHAT ADVICE WOULD YOU GIVE TO A BEGINNER?

Work with respect for all, including the humanitarian imperatives of neutrality, independence, and impartiality. From the start of your career, decide on what issues you are not willing to compromise.

JUDITH

She is glazed-eyed; fertile with ideas and seemingly ready to spring into action.

CAN YOU UNDO THE SEPARATION, AND UPHOLD EQUALITY AS A CONDITION AND CONSEQUENCE OF ARCHITECTURE?

The basic idea of human rights is that each one of us, no matter who we are, or where we are born, is entitled to the same basic rights and freedoms. That may sound straightforward enough, but it gets incredibly complicated as soon as anyone tries to apply the idea to architecture.

The slow pace of human-rights-based development cries out for an alternative framework under which architects could collaborate on goals that advance human rights in the cities.

What you propose represents a set of design standards that comes from human rights, and not from political ideas, religion or dogma, or other similar sources. I think it's healthy to continuously reflect and actually ask yourself what are we doing and whether we are doing it right.

There are some urgent issues about transferring skills of the architectural profession to marginalized groups and communities. A more diverse and inclusive design process taps into neglected talent, uses human resources more intelligently and is therefore more economically resilient and socially vibrant.

And the whole point about this idea is to get people thinking about how architecture can work for them. Meaningful participation requires access to information and know-how—not just about their rights but also about architecture.

Focusing on cases of real urgency where people's living environment is being factually destroyed and reconstructed, allows us to work closely with local communities to address their sustainable needs through architecture.

The problems of widespread housing shortage and people's vulnerability to natural disaster and to estate markets can push architects toward urgent solutions: for example, to create more sustainable and innovative houses that are designed to be fully self-sufficient by drawing energy from the sun and wind, collecting and recycling rain water, treating household sewage, and also producing food. The opportunity to actually shape the new paradigm is a big responsibility. When design goes beyond existing forms, spaces, or material systems, it can converge with human rights to achieve innovation and preserve the goal of being optimal.

WORKING WITH WOMEN AND MEN OF DIFFERENT AGES AND IN VARIOUS CULTURES MIGHT REQUIRE DIFFERENT APPROACHES AND DIFFERENT WAYS OF DESIGNING?

Human rights contain few surprises, but implementing them is not an easy task. Almost all of them require architecture to carefully balance competing interests. Mirroring the diversity of the society they serve gives the work of architects a much greater chance of creating a built environment that suits that society.

BRIDGET
Listening to others seems to her like placing her nerves on the line.

A construction worker employer is normally also the same as the architect's. We architects could make claims in our contracts, otherwise they rarely translate to worker protections in practice and with relative impunity. We should include clauses protecting workers' rights in contracts, that it employs a third-party project manager to monitor compliance of contractors and subcontractors with such provisions, and that any violations by contractors are subject to penalty or legal sanction.

DO ARCHITECTS HAVE CONSTRUCTION MANAGEMENT RESPONSIBILITIES?
Workers are mostly hired by contractors operating on those sites or by employment agencies, rather than directly by the architect companies themselves.

HAS ANY OF THE BUILDINGS YOU HAVE DESIGNED EVER LEAD TO A LOSS OF LIFE?
Not that I know!

Construction workers in developing countries often report to Human Rights Watch illegal and arbitrary wage deductions for things like visa costs, bedding, food, or health care. They also report denial of free movement and lack of access to medical care. All workers sleep in bunk beds, and some workers said they did not have drinkable water in their own camp. Some said their air-conditioning had been broken for weeks or months without repair, despite the high temperatures, and some lived in windowless rooms that stank of mold.

WITHOUT IMMEDIATE AND SIGNIFICANT REFORMS, THE MIGRANT WORKERS UPON WHOSE LABOR THE FIFA WORLD CUP 2022 DEPENDS, REMAIN AT HIGH RISK.
Obtaining contractual guarantees for workers' rights could be a critical and significant first step towards ensuring better protections, if the clauses are comprehensive and enforceable. As architects, we should stress the matter of worker safety.

INADEQUATE MONITORING AND REPORTING MECHANISMS ALLOW VIOLATIONS OF LABORERS. CONSTRUCTION WORKERS SAFETY IS A BIG CONCERN AND RESPONSIBILITY.
Fear of losing their jobs and deportation prevent many migrant workers from using many of the current mechanisms by which they may enforce their rights.

If the Qatari government wishes to avoid human-rights abuses while building world-class stadiums, ambitious transportation links, and luxury hotels in the tight timeframe ahead, it should take steps to meaningfully enforce any laws protecting workers' rights it may currently have on its books, and it should amend laws to meet international labor and human-rights standards, in particular by allowing migrant workers to exercise their rights to free association and collective bargaining.

In the end, it is uprisings by workers and revolts by cultural activists around the world, not fines or negotiations, that will fuel social change in the Gulf. It is clearly not acceptable. In such cases, as an architect, I would find the use of a boycott a legitimate option.

The construction workers are among the poorest, and are often not aware of their rights. They have experienced rights abuses, including long hours and dangerous conditions.

We should bring labor rights to the foreground of architecture and allow nobody to die in construction. No human being should ever have to die in the name of architecture.

CAMERON

Both his thoughts and emotions are visible and palpable in his temple.

DO YOU CONSIDER HUMANITARIAN DESIGN A FUNDAMENTAL RIGHT?

It really is. I have learned how little separates the world of justice and dignity from that of house design and human rights.

ARCHITECTURE FOR HUMANITY PROMOTES ARCHITECTURAL AND DESIGN SOLUTIONS TO GLOBAL, SOCIAL, AND HUMANITARIAN CRISES: HOW DOES YOUR ORGANIZATION WORK?

Through competitions, workshops, educational forums, partnerships with aid organizations, and other activities, we create opportunities for architects and designers from around the world to help communities in need. We ran the organization and grew it from just a small circle of volunteers to an international organization in 25 countries.

THERE IS NO SINGULAR OR UNIVERSAL DESIGN SOLUTION TO RESPONDING TO CRISIS AND THERE IS NO DEFINITIVE PRESCRIBED ANSWER TO A COMMUNITY NEED?

We speak about design process rather than design. Our design process encourages community groups to set goals and work together to achieve them. We have four main practice areas: disaster mitigation and reconstruction; poverty alleviation; design innovation in conservation; and wildlife protection and design activism. Typically, each area requires different approaches to working and team members. We strongly focus on the removal of typical barriers to participation, such as formal hearings or forced locations. For us, design should not only be environmentally but also culturally appropriate. Responsible and innovative design can make a difference; it can improve or worsen the community you are designing for. Design is the expression of a community's vision for change.

ALL PEOPLE AND PLACES HAVE A RIGHT TO WELL THOUGHT-OUT, SUSTAINABLE, QUALITY DESIGN, IRRESPECTIVE OF THE RESOURCES AVAILABLE.

When you live on survival, you have issues with water, issues about food, education, skills . . . so the design is about these issues, never about catastrophe itself.

HOW CAN AN ARCHITECT RESPOND FAST TO COMMUNITIES IN NEED AND TO HUMAN RIGHTS VIOLATIONS?

A synergy can drive a pragmatic methodology that often requires only a small amount of resources to implement. Due to the pro-bono nature of the organization, employing designers for specific projects was not a viable option. So we began hosting competitions for designers to produce projects and the most suitable of these would be implemented in the community in need. So we opted for an open-source model allowing local chapters to independently join and become the first to utilize our Creative Commons Licensing system on a physical structure.

WHAT IS YOUR TSUNAMI LESSON?

I learned that disasters can expose and amplify a community's existing vulnerability, as much as it can engender an environment for alternative visions and strategies for human settlements.

WHAT ARE HUMAN RIGHTS FOR YOU?

Human rights are about treating people with dignity and respect. To make these values basic standards for any architectural solution and service is very simple and very difficult at the same time. It is the fact of our shared humanity that requires each of us to take an interest in humans and in their rights as we contribute to the built environment, and give meaning in their habitat. We must be concerned with the human landscape that we traverse.

ARIANE

Like her eyes, her hands also seem to move in tandem.

CAN HUMAN RIGHTS PUSH ARCHITECTURE INTO MORE BOTTOM-UP DESIGN?

Human-rights based approaches to architecture are as much about how architecture is done as what is done. My work focuses on micro-urbanism in urban leftovers, third spaces, queer-spaces, reclamation of landfills. Fundamentally, communities should engage in systemic change, change made by the community. Networks of people committed to improving the lives of slum dwellers need to be developed and strengthened.

Terms such as 'informal,' 'illegal,' 'squatters,' and 'unplanned' all serve to distance the majority of the low-income and poor urban population from state services and civic rights. They also permit manipulation to the advantage of different influential groups along the formal/regulated—informal/irregular continuum.

Most informal housing is an outcome of a slow, incremental, internally driven bottom-up process that mixes residential, commercial, and industrial units. The informal sector has clear and profound spatial properties. Its spatial network cuts across the city, consisting of multiple relationships and deliberate choices and actions not prescribed by any 'formal' institution or plan. Local action and architectural knowledge can be strengthened by the support of networks of actors at all levels, including slum dwellers and their organizations.

The ways that some informal settlements are risking the hazards of topography and climate—landslides, floods, and fires, for instance—and risking the pathological outcomes of high density housing, such as inadequate sanitation, proximity to toxic industry, and outbreaks of disease, make in situ improvement virtually impossible.

People are demonstrating survival strategies that make life not only bearable, but in some places and in some respects, quite manageable. The challenge remains to find a framework of best practices for upgrading informal settlements. Slope stabilization, new circulation, composting toilets, public spaces, and recreation facilities, however laudable, aren't going to remake these communities entirely. Such measures have to be paired with massive upgrades to sanitation, transportation, and employment infrastructures, which can only be orchestrated at the national and international levels. Cities are becoming the dumping ground for a 'surplus' of humanity.

Human-rights thinking ensures that the dignity and rights of people are properly given importance, so that the conclusions reached most accurately reflect the reality of the situation. It also ensures that the design is the most appropriate;

however the efforts to manage projects through dwellers initiatives often get stalled by problems of development finance.

I am totally in favor of adaptive, bottom-up design. Even though bottom-up and bottom-down design models differ drastically in their application, they rely on traditional solutions encoded into the built environment, which represent the product of our collective intelligence. Implementing this realization to rebuild our world can lead to an unprecedented degree of support for human life from architectural and urban structures.

HOW DO LOW-INCOME CONTEXTS AFFECT DESIGN PROCESSES?

We have a lot to learn from squatter communities—about making do with less. But designers can bring a great deal of expertise to the alleviation of slum conditions, mediating among various interested parties and giving spatial form to their ambitions. Above all, they can achieve this with on-site energy generation, storm water collection, and sewage treatment wetlands solutions.

HOW CAN URBAN INTENSIFICATION BE CONTROLLED AND MANAGED IN A WAY THAT SUPPORTS SOCIAL SUSTAINABILITY AND REDUCES SPATIAL INJUSTICE?

I understand development must respond to uncertainty and must address the lack of attention paid to the role of communities in creating and enhancing the sustainability and prosperity of cities.

I will point out that the use of road closures and boom gates has the potential to violate a number of rights and that these measures cause social division and dysfunctional cities, and lead to further polarization of the city.

HOW CAN WE ENSURE THAT IT IS LEAST DISRUPTIVE TO THE COMMUNITY?

Slum improvement projects on the ground are actually plagued with delays, because there are too many different agencies involved in sanctioning, financing, construction, and the approval of building design, as well as later changes and sanction of housing loans. Formulating policy based on incentives is a tough task.

OLUFIKAYO

His breath warms and moistens the air, as if to keep the conversation open. And friendly.

By looking at architecture, it is possible to trace an important and unarguable insight—that many of the problems which disabled people face are generated by design arrangements, rather than by their own physical limitations.

Disability is something imposed on top of the impairments, by the way they are unnecessarily isolated and excluded from full inclusion and participation in urban social life. They find themselves isolated and excluded by such things as flights of steps, inadequate public and personal transport, unsuitable housing, and a lack of up-to-date aids and equipment.

WHAT ARE ARCHITECTURAL BARRIERS?

Architectural barriers are physical features that limit or prevent people with disabilities from traversing the city as people without disabilities can do. They include parking spaces that are too narrow to accommodate people who use wheelchairs; a step or steps at the entrance or to part of the selling space of a store; round doorknobs or door hardware that is difficult to grasp; aisles that are too narrow for a person using a wheelchair, electric scooter, or a walker; a high counter or narrow checkout aisles at a cash register; and fixed tables in eating areas that are too low to accommodate a person using a wheelchair or that have fixed seats that prevent a person using a wheelchair from pulling under the table. I see architectural barriers as a deprivation of the equality and liberty of persons.

THE TRUTH IS THAT AMONG PEOPLE THERE IS, AND ALWAYS HAS BEEN, A PLURALITY OF APPROACHES.

People with physical disabilities are seen as recipients of services and a burden rather than as equal members of the community or society. To a disturbing degree, barriers in the built environment can prevent people with physical disabilities from visiting social, commercial, and recreational establishments for fear of not feeling safe. Likewise these barriers can render them unable to enter a facility that has stairs, narrow doorways, inaccessible bathrooms, and numerous other unforeseen, potentially hazardous architectural barriers. As a result, these obstacles and barriers force people with physical disabilities into isolation, which consequently prevents them from thriving in their life and in society in general.

CAN ARCHITECTURE REPRESENT THE DIVERSITY OF DISABLED PEOPLE? CAN IT AVOID REDUCING DISABILITY TO AN INDIVIDUAL MEDICAL PROBLEM, AND AVOID NEGLECTING THE PREDICAMENT OF BODILY LIMITATION AND DIFFERENCE?

Over at least four decades, and in many different countries, architects have regarded disability as being bound up with the context of design, and have drawn attention to the disadvantages. We can promote independence and equality by working to create environments where people with disability can enjoy access to the workplace, businesses, and public facilities, and can move as freely as possible within the community. But first we need a more progressive way of understanding disability.

If we aim to understand the critical role of architects and designers in relation to impairments, the focus should be on independent living!

Architects, professionals, experts, and landscape designers must first de-medicalize disability and be much more committed to promoting control by disabled people over their own lives.

Disability is a situation, caused by social conditions. Its elimination requires that no barriers to mobility, housing, recreational facilities, work, or commercial spaces should be put in place. We cannot approach disability issues with just regulations and compliance.

Removing isolation-causing barriers that prevent those with disabilities from being fully active members of their community is just the first step. In evaluating what barriers need to be removed

we need just to look to the Standards for Accessible Design as a guide. All of these approaches reject an understanding of disability as an individual and they exaggerate the challenges into a set of crude dichotomies which are ultimately misleading.

Seeking input from people with disabilities in your community can also be an important and valuable part of the barrier removal process, because it can help identify and provide a source of advice on what solutions may work. It doesn't matter if you're paired, unpaired, gay, straight, pink, purple, orange, polka-dotted, from Mars, from the Moon, or any other place: If you think you want to become somebody, you should be able to step forward to achieve this.

Disability results from the interplay of individual and contextual barriers. In other words, people are disabled by architecture and by their bodies.

There is no greater disability in society than the inability to see a person as more. Architecture should bring us up to consider disabled people the equal of non-disabled people and to help them reach their high aspirations by focusing on their specific approach. We are only at the very beginning with design, but having safe places for anybody to function and do what they need to do, no matter who they are, should be our first step.

MORALO

His fingers move slightly. An almost invisible movement adds elegance to his direct look.

HOW DID ARCHITECTURE BECOME SO CENTRAL TO OUR EXPERIENCE OF BEING RELIGIOUS?

Churches, synagogues, mosques, temples, cathedrals, and gurdwaras are plainly visible in the public sphere. Part of the purpose of architecture is to construct new forms of knowledge that relate to the enhancement and advancement of the discipline itself. In a way, this is inseparable from the performance of architecture in terms of its responsibilities to engage with the society at large.

DO PUBLIC SPACE AND ARCHITECTURE PRESENT OPPORTUNITIES FOR EMPOWERMENT THROUGH RELIGIOUS PARTICIPATION?

The right to display religious symbols and to construct religious edifices is protected by many states; as is the right of people to preach their religion in public places and to go door-to-door to spread their religious messages. Public space is where people come to know one another, through buying and selling, social-izing, playing or protesting, expressing opinions and ideas through art, performance, or prayer, and interacting with strangers, family, and friends.

Public spaces are the lynchpin of communities and the foundation of a democratic, egalitarian city. They are the 'front porches' of civil society—public libraries, community centers, public schools, and places of worship.

Parking lots are often public but by no means are they effective public spaces. The space must be comfortable and useable, safe and clean for women and men, children, and the elderly. Finally, a public space must be sociable. There must be something to do so people have reason to return.

Architecture can pose a physical obstacle to a religious group's freedom of religious exercise—that is, their actual conduct of rituals, ceremonies and other kinds of worship to fully exercise their right to establish and maintain places of worship, which is a constituent element of the right to religious freedom as guaranteed in international human-rights law.

The ability of religious communities to express their beliefs depends largely on their built structures. The buildings encompass not only the right to believe or not to believe, but also the right to express and to manifest religious beliefs.

ABUNDANT RELIGIOUS SPACE IS INDICATIVE OF A FUNCTIONING DEMOCRACY?

Although public spaces should not force people into prayers or religious ceremonies, they should also be respectful of the religious beliefs. When the design of proposed places of worship is subjected to architectural design controls imposed by planning authorities, such design controls can impinge on the freedom of religious expression.

By designing high quality and sociable public spaces, the architect has made a commitment to protecting the social fabric of the nation. The development of urban public space, as part of a larger public sphere, addresses the tensions inherent in the contemporary transformation of the urban public realm and contributes to the emergence of an urbanism that promotes social integration and tolerance.

THE RIGHT TO A SACRED PLACE IS NOT AMONG THE MORE CONVENTIONAL HUMAN RIGHTS, EVEN IF IT IS CONNECTED TO THE FREEDOM OF RELIGION OR EXPRESSION.

Communities know what to expect when a particular faith is building, as in the case of Christian cathedrals, Muslim mosques, Jewish or Buddhist or Hindu temples. A religious building is a machine for worshipping in. Less clear is when the place is just holy. Here we refer not exclusively to the way specific faiths address the world and its possibilities, but rather to places where members of specific faiths find an atemporal space, a space beyond time. This is a place we could call non-descript, which means 'neither here nor there.' A spiritual place! This involves an awakening to the natural environment instead of to the human impulse to gather under a roof. Such a location should also serve both the individual's and the group's needs for a place conducive to meditation or for meetings among those who share common quests, symbols, stories, and ethical impulses.

Authority's maintenance of power and 'order' through the control of public spaces is an explicit attempt to limit where people can move and to favor private developers in matters of land use in the city.

By soul we mean a ghost in a machine ('soul' inside 'body') and not a pilot of a ship. Instead this means the integrated vital power of a naturally organic body. Soul probably means the possibility of an ever-greater awareness of and an openness to the world, and an ever greater freedom in the world.

Citizens are entitled to enjoy free and smooth access to general public spaces and holy spaces. For a space to be truly public, it must be accessible to all citizens, regardless of race, age, gender, income, or religion.

Spiritual freedom will help develop 'free spirits' in the best senses of that term. Freedom of religion builds on the other kinds of freedoms on which democracy depends and which we should enhance—political freedom, academic freedom, freedom of choice, freedom to pursue diverse vocations and careers.

PHUMELELE

Smiling his Stan Laurel smile while pleased that he has the answer.

WHERE IS THE CONVERSATION ABOUT LOVE IN RELATION TO BUILDINGS?

If we're routinely designing the buildings in which love happens, then you might expect us to spend more time thinking about it. Buildings frame and house our relations.

There are all sorts of different types of love. Yes, there is familial love and romantic love, but also love of pets, love of work, love of God, love of books and movies, love of food, love of peace, compassionate love, and more.

WHY IS LOVE SO IGNORED BY COMPARISON WITH OTHER AREAS OF PHYSICAL OR INTELLECTUAL ACTIVITY?

Where architecture ends, life begins.

IS LOVE A HUMAN RIGHT?

There is a very clear human right to family and a right to protection from interference with family life and the right to food, the right to adequate housing, the right to health, the right to education, and the right to assembly are all interdependent and interconnected with a right to love. If you do not have food, shelter, or your health, it sure makes it difficult to go about getting some good loving. In the end, it seems that love is a central part of human rights and that human rights protect love.

It's odd how little architects have had to say on the subject of love. Yes, the availability of private or semi-private spaces allows sexual lives to exist; and their absence inhibits them.

The right to marriage, at least between women and men, is also clear. The Universal Declaration of Human Rights provides for the right to marriage: women and men of full age, without any limitation due to race, nationality, or religion, have the right to marry and to found a family. They are entitled to equal rights as to marriage, during marriage and at its dissolution.

Most architecture sets out to make us civil and efficient. Buildings represent a social life, defined by emotional reserve and obligation. They tell us where and when we can, and cannot, have sex, and with whom. We live such long and varied married lives, we deserve architecture that enables and supports us. We are living in a time of gender revolution and new modes of relations.

WHERE ARE THE HOMES THAT GIVE US PASSION AND PLEASURE? WHY IS LOVE SO ABSENT IN ARCHITECTURE?

Making people feel accommodated—we cannot approach love and sex issues in the same way, with just conventional roles and compliance. Identity is no longer clearly defined as female or male, but by increasingly visible manifestations of sexuality or lack thereof. Traditional feminine and masculine roles are being challenged by cultural shifts stemming from issues of women's and gender rights. But they are also being challenged by issues of living room, which represents so many centuries of traditional family living; yet the goings-on inside the house are an utter inversion of the sexual-societal norm.

The claustrophobically enclosed space in which people are forced to relegate their hearts and souls fails our rights to express love and joy. People are typically assigned a gender and a history, but they can decide what gender to identify with beyond this.

THAT'S HUGE. WHY IS IT THAT IN SUCH A LIBERAL, OUTWARD-LOOKING, AND WELL-INFORMED DISCIPLINE AS ARCHITECTURE, AN ISSUE SUCH AS LOVE HAS REMAINED SO TRADITIONAL?

House design is still deeply rooted in modernism, a movement shaped by a predominantly male perspective. Designers, who should focus a critical eye on society's issues, need to work within this discourse and help to promote it.

Male necessities dictate the design of prime spaces, while the female occupies ancillary areas. In one sense, architecture and gender are fundamentally related, simply because architecture by and large frames our sexual lives, contains them, provides images of them, and to some extent limits them.

Moreover, does architecture help to respect, protect, and fulfill other rights that set us up for love? Architecture as

love is a strange emotion. It can bring us close, and yet, at times it can push us further away. Balancing togetherness and space perfectly is not easy, but it's worth the effort.

CRITICAL

VERSATIC

ARCHIT

& HUMAI

DAKOTA

SIOUX'S

VERSA

C.

CON-

ONS   ON

ECTURE

N RIGHTS

(THE
CON-

TIONS)

BENJAMIN

His eyes are large and black and he wears an unseasonably short-sleeved, open neckwhiteshirt.

YOU HAVE CHOSEN TO MAKE THE NATIVE AMERICAN VOICE HEARD, AND IT IS THEIR HUMAN RIGHT TO DO SO. WHO ARE THE NATIVE AMERICANS?

I went into the Standing Rock protest as an individual, but through the protest, we emerge as a community that has once again reaffirmed its sense of place on the planet.

THE OUTSIDE WORLD IS PUSHING TO HAVE THE DAKOTA ACCESS PIPELINE INSTALLED.

The Dakota Access Pipeline project is a major response to minor needs. Their argument is energy and job creation. But that shallow economic interest shouldn't suggest to anyone that we have all of the answers for all of the questions that will confront us in the ensuing millennia. Now, let's move on. The next chapter begins with first of all asking the fundamental questions. And it is not: why? That I know, and you know. The answer is stuck in their economic interest. If you ask them to come out with alternatives or better ideas, they are not going to, because they benefit from the project. They wouldn't move one foot. The right question is: What is a nation? A nation is caring about the people and representing the people.

WE'RE LIVING THROUGH A TIME WHEN VIRTUALLY HALF OF HUMANITY'S INTELLECTUAL, SOCIAL, AND SPIRITUAL LEGACY IS BEING ALLOWED TO SLIP AWAY.

We, the Native American, are the invisible people in this country. But it's people like these that know things that we don't, and they have lots of lessons to teach us. We can learn from them the wisdom to help us leading balanced lives and to honor the land.

When you tell a story, you awake the spirit in every one. Because there is the story of yourself, the story of us, and the story of now.

The powerful tell tales about why they deserve their authority—so that they can feel better about it. So do the powerless. Their narratives offer an alternative to the dominant storyline of why things are the way they are. I am American. I am a U.S. citizen. I walk on concrete as you do. I am city-bound. But I am Lakota first. Being Lakota is the opportunity to live amongst those who have not forgotten the old ways, who still feel their past in the wind, touch it in stones polished by rain, taste it in the bitter leaves of plants.

My ancestors spent all their lifetime trying to understand how to connect with

nature and honor the Earth. I've always been interested in their relationships; they literally believe that the Earth is alive, responsive to all of their aspirations, all of their needs.

IF I SAY ARCHITECTURE WHAT COMES TO YOUR MIND?

Have you ever been inside a teepee? Your thoughts are like the wind. Completely free.
You can take down and set up a teepee in minutes. It is so quick. You tie the poles together at the top and spread wide at the bottom to make the shape of an upside-down cone. When you put good things in your circle, good returns to you multiplied. If we spend all of our nature resources, we all lose.

The pipeline travels underneath the Missouri River.
And that is the primary source of drinking water for Standing Rock Sioux, a tribe of around 10,000 with a reservation in the central part of North and South Dakota. My daughter's name is Pi-Ya. It means water. She and her brother use the waters where the pipeline poses a threat to swim, fish, and bathe his horse. This is personal.

I knew that something has gone fundamentally wrong with the decision on the construction of the Dakota Access Pipeline the day they bulldozed a section of land the tribe had identified as sacred ground. Now, 380 archeological sites face desecration. These are places of prayer. If you erase our footprint from the world you erase us as people. You erase our ancestors, our hearts and our souls. A body of knowledge about the natural world that had been empirically gleaned over centuries goes away, if we let it go. Is that not genocide? My peoples are not failed attempts at being modern—quaint and colorful and destined to fade away, as if by natural law.

CAN A DIFFERENT VISION OF LIFE MAKE OUR CONTEMPORARY URBAN EXISTENCE DIFFERENT?

A Sioux could sense the presence of a deer beyond the visible horizon, simply by watching the reverberation of grass waves across the great plain, knowing full well that every animal has its unique refractive pattern that can be read with the same perspicacity with which today we read a book. You can live without money. You can live without oil. But you can't live without water. If the pipe breaks you can't do much. The river is very, very easy to affect. But you can learn to respect water.

IF I SAY POWER?

Power is no more inherently good or evil than wind or fire. It just is. The difference is whether we will try to harness it.

WHAT WILL ALLOW THE NATIONS TO TAKE CONTROL OF THEIR ENVIRONMENTAL AND CULTURAL DESTINY?

If you appropriate something that doesn't belong to you there is a consequence. We have had enough lands taken away. The police say we are on private land. This is our land, rightfully under an 1851 Treaty. The pipeline was unfairly rerouted towards our nation and without our consent. Consulting with us is a requirement under U.S. Law. Back to the beginning: We were eight million in 1492 and less than 250,000 in 1900.

The American Dream of individual land ownership turned out to be a very clever way to divide the reservation until nothing was left.

MY LAST WORD IS WORLD.

The world may not have been made just for us.

A R C

T E C T

E C

AS

WAR

R

SYS

HI-

TURE

EARLY

N I N G

T E M

ARCHITECTURE AS EARLY WARNING SYSTEM

We are altering the planet. Architecture is part of the altering process. How do we keep humans from manipulating everything? The world is changing so fast that we urge all decision makers to steer a path for humanity away from the worst of global climate change and social inequity.

The realm of human rights is the crucible for our global future. Designers should embrace them, not disown them. They will help us to design better interactions between humans and the natural world and better interactions between humans everywhere. I believe that human rights can become the most important and long-lasting effect of urbanization, because they pave the way for socioeconomic development at the global level. If neglecting of rights creep up in the urbanization, we lose our ability to survive. When rights die off, we die off. The ongoing challenge for urban growth is whether human rights can keep developing fast enough to sustain ever expanding urban populations. As long as this trend has been established, cities will grow ever larger and will become the inevitable future manifestation of a more just and prosperous humanity.

Today's urban landscape is characterized by an unprecedented, accelerating, and complex mix of risks and opportunities. How we react to them will determine the world's future. If inequality grows, we may see more roundups, raids, deportation, camps, secessions, while injustice will get worse and worse. We cannot wait forever. The elevation of human rights to the forefront of urban design and planning would not just highlight the changes that are underway, but also help architecture to develop a new sense of a collective purpose based on a shared sense of destiny. When something terrible happens, we want to know what are the factors that lead up to it and whether there is something about it that we could spot beforehand. And by doing so we may head troubles off the pass.

Human rights cannot take place in a vacuum. Rather, they thrive in an environment that offers inspiration and the necessary framework for rights to thrive. We are in a phase where transformative change is necessary; this change opens windows for innovation and a new paradigm for architecture that is fully grounded in human rights. The emphasis on human rights and on community development is fundamental to the creation of innovative, fair, and imaginative cities. The implementation of human rights is a design challenge now, maybe the biggest one we currently face.

0) Who were the people who came before?

People remember their homes long after they've forgotten the name of their street. Most of the time, memory systems run quietly in the background as we go about the business of everyday life. Architecture works both as semantic memory, when its buildings, monuments, and ruins refer to general facts that have no real bearing on our personality and are independent of our personal experience. It works as episodic memory when it recollects our real-life events or experiences; the first kiss under the arch, the street of the incident, the building where our best friend used to live, the station of his last departure. All our decisions get integrated into a system that has evolved despite the past. The present is a process where we have to resist different ways of thinking for every decision we are going to make in the future. In the process, we have also to resist fears. Among what we fear (which is a survival process) fearing each other is becoming a very big part of (we do not fear lions or cold weather, etc.).

Monuments may engender a sense of national pride among ourselves, but they also serve as a source of rage or offense for our enemies. We fear the world that others create and we are amazed that outsiders fail to recognize us for who we consider ourselves to be. We see many of the consequences may disconnect us in our ever-changing cities.

Like linguistic communication, architecture consists of codes, meanings, semantic shifts, and syntactic units. We know architecture in terms of conceptual space, perceived space, and lived-in space, all of which supply multiple levels of meaning.

And here begins the struggle to discern between lived events and myths, between memories and the product of someone's imagination. Inside a solid world, such as the architecture of a city, our brain does not question what it sees: there is no reality check, no automatic search for objective evidence or meaning when we view a monument. Likewise, when looking at a city skyline, we lose our ability to desegregate architecture as illusion. We may instead get a sense of unfamiliarity.

Even simple acts like crossing a road may cause frustration, sadness, confusion. Similarly, street and building names are marks of authority that mask the experience of the city and organize the contradictions and complexities of our daily lives. Architecture shapes our sense of history and reflects who we are as a society and as individuals. Buildings and cities are historical documents, containing a lot of information. These documents, of course, are written largely by those who won the war, not by the tribes and people which have the better stories. This leaves many people, especially the disenfranchised—history's losers—feeling that history is moving away from them. But future events are not exact replicas of past events; and an architecture that celebrates the past at the expense of the present, as lived by a city's inhabitants, may not be well suited to stimulating a future that is hospitable to all.

How could we define a boundary that respects the present and the future as well as the past? How could we construct a safe fence within which we could have a safe operating space for both memory and identity of a city which belongs to all its inhabitants and respects all its narratives? In order to make a city such a place of concentrated diversity, where various peoples' cultures and languages and lifestyles comingle, we must find ways to consistently absorb new infusions of history and memories and identities; and we must learn to dissolve the historical fears and uncertainties we hold about one another so that we can work toward a true exchange of values.

What can architecture say about the future, from cultural to linguistic changes to the lessons of the deadliness of wars?

If cities were part of biology, they would die. Yet the truth is that very few cities fail. Even if they collapse under an earthquake or get sacked by invaders, or suffer destruction under the bombing of an enemy, after a relatively short while they rise again. For cities are organic in a human way; they repair themselves and regrow via a series of human interactions. So, what about the future of architecture now? Well, the future poses a massive challenge to humankind: to provide a physical form for interpretation and experience that does not celebrate defeat, exclusion, and does not dictate the path of a singular meaning, but rather offers a variety of multiple collective narratives. Architecture also must expand, not erode, the boundaries of universal recognition for all people, for all histories. The architecture of the future must create space for new and better human narratives. It must recognize that humans are much more than the sum of their memories.

1) The human rights ecology.

Right now, humans use half of the world to live, to grow their crops and their timber, and to use as pasturelands for their animals. If you added up all the human beings, we would weigh ten times as much as all the wild mammals put together. We face over the next two decades a fundamental transformation that will determine whether the next 100 years will be the best of centuries or the worst: fifty percent of us now live in urban areas; that's going to increase to 70 percent by 2050.

Urbanization, the dominant demographic event of our time is putting a big squeeze on planet Earth. All people need living space and eco-cultural systems in which they can thrive. Urbanization is bringing people into ever greater contact, where collectively they act as a giant physical, biological, and cultural force.

The majority of earthlings aspire toward development; yet such a large-scale aspiration means that we are aspiring toward an unsustainable lifestyle. Our present course is not sustainable, and therefore cannot be maintained. We still do not understand, and haven't reconciled our lives to the conditions needed for a stable society, an inclusive economy, and a long-term peace.

Will it improve our lives to promote inclusive and sustainable architecture on a global scale? This is not just about numbers or statistics, it is an equity issue as well. A transformative change can deprive humanity of its heart and soul or it could lift humanity to a new collective and moral responsibility based on a shared sense of destiny and dignity.

In the case of architectural design, that means balancing human rights with technical feasibility, environmental sustainability, and economic viability. We can stretch that balance to the absolute limit. And it is better so, because either we will resolve the problem of non-sustainability in smart, strategic ways by taking innovative actions or else conflicts are going to get settled in other ways, largely outside our control, namely by war, disease, or starvation.

Obviously, ecological urbanism without ecological architecture is impossible. Architecture has also real human, behavioral consequences even if we are just beginning to learn what they are. This makes us the first generation of architects to be aware that the chronic human-rights challenges associated with urban development may undermine the stability of the planet and the ability of the humankind to support its own long-term development.

We are all connected and it is our relationships with each other and with the environment that makes us part of a healthy ecosystem. We now need to restore these connections to a healthy state. Inequality can affect the stability of society because its inherent stresses can spread through the urban system like an epidemic. In the 21st century, the most effective way to improve these relationships is by rethinking and redesigning our urban habitats.

The planetary risks we are facing are so serious that building as usual is no longer an option. Architects now must become system thinkers, who can help to reinvent the world. That happens through the application of their design to the new, 21st century challenges of global warming mitigation, genocide prevention, increasing security, providing clean water, guaranteeing freedom of expression, resolving gender issues, and practicing sustainable agriculture. The looming problem of climate change is a measure of humankind's vulnerable present position; the challenge of eco-sustainability is now foremost when talking about architecture.

Without human rights, our societies will be nastier, our future bleaker, and all our great technologies wasted. Human-rights standards can help us establish modern architectural requirements of availability, accessibility, acceptability, and quality. And that means that the old idea of architecture acting in isolation, unconnected with people, and not serving to connect us as a society, is no longer a viable proposition.

So how can we best design new human settlements as catalysts for people-centered and environmentally friendly cities? One of the most practical ways is by compiling more accurate information on social sustainability issues. We can also scrutinize closer the impacts of buildings on people and communities. Then we can begin to address the underlying pressures of most serious human-rights risks and problems. Architects must identify these problems and search for unusual design alternatives to solve them. In this way, architects can use structural methods of thinking, apply them to real-world problems, and develop a new architecture that is both informed and driven by a universal recognition of human rights. Such a human-rights-centered architecture may integrate technology, biology, engineering, anthropology, psychology, oceanography, economy, while always keeping human dignity as its guiding light.

The chronic human rights challenges inherent in development undermine sustainable growth. They incorporate the most complex of all current architectural challenges: architects must prevent and confront violations that overwhelmingly affect those who have the least; they must advance existing rights of the disenfranchised; they must help them adapt new rights; they must facilitate the strengthening of the production and the management capacity of those seeking to implement these rights; and they must promote equity and environmental sustainability in the building of new habitats. So the task of modern-day architecture is to envision alternative ways to develop cities and other human settlements, to evolve a bottom-up perspective on development while, supporting and nurturing the livelihoods, assets, and settlements of the poor, and facilitating their integration into the city.

In other words, we need to think more creatively and subtly, about when and how we can shape, rather than control, unpredictable and complex human situations. Those with a tragic or historical vision of the world think that while progress is possible, justice is not. Others feel that any progress has benign consequences, as well as inherent dangers. We must accept such risks.

In fact, architecture is now at a remarkable moment. Sustainability demands the evolution of innovative solutions and never before has architectural creative thinking been in such demand.

The good news is that such difficulties and obstacles can actually improve our design. We already know how to make buildings that are greener and smarter. Facing the challenges of climate change, architects were able to break down large-scale problems into smaller fragments and design houses accordingly. On a wider scale, they have grappled successfully with problems such as nitrous oxide, methane, deforestation, and land degradation, working with experts in the field of ecology who provided vital insight as to how design could adapt to these challenges. Architects, like their ecologist colleagues, have learned to no longer look at individual species separately, but rather they now see the bigger picture of the relationships between living beings and their environment. They look at how all the diverse parts of the ecosystem are interconnected, to see how this balance, this web of life, can best sustain life in the long term.

Just as in the natural world every life form needs its own habitat and a wider ecosystem to survive and flourish, so it is for people. On our interdependent planet, *urban communities and global human rights* are co-extensive. When this relationship is disrupted, development becomes unsustainable. But architecture is the key. Witness the impact that architectural solutions have on climate change and on the production of energy: the solar panel concept, for example, was a true innovative. The likelihood of failure was massive. It was the scheme of dreamers and innovators, and it worked.

2)
The survival of each of us is tied to the survival of everyone else.

We all aspire to a place we call home and being as valuable as all others. But what is interesting is the unique way we bring our village and our distinctive lifestyle to the city. Some have called this cultural web of life the *ethnosphere*; the sum total of all thoughts and dreams, mythos and ideas brought into the global space by the human imagination. All this diversity teaches us that there are other ways of living, other ways of orienting ourselves in the world. Human culture is as vital to the wellbeing of the planet as the biological web of life that we know as biosphere.

As the volume of strangers and acquaintances in our cities rises, so do opportunities to improve their rights. Human rights are tremendously important to the way we build, yet their consideration seems extremely remote to much of today's urban planning. Understanding human rights must begin with a deep understanding of why people of a different culture do some things different from the way we do them. This process ends with us coming to appreciate their humanity. Cognition is about understanding the world, emotion is about interpreting it. In our globalized world, the fact that we are now locked together like never before means that we now must share a common destiny. The future of our cities is practically the future of humanity. Massive destruction of both biological and cultural diversity is now putting all of us at risk. It is not change that threatens identity and culture. It is domination.

Aspirations for human rights are rising as never before all over the world. With this rise, the fundamental question becomes whether we are heading toward a situation in which aspirations are linked to opportunities? Are there new ways of thinking about how we might meet these aspirations? Human rights are based on everything we do and everything we feel as individuals and as an entire race. It is when the other's freedom is conducive to our freedom that we decide we are all in favor of his/her freedom and we witness the development of tolerance. It is also when the other's welfare is conducive to ours that we see the development of justice. Simply put, these challenges may be conducive to good architecture.

Social sustainability is about identifying and managing architectural impacts, both positive and negative, on people. If equality is the issue of our century, let's evaluate and criticize our architecture by how it treats the poor. If we truly want to move beyond the dominant urban narrative of "us versus them," we must begin by listening, identifying common ground, and speaking to shared values. We *can* see world-changing values in something as humble as building a house. Human rights are the basic rights and freedoms that belong to every person in the world, from birth until death. They apply regardless of where you are from, what you believe, or how you choose to live your life. These basic rights are based on values such as dignity, fairness, equality, respect, and independence. Architecture is a way of talking about human rights in concrete physical terms that everybody can see. If we reframe architecture into a more rights-empowering practice, and thus engage in more critical reflection, we can set ourselves on a course toward a more just model of global development. Humans can adopt physically to the environmental and to social changes through architecture. The cost of disregarding human rights and the cost of disregarding nature both extend to our quality of life and to the quality of our future. Architecture stays at the crucial point between human population and the natural world, because it is so engaged with the planetary process of environmental and social progress. Exactly how architecture meets the need to reduce climate change and inequality could significantly affect how much space we have at our disposal. The possibility of improving people's lives and the lives of the many who are now discriminated against is a powerful reason to become an architect.

3) Where people go, architecture follows.

Theoretically, there are 51.7 million square miles on the planet where people could live.

The rule of history is that where people go, architecture must follow. Given that a dominant phenomenon of our age is the globalization of architecture, it follows that one of the great challenges of our age is to honor diversity as we bring architecture to the global space.

I believe that the turbulence of the decades ahead will depend on how we pursue that aim: Can we bring architecture to the global space without marginalizing the heritage and culture of people? The loss of cultural diversity, including architecture, is intricately linked to the loss of human rights. The urge for diversity has always been a part of mankind. Human life is expressed in a multitude of diverse peoples created by geographical and social adaption over the course of millennia. All the tribes of the planet—all 15,000 tribes—are today in touch with each other. They each have a right to preserve their own unique expression of humanity, the right to maintain and enrich their unique culture. They have the right to live in a harmonious habitat created in their own image, true to their own values and spirit.

Today we understand that reduced diversity poses a threat to global stability. Conflicts emerge not because people are different, but because they are not allowed to be different. Architecture must commit to the preservation of building diversity, because all people have the human urge to express their essence in the form of their places, art, music, culture, religion, traditions, and societal structure.

How can architecture support diversity? Diversity is a source of innovation, creativity, and exchange. It is never defined as a pure preservation; it is a setting for continuous, unifying dialogue between all expressions of identity. This is the process that forges diverse people into a common place that becomes familiar to us all. It leads to the discovery of street corners, where we encounter an irreplaceable sense of ourselves in the other.

If we have come to occupy every corner of the earth, and in the process generated all of this diversity, these different ways of life, these different appearances, why is that nowadays cities all over the world look the same? Why are so many shiny towers of concrete and steel covered with glass mushrooming up like a toxic species everywhere we go? The sustainability of the global space and the global city depends on the capacity to bind architecture to plausible and specific world visions. Sustainable building requires that the vision of human beings be harnessed in harmony with local cultural aspirations wherever possible. Architectural diversity provides an enabling environment for this.

4) We are a city planet.

How can universal human rights exist? The most obvious way in which human rights exist is as norms of national and international law created by the enactment of judicial decisions.

The second is architecture.

When we think of human rights, we don't automatically think "architect." That's because most people think architects design buildings and cities. But what they really design are relationships. Tightly-knit houses, interwoven alleys and streets mean that villagers' lives are constantly intersecting. Cities are defined by how people interact with each other. They're places where people come together for all kinds of exchange. Cities are complex natural and human realities. Defense and social cohesion has long since defined their design. Today climate change, together with political and economic troubles, are adding stress to cities and to the relations among city dwellers. We are faced with cataclysmic food, fuel, and water shortages. We are bogged down in a morass of multicultural conflict, and people everywhere find themselves caught up in the tangled web of the global marketplace.

Still something universal is going on here. Every week, at least until 2050, will bring an increase of more than a million people to our cities. This will significantly affect the urban architecture of the future. What's the value of architecture if our cities become unlivable? On an urbanized planet, we may soon reach a point where, for the first time, social equality becomes architectural equality. Architecture can be the slow variable, the creative strategy that regulates and buffers our capacity for human rights. We live in a world in which collaboration and interaction will become far more important than maintaining divisions. Through architecture, will we be able to use these changing conditions as a driver of social change?

A city is more than the sum of its buildings. It is a system that shows a behavior which cannot be understood or predicted by looking at the aggregation of its buildings and streets. Networks are but representations of complex systems. Architects intuitively know how to break down complex things and then bring them back together again. Through architecture, we produce and reproduce identities and social practices, continuously generating links between people and places. Architecture gives us the tools to imagine or to fear the future.

And this is where architecture and human rights are a necessity. We now live in a world churning with human migrations, proliferating technological connections, global trade, and policy shifts. Forward-looking realities are often overshadowed by suffering, abuse, degradation, and marginalization.

Universality defines us now, through our interactions and the clustering of those interactions. This is one reason why we might, in the not too distant future, see the creation of the most equal or most unequal societies that ever existed in human history.

The largest questions of human life are also questions of city life. So, what do we know about the complexity of systems that drive our cities? Well, it might turn out that what looks like complex behavior from the outside is actually the result of a few simple rules of interactions. A city has a periphery and a center which contains about 75 percent of all players. Who are the key players? Are they interconnected? What is the overall distribution of control?

We live in communal times, where all of us must choose to take an active role in the running of our cities. We must participate and take responsibility. We must choose to be city developers, we must choose to make our city sustainable. These are choices that shouldn't be made by just one part of society. This may sound wildly idealistic. You many think "That's never going to happen." Yet this was the same response to the ideas of the architects who decided they would end apartheid. It began with a small group of committed people. Human rights initiated through architecture has already worked for a group of forerunners in the global movement of cities. *Architecture is about more than clever plumbing. It's about using imagination in form, giving scale, giving order, giving rhythm, giving a living space in which people can exercise their human rights.*
Architecture, at its most imaginative, somehow transforms the lives of dwellers

and can relate to individuals and communities in a very profound way. How
do we come together and why do we stay
apart? In addition to individual narratives, every space represents a collective
narrative about sharing. We are interdependent on a global scale. We share
the planet and we share the cities.

5) Housing a world of 9 billion people.

Right now, we are 7 billion people, soon to
become 9 billion people. With 83 million
more people appearing on the earth every
year, there are no demographic voids on
the earth; people are everywhere.

Sooner or later, architecture will follow them. Each of these people will
need somewhere to live, and fertile land
to provide them with food. And if it is
therefore the case that one of the major
phenomena of our time is the urgent globalized need for housing, then it follows
that one of the challenges of our time is
to build houses in the global space.
The projection suggested by architect
Alejandro Aravena is that we will have
to build a one-million-person city per
week with 10,000 dollars per family during the next 15 years. Yes! That fast!

The only thing that it is not becoming
faster is our ability to respond to this
demographic explosion. Neither have
we come up with any radical reinven-
tion of social housing models: A little
bit of roof, a little bit of green, a little
bit of heating and shading? The clock
is ticking. If we have that many people,
there will obviously be a much greater
demand for food.

We need buildings designed to take hunger out the equation. What we eat, how

we grow it, and how we eat it will all become part of the challenges of housing. Such challenges might provide design advancements with wide-ranging repercussions on how a building might be used to mitigate against starving. A house is a powerful engine for making sustainable choices.

A house will become both an architectural act and a human-rights issue if we are to start looking at housing from a broader perspective and addressing the challenges of food production, food consumption, income generation, and social relations.

Besides not having much time, we do not have much land, nor much money to tackle these issues. The way we now use land and grow crops is extremely inefficient.
So, what are the human and natural boundaries within which architecture can safely operate? A hundred million people are homeless; how we solve this problem seems to propel us toward a head-on collision. It is misguided to just focus on population numbers and where we will find enough space on the planet to fit us all.

Put simply, cities that do not house people efficiently are not sustainable. Houses which not feed people efficiently are not sustainable. Tackling the problems of housing on a global scale won't happen through the creation of condominiums. I'm guessing it will actually happen by the powerful coming together to initiate the design of new building systems that will eventually govern the global space. Empowering locals has proven to

be a very successful strategy, as it allows local knowledge to be gleaned and used, and thus enables inhabitants to imagine and implement the housing programs themselves. The design of housing offers contemporary architects an occasion to encounter the urgency of these issues, and to solve them with designs that incorporate greater social-environmental justice.

Access to safe, decent, and affordable housing is a basic human right that should be available to everyone. Architects must now address a growing list of global challenges in their long-term work: rising oceans, dying farm fields, starvation, a rise in poverty levels, the threat to human rights, killer storms. Changing weather patterns has already influenced building design, as we've seen in the "floating city" designs coming out of the Netherlands.

A crisis can be a good catalyst. Right now, major demographic transformations are happening. But our response to those transformations, how we approach future housing and design challenges, is up to us. While housing is a human right, that doesn't mean it's free. It will only become a universal human right if we're all willing to help each other get access.

6) The implosion of human rights and the making of cities.

On a global level 1:7 million people live in unplanned settlements, favelas, refugee camps, or camps for the internally displaced. The kind of turbulent and authoritarian urban planning of Addis Ababa is typical of the accelerated urbanization taking place in Africa. This process gives thousands of households no choice but to abide by the rules and move elsewhere. The massive influx of people into cities takes place against a backdrop of geopolitical, economic, social, technological, and architectural changes. These changes pose new challenges for the disenfranchised masses, but also opportunities for the introduction of human rights in people's daily lives.

Rapid urban transformation accompanied by disregard for human rights enhance poverty and widen the gap between the city's poor and rich, in terms of income as well as in social, cultural, spatial, and political terms. Land can be sub-divided and owned. Space is a commodity. Entitlement to occupational use means that space can be sold and traded. Inequality, architecture, and real estate development are intimately connected, each unable to exist without the other. Terms such as 'informal,' 'illegal,' 'squatters,' and 'unplanned' separate most of the low-income urban population from state services and civic rights. These labels also allow the poor to be manipulated to the benefit of influential groups along the formal/regulated–informal/irregular continuum.

In more than 5,000 years of urban settlements there has rarely been a truly equalitarian culture without a privileged class controlling all others. We learn social behavior and attitudes from the physical patterns of cities. We have an elaborated code of behavior, cued by the buildings and streets. These spatial practices inform our daily use. Furthermore, narratives of cities change over time to suit the needs of society, certain groups, or individuals. Social sustainability is about identifying and managing architecture impacts on people, both positive and negative. Is home a physical place? In many parts of our cities, the opposite of a favela is not wealth. In too many places the opposite of poverty is architecture. Architecture will ultimately be judged not by technology and design, but by how it treats the poor. While GDP only accounts for a country's economic performance, architecture accounts for the dignity, freedom of choice, freedom of discrimination, and access to opportunities of citizens, visitors, occupiers, and users.

The urbanization we are witnessing on a global scale is a striking reflection of the urge for freedom and for recognition of the fundamental and inalienable rights of all people. The numbers are considerable. A billion live in squatter cities now.

Another billion are expected. That's more than a sixth of humanity living in a state of disenfranchisement. And that will determine a lot how we function as a future society. People living in resource-constrained areas aren't less than, and they aren't other. They do not need an architecture which will merely help them, they need an architecture which will ultimately empower them.

7) Architecture is bigger than architects.

Cities are a permanent force for change; the idea that we can fix a problem and then walk away is the exact opposite of what we need to be thinking. Instead, architects are involved in an interactive creative act that is fluid, that's going to continue to be in motion, and one with which humans are going to continue to interact. The designers of today's world must ask themselves: will future generations want to live in the cities and in the buildings we're leaving to them?

As we shape the global development agenda and frame our thinking at this historical juncture, we must reflect on the architecture produced up to this point, and be mindful of our thoughts, actions, and motivations moving forward. Instead of "I'm here to help," we might try: "I'm here to work with you, to leverage both of our skill sets."

As architects, we now have to rethink the oppressive notion that the global community "needs our help" and that we are uniquely qualified and able to contribute. Most innovation isn't driven by a few isolated visionaries; rather, it is driven by millions of people empowered to imagine and implement new ways to live, and to adapt and improve

existing ones. It's a great example of how architecture, as living things do, evolves and adapts to its surroundings and the social circumstances.

From a mathematical point of view, cities are the physical manifestation of interaction between masses of individuals, and the subsequent clustering and groupings that result. Architecture frames both our interaction with the planet as well as our interactions with each other. In order for neighborhoods to be safe and lively, they depend on people who are able and willing to invest time, energy, and creativity toward improving and enlivening local conditions. They also depend on extended social networks: If neighborhoods are to be safe and supportive environments for children and other dependents, neighbors need to know and watch out for each other and feel a basic responsibility for their environment. Social cohesion and mutual understanding are the basis of good neighborhoods. So the architecture challenge will be to effect a monumental transformation. If we manage it in a negligent or a shortsighted way, we will create waste, pollution, congestion, destruction of land, and inequality. What about if architecture is used to strengthen social resources and human capital, rather than just to build physical structures? This would indeed constitute a profound architectural change.

A city is primarily all of us together. A successful city will accommodate people who are constantly adjusting to changes and difficulties by adapting the existing architecture to their future. Building often effects lives in a very real way; it can rip families apart, foul rivers and pollute the air; it can intensify the calamitous effects of climate change, imperil the planet, and exacerbate inequality. As a collective act, architecture is inseparable from society and from the Earth.

The architecture of the future will be about ideas and more and more about people's decision-making and power. It will be less a space of representation and much more a space of interaction. There is a growing understanding—especially by architects and progressive urban planners—that it is not enough for architecture to concern itself only with short-term profits, because natural disasters, social unrest, or economic disparity can damage long-term prosperity.

The architects that understand this challenge and take action will be a step ahead. Architecture, not architects, is potentially positioned to lead the way in limiting inequality.
Today, the competitive advantages of cities that attract the best and brightest minds from around the world include increases in freedom, diversity, tolerance, culture, and dynamism. Still, many current urban redevelopment schemes fail to address the needs and priorities of the urban poor, and end up impoverishing and marginalizing these communities instead.

8) Everyone else's lives are as complex and as unknowable as our own.

The main purpose of this book is to weave a complex web of ideas and thoughts to show that the world's future depends on architecture. That is a terrifying and exciting thought. I am very grateful to have had the opportunity of addressing these issues by giving voice to the people of Addis Ababa. I hope my book creates a safe space for this type of honest exchange, and gives people an opportunity to engage one another in real and necessary conversation.

It is hard to believe you deserve respect when you don't have a home, when your country of origin rejects you, when you must leave the country or city you grew up in to escape persecution or hunger, or when your city is completed destroyed.

The idea of human rights has inspired many of the world's greatest reformers for centuries. It is notable that today many architects seem to believe that the high and rising levels of inequality in the way we shape and construct cities is objectionable in itself and it is worth asking how things could be done differently.

If the only people who can protect themselves from the gaze of urbanization are the rich and the powerful, that's a problem. And it is not just an economic problem. It is a human-rights problem.

Architecture coupled with human rights is probably the best way to give a human face to the new phenomenon of urbanization. Inequality brought about by architecture can undermine the legitimacy of architecture itself. Any architectural explanation which seeks to untie the connections between the poor and the rich, will inevitably cast the poor as responsible for their own lack of empowerment. It lays inequities and alienation squarely at the feet of the poor. But if cities are to be 'inclusive, smart and sustainable' we should all be part of the conversation about architecture and human rights.

Is poverty a lack of basic resources or the unequal distribution of space, resources, and opportunities? In fact, we redefine what poverty means all the time. In rich countries, the majority of people on the poverty line still have electricity, water, toilets, refrigerators, television, and mobile phones. While the ones under the poverty line do not have homes.

A trophic cascade of poverty is an "ecological" process, which starts at the top of the building chain and tumbles all the way down to the state of homelessness. In our comfortable, safe, crowded cities, we build and harm people.

Many, including philosophers, architects, and ordinary people, believe that human nature is fundamentally selfish, that we're only ever really motivated by our own welfare. But if that's true, why do some have the fortitude to stand up to some of the world's greatest injustices? Because who we are, and the extent to which we are human, depends on how human everyone around us is.

9) Going to the root of the matter.

I don't think we account enough for the effect of architecture on human history. A major turning point in human history came when tribal/village organization developed with the advent of agriculture. That is where private property began, division of labor began, issues of power and economics began. Architecture began. And soon architecture became our main interface with the earth; it became the dimension through which we interact with each other and organize and are organized by larger systems of political, legal, and economic class structuring.

The real break in future human history will be a planetary urbanization; we are already evolving into a global network civilization. Cities are the infrastructure that most define us now. This is a new way of human living which has never quite happened in the way it is happening now. The world's urban population currently stands at around 3.5 billion. It will almost double to more than six billion by 2050. Under the effect of this boom, cities and towns across the globe will grow rapidly and re-develop. Instead of thinking about what to build, we are now building in ways that reflect how we think.

What's happening today is that architectural interventions have now migrated in very large measures onto the global stage, which is largely unregulated and not subject to considerations of human rights. In this global structure, those who hold power may act largely free of constraint.

At this stage, there is no property-defining status at all for many urban dwellers except their very existence in unauthorized spaces. Only their presence in such spaces gives them any effective right to be there.

Who are the poor? The logical explanation links the rich directly in opposition to the poor and by doing so casts the poor as responsible for their own lack of empowerment and the resulting inequities and alienation. Yet the poor are not a mass of people with abject lives who are owed something better. These people are valuable as a group. They have perspective, experience, priorities, aspiration, and their own realities. They are communities currently denied the political, civil, economic, and cultural rights that they should have according to internationally recognized principles human rights. These are not simply people crushed by poverty. These are people busy getting out of poverty just as fast as they can.

The poor are helping each other in their efforts to escape their poverty. They're doing it by transcending the laws, by becoming outlaws in effect, by operating in the informal economy. Most of all they use their social organization, a complex system of friendship, kinship, acquaintanceship networks, and associational ties rooted in family and social lives.

They engage in neighboring activities with one another—including borrowing tools or food, having lunch or dinner, or helping each other with problems. It is not the case that slums undermine prosperity; they help create prosperity. Where everybody is connected to everybody else, the most important thing is that everything a person can do they can do with others. We don't understand yet how it works, but architects will need to learn this lesson soon.

10) What's architecture?

There is no single and exhaustive definition of architecture, nor is there a delineation of its scope that commands universal acceptance. The word architecture is used with great flexibility; this is an advantage, but it also creates confusion when it comes to practical application. Whether architecture can be defined at all has long been a matter of controversy.

And to make things worse, the definition of architecture is controversial in contemporary philosophy. Moreover, the philosophical usefulness of a definition of architecture has also been debated. Contemporary definitions are of two main sorts. One distinctively modern, conventionalist, sort of definition focuses on architecture's building features, emphasizing the way architecture changes over time, how modern buildings appear to break radically with traditional architecture, and how the relational properties of an architect's projects depend on their works' relations to architectural history, style, etc. The less conventionalist sort of contemporary definition makes use of a broader, less traditional concept of aesthetic properties and includes more social-relational ones. This focuses on pan-cultural and the trans-historical characteristics of shaping social space and solving problems with buildings.

In the final analysis, architecture is any creative act which will transform a place into a somewhere human beings live. Without architecture, I fear I should not be able to find my way across the world; nor know how to conduct myself in any circumstances, nor what to feel in any area of life. There is no enterprise that connects us to each other, moves us to action, and strengthens our ability to make collective choices more than architecture. There is no approach that breaks barriers, connects across cultural differences, and engages our shared values more than architecture and human rights.

Architecture is about disclosing relations through the alteration of space.

Such an approach would transform both the relationship between human beings and between humans and the planet. That's what *climate* change does. It limits the Earth's capacity, to the point where there's not enough capacity to support its population. That's what negative *social change* does. With no human rights, it makes all of us victims of global injustice. The true test of architecture is the degree to which it delivers on the promise of human rights; civic, cultural, economic, political, and social. Architecture will ultimately not be judged by technology and design, we will judge it by how it treats people. That is when we'll understand all the truly profound aspects of being an architect.

Architecture holds that just as there are reliable ways of finding out how the physical world works, or what makes buildings sturdy and durable, there are also ways of finding out what individuals may justifiably demand of architecture. Mainly because space alteration can deeply transform the relationship between the poor and the rich.

In a way, I feel like this is the choice that faces us today. If we dismiss these tasks as unacceptable or impossible or none of our business, we might as well just pave them over. Now it would be easy for us to dismiss architecture as excessive, as unnecessary, a waste of money and resources when compared with the destitution, ills, and social injustices ever-present around the world. If we do this, we would be missing the point of architecture. Architecture is the dominant strategy by which humanity's landscapes are shaped for social life. It is our interface with the earth and the space through which we interact with each other and organize and are organized by larger systems of political, legal, and economic class structuring. And in a world where everything is changing, we need to be very smart about how we define architecture.

And so, I believe that architecture is not just those buildings and spaces that are designed by architects, by women or men. I think that architecture is anywhere that life thrives, anywhere that there are communities, people, and other species together, anywhere that's under a blue sky, filled with life and growth. So where does this put human rights? What counts as human rights in a world where everything is influenced by architecture?

Architecture is the beginning of something.

11) When an architecture project is evicting or displacing, "the truth of its architecture is temporarily unavailable."

Why do so many architectural projects build a fragile social edifice based on disdain for rights, rather than a building that incorporates a critical viewpoint? Although we acknowledge development to be necessary and beneficial, all development is bound to displace something or someone. It may be the flora and fauna of the natural environment; it may be the cultural heritage of a people; it may be the people themselves.

One of the tragic and yet regular consequences of urban transformation is forced displacement. Displacement is a threat to the peace; it gradually expands into violent conflicts, human-rights abuses, proliferation of violence, and ultimately terrorism. In the context of a changing geopolitical community, displacement is tied to aspects of human security—the challenges of climate change, poverty, illness, economic under-development, and interdependence.

One of the reasons why displacement is so commonplace may be due to the feelings of many architects about their profession. This can be translated into a belief that 'my building is worth more than the rights of people.' Such thinking is "corrosive" of our sense of justice and our democracy, because it has disastrous consequences, particularly for the most vulnerable. It's also terribly narcissistic.

Architecture can easily become 'me space,' a place for individualism, for people's nascent and by now overwhelming urge to claim space for themselves, and to claim that space from others, from society and from the state by emphasizing privacy over communalism and denying strangers access to the community and its resources.

I associate architecture without human rights at its core to psychopathy. Architecture without human rights is cold and uncaring. This kind of architecture results in antisocial and sometimes very violent acts against humanity. Think of the dictator Ceaucescu in Romania razing many city blocks and displacing hundreds of residents in order to build his monstrosity of grandiose architecture, the so-called "House of the Republic." When an architectural project ends up evicting or displacing people in this way, "the truth of its architecture is temporarily unavailable."

This is post-architecture, its borders blurred between racism and indifference. It happens through a selective clearance approach, in the demolition of neighborhoods. Forced evictions can have catastrophic effects, particular-

ly for people already living in poverty. The evicted do not just lose their homes and possessions, they also lose their livelihoods, their social networks, and the basic services they rely on for survival. They struggle to find clean water, food, and toilets. They struggle to find work and schools for their children. And they struggle to rebuild their shattered lives, often with no help or support from the governments that uprooted them.

What does architecture mean in the context of such transformation, great social changes, ethnic conflicts, urban inequalities, environmental threats, and economic problems? The answer is a widespread sense that much of what we have built can't be tolerated, because at the root of the human-rights concept is the idea that all people should be able to live with dignity. Accepting eviction, or rights deprivation, or outright rights denial as inevitable, or acceptable if it gets things done faster, is horrifying, and how many of us would want to live in a world where that's the norm?

12) The future tense of architects.

Buildings naturally resist change, especially when they are built solidly. But architecture can make change even harder for people than it needs to be. First of all, planners often wait too long to act. As a result, planning and design then happens in crisis mode. We seem unable to marshal an appropriate design response to the dangers that lie ahead. Dealing with present stresses and social traumas can cloud visions of what lies ahead. We're just cleaning up our messes over and over again. Alternatively, architecture can be less reactive to present circumstances and more focused on meeting our future needs. We are always going to create and repair and rebuild. But design can go much further than that. With imaginative and innovative design, we imagine things that don't yet exist. This is a visionary step beyond simply making a building. The future is more of a verb than a noun. The future requires action. If we don't act on the future, we're only working in a profession that's about remediation. The world is changing so fast that we need to steer away from the worst of global climate and social inequality. There is a risk of the elite doing things that would bring the society down in the long run and insulate themselves from its consequences by living in gated compounds.

We build as if we were only 20 billion in population. That's why people migrate to cities and slums and shanty towns. Data on economic inequality shows the things that go wrong when poor and rich are too far apart: real effects on health, lifespan, even such basic values as trust, collaboration, self-determination, and respect. Designing for "some" and letting the others adjust to this new reality isn't smart, because we will be left with results that will make the vast majority of the global population unhappy.

Our global problems are so vast that we need to open ourselves up to change and changes in our way of thinking. Human culture and sustainability are only possible if we can anticipate our future. Bees build dwellings because they are genetically designed to do so, not because they agree on a blueprint.

Projecting the future enables architecture to become knowledgeable not just from our own experiences, but also from those of our fellow humans. Most architects are ready for this challenge. We see why it's necessary.

Discrimination through architecture, urban planning, and landscape design amounts to a bleak view of our immediate future.

This future is not far-off. It is fast approaching and will soon be with us; the effects of discrimination are already happening and are already affecting us.

Inequality is nothing new. What is new is that the narratives and data that make inequality intelligible as rendered tangible through architecture. Inequality begins when a line is drawn that separates inside from outside and ultimately one house from another.

It is easy to understand why people want to be better off than they are, especially if their current situation is very bad. But why, apart from this, should architects be concerned with the difference?

If architecture contributes to socioeconomic disparities, it can also do the opposite. It can generate positive design solutions to rectify specific human rights offenses, based on an understanding of the design decisions taken by offenders. The challenge facing the design sector now is to analyze our accumulated know-how and use it to reverse poverty, injustice, violence, inequality, and discrimination.

And, given the urgency, what we can do is to ask architects to envision more positive outcomes. Equality doesn't emerge magically from a womb; it is built. The architecture of our future cities is going to depend on the capacity to 'invent' the future of the people who shape it now. Looking into the future is a central function of social change for the reasonable logic that what makes humans thrive is considering their prospects. The people who plan our futures need to consider how architecture can help us all prosper: After all, planning a new building is much simpler than solving problems of poverty, starving, unemployment, and crime.

13) Ensuring that no one is left behind.

Many of the world's resources are located on land owned or controlled by indigenous peoples. This means that when we build we are frequently in close contact with indigenous groups and so improving our relationships with these groups is becoming increasingly important.

There are many opportunities to involve indigenous people as decision makers, owners, builders, suppliers, contractors, and final users. This can contribute to the long-term success of projects and help embed design into the local community. Yet many of the world's indigenous people have suffered abuse, eviction, discrimination, and marginalization, sometimes because of adverse architectural plans.

Architectural change is altering the pattern of life for indigenous peoples, causing widespread extinction, migration, and behavior changes. As a result, many indigenous people live in poverty. Their cultures, languages, and livelihoods are threatened. In some cases, the damage they've experienced cannot be undone. Human rights are universal and every person around the world deserves to be treated with dignity and equality. Basic rights include freedom of speech, privacy, health, life, liberty, and security, as well as an adequate standard of living.

The UN estimates that there are over 370 million indigenous peoples living in over 90 countries. They are particularly vulnerable to the impacts of commercial development and business activities.

When architecture treats indigenous people with understanding and respect, these people are also more likely to fulfill and maintain their ability to operate as a society. As we shape the global development agenda and frame our thinking at this historical juncture, we must be reflective about the architecture of the past and highly mindful of our thoughts, actions, and motivations while designing the architecture of the future. Instead of approaching architecture with an attitude of "I'm here to design," we might try: "I'm here to work with you, to leverage both of our skill sets." We have to rethink the oppressive notion that the global community needs our solution and that we are uniquely qualified to help them.

Wouldn't it be great if we could find in cities the vast diversity of landscapes and experiences that exists across the natural world? For one thing architects have largely ignored the global diversity of human living and thinking. The tacit assumption of much modern architecture is that living in a condo represents the assumed belief that this is a universal aspiration and that all people are basically the same.

14) Architecture molds our minds.

We need a theory that explains why different populations have different architecture; we need to try to understand the kaleidoscope of different ways of living and thinking in different architectural settings. While architectural forms appear largely static, they continually change through our vision and use. I would not be surprised if our ways of thinking reflect the local architecture we grew up with. While identities link our inner ideas with the outer world, architecture links the outer world with our inner ideas.

In architecture and cities, we encounter the "other," both in terms of people and objects.
We see who others are, what they think, feel, and believe by what is expressed in buildings and places. Some of the most remarkable differences of neighborhoods revolve around the concepts of individualism versus community-building—whether spaces make their inhabitants consider themselves to be independent and self-contained or interconnected with others. These differences translate to a more collectivist or individualistic architectural mind-set.

Some architecture makes us more individualistic, prouder of success, more ambitious for personal growth, and less connected to others. Architecture fostering individualism tends to influence people to value personal success over group achievement. This search for self-validation can be seen in design as well as in the emphasis of people living in individualistic environments to stress personal property and freedom.

Where architecture fosters community, people tend to have a more collectivist and holistic mind-set. Living in a slum, for instance, requires far greater cooperation. Where poverty compels innovation, locals get together to help one family by improvising floor space enhancements. Our thinking may have ever been shaped by the kind of architecture that surrounded us. A skyscraper is vertical, a profoundly hierarchical structure, with the top always representing the best, the bottom the worst, and the taller the building the better. Buildings touch the way we think, feel, reason, and compare ourselves with people living elsewhere. They can make us sensitive to being looked down on, or they can boost our self-esteem. Values and identities are represented in all architecture and cities, and furthermore, some collective sets of beliefs are more apparent than others.

Until the invention of cities, humans had their eyes on the natural world around them. Their world included rivers, forests, animals, and plants. Today 90 percent of what we see is architecture, 90 percent of our time we spent inside architecture. We are surrounded by architecture. Architecture influences the way we see the world and understand it.

15) Architecture molds our morality.

The word ethics comes from the Greek word ethos, which means custom or behavior. Ethics defines the way we do things and the way we act. The meaning of 'ethics' is more or less equivalent to that of 'morals,' which comes from the Latin 'mos, moris' and also means custom or behavior, but at a more personal level. Morals infer that ethical values are rather personal interpretations, deliberations or preferences and not general principles that can be proven true or false. Morality evolves, through decision-making and choices between what is right and what is wrong, just like any other field of human knowledge.

We have seen morality progress over time. In the Bible's law, it was perfectly acceptable to own, beat, and rape your slaves. Some 2,500 years ago, members of one Greek city considered members of another Greek city to be sub-human and treated them that way. The bricks used by ancient Romans to build an arena in which gladiators would fight to their death for the public's entertainment are still in place—and will be until the Coliseum crumbles.

The problem with morality, and therefore with human rights, is that not everyone agrees on what is moral: until there is some conventional acceptance as to what constitutes right or wrong, confusion will reign. For most of us the task of taking care of human rights is very definitely the responsibility of the government. We might have worries, we might have rage, we might have standards, but we expect legal and political enforcement from our representatives. *That has to change.*

Building is based on an embedded set of goals, values, functionality, and spatial relationships, and on a clearly defined set of environmental and social issues and priorities.

When we design to accommodate cars, we express a dominant vision of our values.
Morality may be understood as our ability to model, sense, monitor, and set up a new form of design, one with humanity at its center. By doing so, we begin to imagine new goals for architecture. In a controlled society, values are well codified and require a critical mind, free of prejudice and open to new ways of thinking. What we can do is turn the problem on its head. Instead of asking "are we right, fair, just, or good persons?," maybe we should ask "which is the right building process that ensures people will live safely and be good stewards of the Earth in the Anthropocene?" By reframing the question, we can focus on what's wrongheaded about our current situation, and on finding alternative solutions. People throughout the world have different moral convictions. The real challenge is not moral pluralism, but the ability to translate ideals into a set of clearly defined solutions that can be interpreted and applied into architectural design.

We often use architecture not to solve the problems of social living but principally to serve the interests of a privileged minority. So those who have greater power in this globalized world are able to disproportionately influence the values of the age—including the ethics of their society, often through the alteration of the common space. The relationship between public and private space is the source of further ethical issues, which are important not only for the economy, but for all sectors of society.
Is homelessness just an accepted fact of urban life? To be ethical we have to learn to be deviant, because we could need to go against the conformity of prevailing values. We also need to avoid always seeing problems through a technological lens. If we push ourselves into inventing solutions for climate change, poverty, homelessness as visions for our futures, we are pushing ourselves into a moral evolution.

There are four ways I'd suggest by which ethics can drive architectural decisions:
1) Approaching each project from the question of its public interest
2) Focusing on sustainability, which means arresting and reversing the degradation of our planet, both natural and social
3) Fighting inequality, that is to say focusing on people rights and bring them into the space
4) Improving the participation of all, especially those in vulnerable situations

Ethical considerations always underpin how we design, plan, and build. They also underpin the vast majority of urban decisions. How do we account for architecture that endorses discrimination, racism, and aggressive or violent expansion? Again, in some important sense, these tendencies are built into the ethical system of our globalized world. Is being homeless just a matter of fact?

The need for a seismic shift in values exists at both the professional and individual level.
The world is, was, and always will be filled with rights and wrongs. Power, or its abuse, often produces the greatest wrongs: intentionally harming people's dignity, hurting people physically, destroying people's morality, killing ideas, not to mention permitting crimes against humanity. Ethical issues include affordable housing, homelessness, the moral status of migrants, violence, and discrimination. Ethics are practical questions relating to daily life. Ethics help us get better solutions, and enable us to do our job better and to help us feel better when we do it.

16)
The bias in architecture.

When we first enter an urban space, we tend to label people living there in certain ways.
"A poor neighborhood" we might think, or "a dangerous street." This common experience suggests that there are some categorizations that spring faster to mind. So fast, in fact, that they can be automatic, or reflexive. The income of people living in that area is an example: we tend to notice whether someone is poor or rich. You can see this in the way people talk about places: squalid buildings, oppressive masses, drab streets, anonymous blocks, human dust-bins . . .

This is unfortunate, because if perceiving poverty is automatic, then it lays a foundation for racism, and appears to put a limit on efforts to educate people and architects to be income-blind or to put aside prejudices in other ways. Do we need to fix their housing? They are poor, but they are intensely urban. And they are intensely creative. The aggregate numbers now suggest that it is really squatters, all one billion of them, who are building the modern urban world, which means they're building the world—personally, one by one, family by family, neighborhood by neighborhood. Of course, cities are hardly homogeneous entities.

We break them up into our city versus their city, residential versus slum, downtown versus uptown, in-group community versus out-group community, and sometimes when we do this, we know we're doing something wrong. Architecture always entails an active taking of sides and it makes this almost inevitable because of its physical connectedness and inclusivity.

The ability to architecturally stereotype people is not some sort of arbitrary quirk of the architect's mind; rather it's a specific instance of a more general process, which is that we experience economies and people within a world that categorizes: so we use these categories to make generalizations and groupings when we meet new instances of these categories. Our stereotypes and biases have real-world consequences, both subtle and important. Stereotypes can go awry. So often they're irrational, they give the wrong answers, and other times they lead to plainly immoral consequences.

We can start with the two most common misconceptions. Misconception number one: this is not our responsibility, not an architectural issue. Misconception number two: the most pressing humanitarian issues on our Earth are located in the south. We have all heard this and might even have thought it ourselves. An alternative way to think is: all architecture matters, north, south, east, and west.

An alternative way to think is: most ingenious and effective solutions stem from resolving intractable problems.

So now that we know about this, how do we combat bias? One avenue is to appeal to our ethical responses, to appeal to people's empathy, and we often do that through stories. The preservation not only of buildings but of communities makes cities viable, makes cities livable, makes cities equitable. We need not just talent but also profound respect for all people and recognition of the importance of our contribution to counter an unethical and immoral view of the world. Conserving cultural heritage, maintaining cultural diversity, defining and establishing cultural citizenship, and enforcing human rights are all of contemporary relevance for architecture. Segregation and zoning enables one group to treat another as inferior and deny that group fundamental human rights. Another approach is to evolve new forms of creativity and creative thinking and to be aware of the responsibilities of architecture as a framework for social action.

17) The truth in architecture.

Architecture has traditionally been understood as a constructive discipline. Actually, we may think more appropriately of architecture as reconstructive. There is always distortion, contamination, and change within architecture. It offers a place we can go to effect change in the world. Or somebody else can go there and bring change. Anytime. Any person. When people move in, they bring a new life to the space. In some sense, design becomes an ongoing layering process that always opposes the status quo: it takes "this is what it is" and asks "why could it not be this?" The act of inhabiting is influenced by various factors including perception, imagination, semantics, and beliefs, amongst others.

There is not just one player in architecture; the stakeholders are many. Is architecture about the place or is it about the people? Architecture compels us to seek the truth. There is always a definite link between the architecture of a place and the character of the community that has settled there.

On the other hand, overestimating architecture's capacity to "create" distorts our perception of what a community actually wants and will benefit from.

Architecture does not work like a video recording of human lives, rather as a reconstructive memory suggested in the absence of other data; it is up to us to fill in the gaps and to make more sense of the space. The "creation" paradigm focuses the action on those who "create," without much thought given to those who receive. It assumes that those coming to "create" always have the right idea, the right approach, and the right tools. The complexity that relates to the urban environment is the same complexity that relates to us.

And when we say "us," "our" or "we," we have to reach out a bit. There are multiple groups called "we" here. What is our stand here? The fabric of reality emerges from our human interactions. No single group should get to decide the destiny of any other. Many projects nowadays reveal how architecture is crucial to dealing with changes in everybody's life and situations. Technology is changing architecture faster than ever, bringing with it brand-new dwelling ideas, while our most pers istent troubles—like discrimination and *the negation of human rights*—haven't been addressed.

If we plant the idea of human rights into the design of future dwellings, we may create space for new discoveries. We are more and more grasping the relevant variable of design. Buildings are prototype ideas about how the space of living, working, and sharing could engage us. There is no end to man-made problems and seemingly no way to stop man-made environmental transformations, but neither is there an end to human vision. Cities are built by successive generations of urban dwellers, each building on top of each other's ideas. The stories we tell ourselves about the places we live in matters. Even more the way we participate in each other's stories.

18) Adaptive is the word.

Being adaptive in architecture is being able to actually develop targeted antibodies to threats that have never even been met before. It is more about building a better world than a better building, addressing issues such as poverty, disease, segregation, access to sanitation, and pollution. Architecture is intended to change the human habitat, not just describing the existing one.

The strong claims made on behalf of architecture and human rights frequently provoke skeptical doubts among those who see the function of architecture as being no more than building a structure of stones, wood, glass, and concrete, all arranged in a pleasing fashion. Concern for equality may at times require us to point out the unjust, but even more it calls us to highlight the sustainability of our organization of space.

Such a claim suggests that architectural decisions are not based solely on the present but on expectations for the future. Concern for the future is a call for a new radical humanism, which prioritizes human respect rather than human domination and celebrates questions instead of answers. At its core, it recognizes that human dignity needs to be respected. In other words, we need to think more creatively and subtly about

when and how we can shape, rather than control, unpredictable and complex human situations. If not, the environment we create will be "unadaptable" to humans.

As central as bodily experience may be, it cannot be the only source of architectural aspiration. Architecture will not ultimately be judged by technology and design, we will judge it by how it treats people. The initial organization of the space does not depend that much on architecture. Nature provides a first draft, which human experience then revises. Built-in doesn't mean unmalleable, it means organized in advance of experience. Due to changes in globalization, due to advancements in technology and other factors, architecture is constantly having to adapt to the needs of humankind. Architecture can be used to help people to find their place in the world both physically and socially.

But let's not just focus on the bright and dazzling things. In the future, our design could be overshadowed by human experiences of suffering, abuse, degradation, and marginalization. Unless we address these realities, then our positive beliefs will be implicated too.

In this respect, architecture may now need to review its well-regarded traditional role. Architecture is usually tasked with the organization of spatial adjacencies—inside and outside, natural and cultural, private and public, sacred and profane; and to this list we may now need to add human and inhuman. This will occur when we understand truly profound things about being human and have no choice but to create more cities based on human rights. Because who we are, and the extent to which we are human, depends on how human everyone is around us.

The human rights properties of a given design are subject to criticism, the very purpose of which is to influence the designer toward further human-rights considerations in that design. In fact, this is the era of "always-on" transformation and architecture is at a remarkable moment in time. The reality is that this transformation is much too important to put the burden solely on the United Nations or governments acting alone. If human rights exist only because of legal enactment, their availability is contingent on domestic and international political developments.

Adaptive capacity encompasses the ability of architects to modify exposure to, absorb and recover from climate and social change impacts, and also to exploit new opportunities that may arise through adapting to our changing world.

19) What are Universal Rights?

We stand today at the threshold of a great event both in the life of the UN, and in the life of mankind.

With these words, Eleanor Roosevelt presented the Universal Declaration of Human Rights to the United Nations. It was 1948 and UN member states, determined to prevent a repeat of the horrors of World War Two, were filled with idealism and aspiration.

The Universal Declaration provides a setting of common standard for legal achievement, and we could consider it a template against which every system of law will be measured. Finally, its words and sentiments have become the lingua franca of how people should be treated.

At the same time the concept of human rights is continually evolving through countries worldwide recognizing and codifying new human rights or clarifying the content of existing standards.

The rights which are laid down in law are called legal rights. Is a human a living thing recognized by law? Or is it rather to be a living thing belonging to the human race?

Rights arising out of general principles of fairness and justice are called moral rights.

While human rights are claims recognized by states according to a moral or philosophical approach, moral rights are necessary to human dignity.

Thus, a moral right asserts that even if it does not have the sanction of the state, it is a right because it is now accepted by human civilization as a basic condition that every human being is entitled to expect. The implementation of human rights can go well beyond legislation. So even if they can and often do inspire legislation, it is a further fact that rather that for human rights to be legal, or pro-legal, ideally their legality—their status as enacted law—should not be their constitutive justification.

Without going into abstract philosophical debates, it would probably be universally agreed that what we normally call human rights are the minimum agreed standards defining our humanity at this point in history.

Human rights encompass a whole set of values, and provide a template against which we should measure our design and ourselves. Are human rights created or discovered?

And at this point you may ask why does it matter? Is this just a game that activist and politicians and philosophers play? The answer is that it matters quite a lot. Because if we believe in sustainability and we get the answer wrong on human rights, we may end up building cities that collapse.

The struggle for rights seeks state recognition but pursues it in society and culture to further realize it in practice. The greatest hope for humanity lies not in condemning human-rights abuses, but in making such abuses obsolete.

The idea that the struggle for human rights is equivalent to street protests is also very limiting. Because although protests can be a powerful public expression of a desire for change, on their own they don't actually create change— at least not change that is fundamental.

In fact, most of the rights that we enjoy today in this country—as women, as minorities, as workers, as people of different sexual orientations, and as citizens concerned with the environment, were not handed to us. They were won by long struggles for change.

Let's learn more about where design solutions have worked and how we can make change more powerful, just like we do with other systems and technologies that are constantly being refined to better meet human needs. Architecture provides a pretty harrowing link between what's happening to our environment and what's happening to our human rights.

20) How can we build without destroying the planet and without trampling over human rights?

When it comes to the current transformation of our cities, you can't help but get a sense of excitement. Urban transformation is empowering and energizing. Growth in the economy and in the population, on the other hand, is putting increasing pressure on our land, on our water, and on our forests. Billions of people perhaps might soon have to move, and if we've learned anything from history, that will probably mean severe and extended conflict.

This is a completely unsustainable pattern. We still seem to lack the depth of understanding of the immense risks of human rights violations. When people's rights are violated, when their countries are occupied, when they're oppressed and humiliated, people need a powerful way to resist and to fight back. Most of us are concerned with the level of violence in the world. But we're not going to end war by telling people that violence is morally wrong.

As stakeholders and active creators of this transformation, architects need to have a vision, a clear road map with agreed-upon milestones, and then they need to hold people accountable for results. In other words, architects need to be directive, committed, and creative. But in order to capture the hearts and minds of people, their architecture also needs to be inclusive.

Inclusive architecture is critical to putting people and their rights first. Too often, our first impulse is to make decisions on other's behalf. Instead, we must offer a tool that's at least as powerful and as effective as violence. The imperative for putting people first is to empower people with the capabilities and the rights that they need to succeed during the transformation and beyond. The classic view is that architects and those who live in their buildings can do their dwelling on one side, while policy does the rest, keeping "social sustainability" as a distinct subject from architecture.

In reality, architecture is never a stand-alone discipline. It is embedded in the larger organization of humanity, and it can work in complete harmony with humanity's social and natural environment, to create an unprecedented level of human-rights protection.
To achieve this however, multi-dimensional thinking is needed.

Architecture is primarily concerned with a body in space. But a person's body and a person's rights cannot be separated like subject and object. We must be physically respected to fully experience rights, freedoms, and equality.

The structural quality of architecture emanates from the human body but the sustainability of architecture emanates from human rights. How can we find a way to design that is contemporary, contextual, humble, participative, and descriptive of these expanded roles for architecture?

Gandhi's oft-quoted advice goes: "How do you know if your next act will be the right one or the wrong one?" He said "Consider the face of the poorest, most vulnerable human beings that you ever chanced upon, and ask yourself if the act that you contemplate will be of benefit to that person. And if it will be, it is the right thing to do, and if not, rethink it." This is why any reflection on the future of architecture should start by analyzing architectural responses to the poor.

If not, I'm afraid to say, the social divide is going to keep getting worse, faster than we imagine. The implementation of human rights is a profoundly complex, nonlinear challenge, full of elusive demands, hidden thresholds, and irrevocable tipping points. Human rights are specific and problem-oriented.

21) What do Universal Rights hold for you, for me, for us?

It is crucial not to narrow universal rights to a juridical debate and to start seeing them as powerful tools to construct better cities. And with an increasing number of urban planners and states reluctant to honor human-rights treaties, it might be also very smart.

Today's urbanization is so pervasive that we cannot fail to notice when architecture is part of the solution or when it is part of the problem. Architects are increasingly coming up against humanitarian challenges and strategically tackling challenges such as climate-risk mitigation, sustainable day-to-day living, development aid, and healthcare. Now it's obvious that what they are dealing with is the practical reality of human rights.

Top-down planning, the communal process of shaping public space, land use regulation, community inclusion, bonding designs, and engagement with a diverse cast of individuals: all shape the way a city is renewed. All involve a choice of whether or not to compromise on people's rights.

In its latest role, architecture deals with global issues and new social trends and, more meaningfully, experiments with potential answers. The urbanization we are witnessing on a global scale is a striking sign of the aspirations of all people for freedom and for recognition of their fundamental and inalienable rights. Another way of putting it is this: In this 21st century human rights can be a positive force for change, by which we can all gain. We all want to get away from the idea that rights must always involve winners and losers—my gain, your loss, or vice versa. In order to do so, we have to change our approach from the architecture of crisis into the architecture of innovation.

The very practical implications of this challenge means that if we want to empower people's rights through our design, we must respect and listen to the knowledge of the people who will inhabit our architecture. The trick is to listen. We can commit to working with people to develop a range of urban solutions; we can address and dismantle any barriers they face; and we can share their ambitions for the changes they want to see. All people deserve no less.

The more understanding we become, the richer our design will be. This means that effective solutions to the problems faced by poor people must be drawn from the experiences of poor people themselves; effective solutions to the problems disabled people face must be drawn from experiences of disabled people themselves . . . and so on.

The same project approached by two very different architects will be interpreted in two very different ways, based on what they know about the people they are building for. Many people worry that aesthetics kills ethics, that inclusion kills profit, that human rights kill creativity, but I don't think this is true at all. It is simply not true that designing something from an ethical point of view diminishes the richness of the design. Quite the opposite.

By putting people at the core, we are building in a way which could break down traditional barriers between different groups and in doing so, create possibilities for meaningful conversations around social justice. How about if architecture doesn't just correlate with human rights, but actually emerges from it?

22) At risk of overload.

These sort of inquires drive architects in some ways toward an attempt to translate the Universal Declaration principles into more detailed guidelines.

The language of the Universal Declaration is special. Because of the philosophical concepts, and also because of all those technical inputs and suggestions that are seemingly embedded and poignant as soon as we transfer them into architectural design. But it also must allow these ideas to be practically applied into real-world disciplines such as architectural design. Universal Rights provide a cornerstone for creating real prosperity within society, but they are legal fiction if not given application.
In other words, rights can signify an individual's as well as a collective set of values.

Values are represented in all architecture and cities, and furthermore, some collective sets of beliefs are more apparent than others. A framework of enacted architecture seeks to identify, explain, and understand the interactivity of people and build form as a practical approach towards a system of values, rights, and duties.

We embed our values into architecture. That is to say, through architecture we develop the conditions of housing,

education, health, work, and the economic, political, social, and cultural life of a society.

Should universal rights be an architecture imperative beyond what is legally required?

The world would be a much better place if architects act as if they were, and if the work of making cities requires everyone's rights to be met. The design thinking that goes into rooms, backyards, streets, sidewalks, subways, buildings, and parks goes beyond the analysis, location and physical design of architecture; it extends into how to bring human rights into the ongoing processes of community-building. If we do want universal rights to become historical facts rather than eternal aspiration, we need to incorporate these ideals into the society of the future through our architecture.

Human rights are much broader than the absence of torture, they signify acknowledgement of equality and fairness in all the relationships of our co-existence. The rights to an adequate standard of living in terms of the health and well-being of people includes food, clothing, housing, medical care, and the necessary social services, and the right to security in the event of unemployment, sickness, disability, widowhood, old age, or other circumstances beyond a person's control.

We know architecture in terms of conceptual space, perceived space, and lived-in space, all of which determine how people's rights and or duties are dealt in daily life. Now we have to consider how human rights fit into a spatial context, a historical context, and, most of all, a human context. The ability to model, sense, monitor, and respond to the challenges of urbanization generates a new form of design, one where we can ensure that humanity takes center stage.

Is it not the obligation of architecture to give all human beings access to facilities that constitute the minimum standards of human rights? These include shelter, education, work, and the possibility of participating in the economical, political, cultural, and social life of a community or nation. As its first obligation, architecture should facilitate these possibilities, especially for disadvantaged and vulnerable groups such as women, the disabled, minority groups, the poor, the homeless, refugees, migrants, nomads, and Romani people.

Architecture is a building culture, and it cannot be framed by the corruption of our ethical integrity that ultimately leads to damage to the very fabric of our humanity.

23)
What's equality?

Equality has two different aspects: equality in law and equality in fact. Many laws establish that we are all equal before the law, even though in practice people living in the same city—women and men, old and young, low- and high-income, migrants and non-migrants—rarely experience this equality.

Architects can lobby for significant changes to building codes. Not just green building codes—but all codes. In such codes, certain measures should take precedence. Rehabilitation of slums instead of demolition could become mandatory. Good codes as we know can quickly bring striking results. We're not cutting emissions in the way we need to. We're not managing inequality as well as we can. The depth of understanding of the immense risks of human rights violations are not yet evident. What has to happen now is a catalyst that will en-able all of this to become the new normal. We have to care and be informed about rights, not needs, where we recognize those "in need" for what they lack, rather than value them for what they have.

Common logic links the rich with the poor and by doing so casts the poor as responsible for their own lack of empowerment, and the alienation they suffer due to inequity. One suggestion is to reflect on Muhammad Yunus' vision: think of all the things you get at your bank and imagine those products and services tailored to someone living on a few dollars a day. Think of all aspects of designing a beautiful house: choosing the right materials, light, color, and then imagine them tailored to someone living on a few dollars. As I stated before, the poor are not a mass of people in need with abject lives who are owed something better. These people are valuable as a group. They have their own unique perspectives, experiences, priorities, aspirations, and realities. They are communities currently denied the political, civil, economic cultural rights that they are entitled to under international human-rights principles. These are not people crushed by poverty. These are people busy helping each other to get out of poverty just as fast as they can.

The poor have their own social organization, complex friendship, kinship, and acquaintanceship networks, and associational ties rooted in family and social life. They engage in neighborhood activities with one another—including borrowing tools or food, having lunch or dinner, or helping each other with problems. It is not the case that slums undermine prosperity; they help create prosperity. While zones, districts, sectors are boundaries imposed by census geography, the ecological properties of neighborhoods are shaped by social interactions. Neighborhoods are interdependent and characterized by a functional relationship between what happens at one point in space and what happens elsewhere.

When we say that a person or a community "needs help," do we suggest that they are less than, and that we as "problem solvers" are inherently better or more capable? Architecture does not create neighborhoods, but it should explore the cultural dimensions and social organization of cities, the interface between the cultural and physical or spatial dimensions of urban areas. It should also explore the role of cultural diversity in terms of ethnicity, language, gender, sexuality, etc. in either bridging or reinforcing the urban divide. Architecture must address a multitude of issues: social and spatial segregation; diversity in social, economic, and cultural life; active cultural expressions in the city by diverse citizen groups; cultural pluralism and tolerance (or the lack thereof) in cities; diversity in gender, age, sexuality, minorities, and vulnerable groups; preservation of cultural heritage (in terms of both built and social environments); urban entertainment; marketing of cities through culture (such as festivals and events); culturally and socially inclusive policies and approaches.

Given this diversity of issues, might it be that equality is simply a set of well-meaning aspirations without legal or philosophical foundations? Could architecture develop a secular and meaningful idea of dignity that can offer wider grounds for human rights? And what is dignity anyway? Inequality opens up opportunities, and we have to look at it as an integrated thought process of building. That's what sustainability is.

24) How does responsibility work?

Rights always trigger obligations and responsibilities, whereas needs do not. Rights cannot be addressed without raising the question of who has obligations in relation to those rights.

Economic, social and cultural human rights involve a three-fold obligation, regardless of resources; an obligation of non-discrimination, an obligation to adopt measures, and an obligation to ensure at least that basic rights are observed.

As to the formal legal basis, human-rights treaties seldom explicitly obligate actors other than national governments to be bound by their guidelines. But as people of conscience, and as a profession dedicated to improving the built environment for all, architects cannot be involved in the design of spaces that violate human life and dignity. A preliminary consideration of the relationship between professionals and human-rights responsibilities immediately reveals that professionals can have an impact on the human rights of others by virtue of their expertise. Architects, designers, and planners definitely have the power to change lives for the better. Like it or not, environment influences human behavior and this is true whether the environment is natural or manmade. Because architecture is becoming our main environment, no architect can persuasively claim to be an impotent and powerless bystander in the face of human rights violations. Architects still have freedom of choice. And their choices could not matter more.

Neutrality is often an excuse that architects use to hide from their responsibility. Rights-based development is based on the ethical premise that everyone is entitled to a certain standard of material and spiritual wellbeing. Rights-based development takes the side of people who suffer injustice by acknowledging their equal worth and dignity; it removes the charity dimension of development by emphasizing both rights and responsibilities. Rights-based thinking recognizes people—including the poor, women, minority groups, diverse people, old people, and children—not as beneficiaries, but as active rights-holders. It also establishes a corresponding duty to ensure that nobody's rights are infringed by design.

When designing for them, an architect should think not just about the bare necessities, but about what it means to be human. This approach counteracts the discriminatory and anti-social provisions of architectural solutions that hinder the development of their users, divide neighborhoods, stand in the way of co-operation, and give rise to political tensions between peoples. Such provisions are contrary to the fundamental principles of social sustainability, and thus seriously disturb peace and security.

We do not expect architects to draw up peace treaties, but they should expose injustice and ensure equality in architectural design. This is a positive obligation requiring professionals to think proactively about how they can achieve these aims in the course of their work. This involves access to knowledge as well as to the way that professionals choose to use their skills. From the smallest home renovation to the largest mega-project, their work has an immediate and lasting impact on people and places.

Architecture can facilitate and empower new participatory community solutions for planning, designing, implementing, and managing more human-rights-centered city developments. Rights, as opposed to needs, make no claim for aid and benevolence, but instead for a duty to support marginalized people as equal human beings in their efforts to claim their rights and address the poverty, suffering, and injustice in their lives.

Architects can subvert these rights, partly by setting other priorities, and partly by ignorance of the relationship between their actions and these concepts. We know all too well that inadequate housing increases the risk of severe ill-health and disability; it can also lead to poor mental health, lower educational attainment, unemployment, and poverty. Rights raise questions about the actions and responsibility of duty-bearers. No building type or architectural style creates inequality on its own. The importance of human rights lies not only in their definition or enforcement, but in the continued discussion and redefinition of the issues. Social and environmental sustainability is a choice and a responsibility. Architects can start by taking a stand against a status quo that simply isn't acceptable, and then dedicating their work to changing it.

Begin with a Charter of Duties of Man and I promise the rights will follow as spring follows winter.

Mahatma Gandhi's understanding of human rights is based on duty, rather than on rights. He did not stand for rights but for duties. He argued that if all insist simply on rights and not on duties, there will be utter confusion and chaos.

He argued for a "Charter of Duties" when asked for his opinion on what is the golden way to be friend of the world and to regard the whole human family as members of one family.

In the 1940s, when the world was focusing on the emerging 'rights-discourse,' Gandhi's contribution was unique because of its emphasis on *duties*. Gandhi disagreed with the rhetoric of rights—at a national and international level—and opted for a discourse couched in the language of duties. What is most fascinating is that he went beyond the obvious correlation between human rights and state duties, and emphasized the duties of *individuals*.

Gandhi's emphasis on the duties of non-state actors in the context of human rights is becoming more and more relevant. Actually, many people are starting to become more conscious of how close the modern law of human rights came to becoming a law of human rights and human duties. We are hearing more and more noises about corporate accountability for rights violations, individual criminal liability for rights violations, the responsibility of armed groups and 'belligerents' in times of war, duties of peacekeepers and human rights defenders.

26) Architecture is a holistic enterprise.

The enjoyment of human rights through architecture addresses questions about the existence, content, nature, universality, and justification of architecture. Many people have looked for a way to support the idea that human rights have roots that are deeper and much more subject to human decisions than legal enactment. One version of this idea is that people are born with rights, that human rights are somehow innate or inherent in human beings. The way we build is a reflection of the way we live. This allows architecture to accommodate a great deal of cultural and institutional variation, and to allow for democratic decision-making and sustainability solutions when it comes to the design of human habitats.

At its most noble, architecture is the embodiment of our civic values. Architecture is an expression of values and architects are serial big-picture thinkers: they apply engineering, ecology, urbanism, poetry, biology, mineralogy, anthropology, technology, sociology, handcraft, and physics to a wide variety of global issues.

If we try to think of urban sustainability as the ability of architecture to reduce environmental degradation and human

rights violations, we should add connotations of sustainability beyond the greening of buildings, energy conservation, and environmental accountability. This is when the conversation between architecture and human rights actually starts to evolve, because it moves away from the easy answers that assumes a right and a wrong. It acknowledges that we need a greater level of analysis and understanding, and a discussion about what we need to achieve. Human rights represent high-priority goals for architecture and assign responsibility for their progressive realization. Let's not miss the obvious, human rights are rights. Human rights contain specific norms (for example, a prohibition on the design of spaces for torturing or killing) and specific values, for example, a respect for human life and dignity.
Architecture and human rights combines a concern for the design and construction of places where human rights can be enjoyed and encouraged.

Human rights can push architecture and engineering to the limit. Human rights demand that we adjust to changes and difficulties and work with the prevailing circumstances.

27) Assessing human rights.

After working at the Ethiopian Human Rights High Commission, the lack of human rights and the widespread discrimination in the built environment became very apparent to me. Most of us are concerned with the level of violence in the world. But we're not going to end it by telling people that violence is morally wrong. Instead, we must offer them a tool that's at least as powerful and as effective as violence.

Today I find myself assessing human rights everywhere I go—looking for demolition sites and gentrification, but also appraising iconic courthouse designs in search of public spaces, where people can gain their right to a public hearing, trying to find ramps, asking for gender-free toilets, surfing the metro from a blind perspective, searching city parks for spaces where migrants can engage and feel welcome, and reviewing the relationship between housing and basic necessities ranging from education to transportation.

In assessing human rights violations through architecture, I put together a checklist of things that I go through to try and understand them. Whom are human rights accessible to? And whose needs are not being accommodated? Who is excluded? People are either welcomed or shunned. They can face fences of barbed wire or cheering locals. The introduction of the BREMM rating revolutionized the way in which architects incorporate sustainable methods; it became a benchmark in assessing a buildings eco footprint. My assessment is a counterintuitive reaction to inequality and discrimination by architecture. I look for human impacts on the built environment, the destroying of resources, of opportunities, of choices, based on what people depend upon or aspire toward.

Human rights are relevant to all of us, not just those who face repression or mistreatment. They are 'rights' because they are things you are allowed to be, to do, or to have. They are also there to help us get along with each other and live in peace. I believe today that it is possible for us as a world community, if we make a bold decision on architecture, to come together and stop destroying the planet and stop trampling over human rights. But it will require three things: commitment, empathy, and creativity.

If we approach certain empirical questions about architecture, we will come to recognize human rights. There is always a connection between human rights and architecture and this connection is verifiable.

The issue of human rights and their relationship to architecture is simply not as obvious to many as it is to me now. A rights-based assessment to architecture is both a vision and a tool-kit: human rights can be the means, the ends, and the mechanism of evaluation and the central focus of sustainable human development. The examples above show just how diverse the array of human rights violations through design can be, despite our high expectations that effective solutions can result from responsible architecture and a regard for communities when designing the built environment. For someone affected by achondroplasia, a bathroom is an example where design infringes upon his or her dignity. We know architecture in terms of conceptual space, perceived space, and lived-in space. These distinctions show the multiple levels at which people are given freedom of choice, freedom of discrimination, opportunities, and rights in their daily life.

In the long run, legislation is not the answer: the law can only do so much. Education and awareness amongst the design community are what will make the difference.
Everyone is starting from a different place and going to a different place. Equality doesn't mean we require the same environment, but an equal opportunity to address our individual needs and wants. Architecture could offer better solutions to global problems, such as the organization of alternative urban farming food networks. By reaffirming its faith in fundamental human rights such as the right to food, or designing public libraries in such a way that the right of free expression, we can positively transform the life of their more vulnerable patrons, the homeless. It is certainly possible to design small, practical but meaningful solutions to combat the feelings of isolation that migrants can feel when they are relocated to a new

country, and must overcome the trauma of displacement, and often war, as they restart their lives.

28)
Hate architecture.

I call 'hate architecture' any architectural project that aims to eradicate 'differences.' Hate architecture serves and is often motivated by a desire of a group to protect their territory or react to a perceived attack against their own group and social identity.

There is no duty or law to legislate against an architecture that incites hatred directed towards a group of people, that is threatening, that is insulting or that aims to stir up racial hatred. Architects should always question whether their design solutions involve prejudice or hostility that may not contravene any legal requirement, but which may result in harm or may escalate into a form of emotional, or physical humiliation.

We can hear inhabitants claiming to suffer health problems and depression from spending time inside certain buildings. We produce identities and develop our sense of reality through our interaction with architecture.

Architecture can be a cruel strategy of institutional violence built into public space at the cost to society's most vulnerable, something designed to be specifically hostile to them yet camouflaged into the normal fabric as permanent barriers.

From an urban poor, immigrant, homeless perspective, architecture is a kind of warfare. People are captives of the spaces they inhabit and victims of powers and biases or exclusions. For those who are pushed toward the outside, an arch is a space alteration that sustains their permanent exclusion. Such architecture achieves a centrality of prejudice. Prejudice is any attitude, emotion, or behavior towards members of a group that directly or indirectly implies some negativity or antipathy toward that group. Does this oppressive ethic count as architecture? In a sense, it does. We use the means of architecture not primarily to solve the problem of social living, but primarily to serve the interests of a privileged minority.

The perpetration of stereotypes is one of the many form of discriminations. The seeds of prejudice are to be found in the way architects process information as they seek to simplify, make sense of, and justify their architecture, for example in the design of a bench that no homeless person can comfortably sleep on.

Hate architecture need not actually be motivated by hatred for a 'victim.' Rather it can be the expression of a more generalized prejudice or bias that probably characterized such an architectural offense.

When architects attempt to make sense of the world around them, they tend to create stereotypes about other people. Such a perspective has several drawbacks. It assumes that design operates autonomously and independently of people and remains unaffected by whether the groups are in conflicts with each other. The victims of hate architecture are often defined by their race, disability, or sexual orientation.

Hate architecture not only alters individual lives, it creates buildings and spaces that can oppress entire communities. Threats can consist of tangible conflicts of interest such as competition over resources or perceived threats that certain groups of people pose to one's own intergroup. Hatred erodes rights and it drives wealth and power up towards the top, so it enables the powerful to further entrench their power.

How do we account for architecture that endorses discrimination, racism, and aggressive or violent expansion? At first sight, the obvious way in which architecture and urban planning can avoid hatred, intolerance, and discrimination is by involving people in the planning and design process. Greater harmony can be generated by cooperating with excluded groups rather than by conflict with such groups. Our emphasis in designing is still too often for people rather than with people.

When confronted with the hate architecture I see so often in our cities, it doesn't surprise me that those who might not have thought very deeply about universal rights might think this is good architecture. Architecture can be used to break down prejudices, enhance sustainability, and transform communities. It can also influence how people treat each other.

29) Building as usual.

What happens if architectural practitioners and consultants fail to address in their work problems that go beyond their formal remit to encompass questions of human rights, bio-politics, fair trade, fair economy, politics, sustainability, technological transfer, and so on? Conflict is always more likely to occur in pre-categorized areas—in places where the "others" live. When such conflict occurs, whole communities of people lose opportunities for a good education, quality housing, living-wage jobs, services, and support systems.

As a practice, just as capable of exacerbating divisions as securing them, architecture has tended to challenge ways of working, thinking, and relating within a given society with the help of historical, geographical, and speculative strategies. We have to be thoughtful about our involvement in global development efforts, realizing that good intentions do not translate into mutually beneficial outcomes. I see too often an architecture driven by unconscious bias and I have learned that a city can have racism without racists.

Apartheid has been over for decades, but cities and towns are still designed to give white people access to the central businesses districts and homes in the leafy suburbs. Black people have to live far outside of the city, only venturing in for work. These living spaces have remained a challenge and socio-economic inequality is still stubbornly divided along racial lines. Can we imagine other ways in which things could be done, thought, or produced?

It is no secret that segregation and inequality persist in much architectural design. We now have the tools to see the cities on a larger scale: aerial photography, the global positioning system, GIS, and computer simulations. Through these tools, we can now visualize the urgent need for change through better urban planning. We can then begin to implement these changes with the effort and attention required by struggles for greater social-environmental justice.

Other links between architecture and human rights are clearly reflected by the fact that residents of slums and informal settlements are often more susceptible to eviction, family breakdown, poverty, food insecurity, ethnic conflict, religious conflict, crime, health, rape, and unemployment. In most of our cities, people in richer areas live anything from five to 13 years longer than people in poor areas. Poorer people have less control over their lives and less access to resources, infrastructures, and economic opportunities. They also get less respect in an urban setting. Increasing homelessness, overcrowding, and declining quality of life for families and individuals all painfully reflect the human costs of this predatory approach to development. Building as usual will just get us further from where we need to be.

When it comes down to it, at the personal level, our living in a city as poor or as rich people, Rome or Addis Ababa– are not that different from each other.

30)
The deviant plac-es.

It's easy to move through our cities without seeing these power plays, enacted through design and policy, that keep the predicament of the homeless, poor, or the impaired conveniently out of view. A lack of accurate information about human-rights issues is one of the biggest deterrents to human-rights empowerment. There are architectural deterrents on every corner and we take no notice of them at all, remaining entirely unaware of the social role of these devices. What are they? Why do we carry on with this approach that doesn't seem to be right? I sat with different people around the world who suffer discrimination and talked to them.

Spikes are a form of homeless deterrent strategy. This is a kind of human-right abuse right under our nose, that we don't even notice. Disabled people face multiple exclusions. We have a large potential workforce of skilled and talented people who are unable to contribute to society—economically, socially or civically—because of arch barriers to full participation. The structural features of urban life, such as crowding, almost automatically contribute to higher rates of human rights abuses, regardless of who is living in these neighborhoods. By inhabiting space, individuals can breathe the injustice that surrounds them. Less trees and buildings constructed from materials that retain heat are health hazards for women, children, and the elderly. Car parking and highways are deterrents to pedestrians and impede a more sustainable urban lifestyle. These structural features can include public buildings and open areas, but also streets and places to gather, meet, and interact, where people affirm their shared rights to the city. They can be labelled as private or public.

Architecture should improve the conditions of these interactions in order to strengthen the minimum standards of basic individual rights. Design is so fundamental in dealing with changes in everyday life and it plays such an important part in influencing, tackling, and improving social issues that human rights should always be prioritized. Every person living in a city should be allowed to interact with the environment in a way that's meaningful to them. The existence of deviant places are a more pervasive problem that can't always be directly observed. These require us to address and dismantle the deviant place or barrier, so that every person is able to access the right to live independently, to feel respected, and to enjoy an adequate standard of living. The places that we hate the most are often the places that are designed specifically for us.

Architecture also enacts power, which is defined as the relationship between two forces and can be viewed as a dynamic of balance or a struggle. Identifying power in architecture and city development opens dialogues about the values and ideologies represented by these types of power and about how we are controlled by and how we control space. Under the privatization of many traditionally public functions and through public/private development projects, public and private realms overlap and blur their conventional boundaries. Furthermore, the public realm includes both collective concerns, meaning shared interests, and community functions, which refers to special interest groups such as a neighborhood or the environmental community. This means creating spaces and buildings that are more affordable, people-centered, peaceful, safe, healthy, green, and more respectful of human needs and abilities, of privacy, of different types of lifestyles, and of different cultural values. That is to say, we must develop the conditions of housing, education, health, work, to enhance the economic, politic, social, and cultural life of the society. As place of empowerment, architecture influences our encounters with strangers and with the others, which is a fundamental condition of cities, places where otherness and strangeness prevail.

31) What has gone wrong?

People can encounter modern-day slavery without even realizing it. They can encounter on a construction site workers under hard hats and hi-vis clothing who have become perfectly camouflaged and unnoticed modern slaves. They clean and prepare construction sites by removing debris and hazards, they operate concrete mixers, they tear down buildings, they dig tunnels and mine shafts, they build highways and roads, they remove asbestos, lead, or chemicals, they carry tools and materials, they work with cement masons, they clean up sites and remove waste. Human trafficking is the use of force, fraud, or coercion to compel another person's labor. It is estimated that there are 27 million slaves in the world today, many of these work in the global construction industry.

Most victims of human trafficking are poor and marginalized. They're migrants, people of color. A very large number of them are escaping a country or a part of the world affected by civil war, ethnic conflicts, kleptocratic governments, or disease. Construction workers are among the world's most underpaid and exploited laborers. Their working and living condition are shocking and the violation of their human dignity heart-breaking. Being vulnerable does not make them slaves. What it takes to turn a construction worker, who is destitute and vulnerable, into a slave is the absence of human rights in architecture. Yet this seems like an overwhelming level of responsibility for architects.

Now we have to ask ourselves, are we willing to live in a world with slavery? If we don't take action, we just leave ourselves open to having someone else use slaves for the benefit of our construction, our design, our architecture. Architects have ways of assuring their clients that nobody had to sacrifice their rights to build the house they love so much.

The global trend towards outsourcing and price-cutting is also not an excuse for human trafficking. Affordable architecture does not need slaves. I believe architects have enough power to bring slavery to an end. Improving the life of vulnerable workers is their responsibility. They are in positions of influence and power and should never turn a blind eye on degrading living conditions, excessive volumes of work, forced overtime, use of threats, or the limited financial penalties imposed for depriving another human being of his or her freedom.

Architects can in response honor ethnical recruitment and fair employment and thus play a crucial role in combatting modern slavery and protecting those most at risk of exploitation. And if there is a fundamental violation of our human dignity then we should all denounce it as horrific, as slavery. If human rights considerations are respected in architecture, this will protect the poor and the vulnerable. The eradication of slavery in construction labour may start just with an architect knowing each worker by name and asking and caring about his or her working conditions.

32) Human rights are universally broken.

The universality in human rights implies that, irrespective of citizenship or territorial legislation, people have basic rights that others should respect. And yet it is hard to avoid the conclusion that people's human rights are universally violated. What causes this? Those who hold a tragic or historical vision of the world will believe that while progress is possible, perfection is not.

While it originated as a comprehensive concept, the universality of human rights became such a popular phrase that it is now used to justify almost any agenda. People mention human rights regardless of what they try to promote.

Rights are described in vague, aspirational terms which can be interpreted in multiple ways. Let's take the freedom to build and raze and displace. We live at a time when the claim to human rights is both taken for granted and regularly disregarded. The central idea of human rights is that they are rights that people have, and enjoy even without any specific legislation. Does this idea make our talk loose? The inclination to rely on legislative rather than design solutions assumes (unintentionally, most likely) that first, the design of the physical environment has no bearing on the well-being of the city. The problem with this model is that it's unsustainable globally. It is unaffordable globally. It is unrealistic globally.

Laws solve problems by a process of analysis whilst design solves problems by synthesis. So, what can design do to help? Let's start with the question of global social sustainability. Many believe that international human-rights laws are among of our greatest moral achievements. But there is little evidence that they are effective. Let's take climate change: we know that summit after summit is not going to reduce greenhouse gas emission. What we can see is that by transferring technological knowledge into architecture, we are actually beginning to reduce the eco footprint.

In the world of Zabrisky a right can be the power of the will or the will of power. And that is the key: it is all about power.

The architecture of the global space, which is largely unregulated, not subject to the rule of law, and in which people may act free of constraint will most benefit the powerful and those who have the most power to operate in this space without constraint. Because it has never happened yet that many, many people enjoy power without having money.

The label human rights is misleading because it lays claim to the idea that these rights are common to all human beings. There are human-rights issues that are little-explored, that may be unconventional, experimental, or challenging, and which arise from diverse disciplinary traditions. These necessitate architecture becoming more inquiring and less prone to ready-made answers.

David Harvey reminds us that the right to the city is far more than the individual liberty to access urban resources; it is the right to change ourselves by changing the city. This transformation depends upon the exercise of a collective power to reshape the processes of urbanization. This starts from the wrong assumption that we owe nothing to others unless we have actually harmed them. This may necessitate new alliances among individuals, communities, at country level, and internationally and require a new role for architecture. There is a line between having a right and not having it. That line is movable and permeable.

Difficulties for some and injustices for others force them to work harder, to think more, to learn more, to speculate on both the past and future of the problem of contravening the human rights of others. Protecting the human rights of others is not out of our control. These are problems entirely of our own making. Whatever we can break, we can also fix. All human rights can be relevant throughout the design process from sketching a house to living in it.

33) Human rights skills.

Human rights require not just knowledge, but the right attitudes and skills. Many of these are not inherent in people; however, they can be developed and refined over time, at both the individual and professional levels. An attitude is the manner of behaving, feeling or thinking that demonstrates a person's disposition or opinion. The attitude of an architect, planner, designer, engineer, landscape designer, or developer can benefit or damage the urban environment, and can greatly affect the upgrading of social and commercial services and related facilities, the improvement of urban and regional transport networks, and the preservation of the architectural and cultural heritage in urban areas. Furthermore, the quality of any human-rights-based solution will empower communities' efforts to counteract the functional obsolescence and future sustainability of their urban structure.

Honoring human rights requires consultation, dialogue, creativity rather than coercion, force, repression, and exclusion. Architects must therefore acquire the relevant skills for building consensus around issues relating to the right to housing and human-rights architecture. Support-based strategies that recognize the role of the informal sector in the creation of housing must be developed and imple-

mented. In the final analysis, the full realization of the right to adequate housing depends on the extent of attitudes, skills, awareness, and actions taken toward this end. Together, planners and architects working toward this goal should explore the potential of space as a platform for social, economic, and environmentally inclusive development.

Human-rights architecture requires compliance with the principals of human rights, and necessitates working with respect for these basic principles, such as the inclusion of the humanitarian imperative, neutrality, independence, and impartiality.

From community mobilization to design of re-blocking plans and the upgraded of houses to negotiations with city government around building regulations and provision of infrastructure and basic services, every project starts with an assessment of how design and planned activities, including those of operational partners, adhere to or violate these core principles. It is up to all professionals involved at every step of the process to ensure that all activities are in line with the core principles of human rights. Planners should inform all actors, regardless of their function, about the core principles and how they can demonstrate them in their work, such as through the Human Rights Architecture code of conduct.

34)
Human dignity.

We can find the basis of human rights in a very simple phrase: human dignity. It means worthiness! A person always has the right to be valued for his or her worth, to be respected, and to receive ethical treatment. The dignity of a human person is not only a fundamental right in itself, but constitutes the basis of the Universal Declaration: *recognition of the inherent dignity and of the equal and inalienable rights of all members of the human family is the foundation of freedom, justice and peace in the world.*

Human dignity means that an individual or group feels self-respect and self-worth. This is characterized by physical and psychological integrity and empowerment. When you talk to the homeless, they speak about feeling excluded. Isn't exclusion a matter of architecture? Through spatial practices, we gain a sense of identity, a sense of power, and a sense of communion. We gain a sense of where we belong as well as where we do not. We evaluate, categorize, and understand the world from this urban identification and division. In what ways can human dignity become naturalized in the contemporary fabric of our cities?

Pain, violence, victimization, and injustice have long been elements of human reality. Can we change, or are we doomed to repeat ourselves and despise one another until the end of time? The answer is not obvious. But one thing is certain: as long as we live in a cave we are not going to resolve this conundrum.

Architecture can prevent the violation of essential *human dignity* and freedoms. Such violation takes place through the imposition of disadvantage, stereotyping, or economic or social prejudices. Architecture can provide a simple reality check to counteract such violations: the architect can ask whether a project looks at the homeless as equally capable and equally deserving of our design concern, respect, and consideration?

Architecture can explore the modern challenges of ensuring dignity and human rights. It can also resuscitate a new and more coherent secular ideal of dignity as a spatially valid guarantee of human rights. While architecture cannot eradicate racism or the stresses that result from it, it might just be able to create environments that provide a buffer for those people who experience discrimination on a daily basis. That buffer can be an architecture that increases the dignity of all people and enhances their ability to express themselves.

Is it possible, therefore, to develop a meaningful idea of dignity in our urban landscapes that can offer new grounds for human rights? And is it possible for architects to view people first in the heart and eye, before they harden into categories, styles, or definitions? And if it is possible to do so, to reconcile the layers of meanings and to pull from all these contradictions some organized space, the act of conferring dignity to all will finally begin.

35) An architect's responsibilities.

In legal terms, an architect is liable for anything that goes wrong with a building. But who is liable if a building is constructed on sacred land and offends a tribe for whom the land constitutes a burial site? What if the design of the room makes access and exit impossible for a person in a wheelchair? What if a potential user or dweller feels scared, uncomfortable, humiliated, offended, or secluded in the space which the architect has designed?

What responsibilities has an architect if a person inside the space he/she designed is starving? Hunger is more than missing a meal. The issue, largely, is that the people who need food the most simply don't have steady access to it. The causes of this can be displacement, dependence on disrupted farming, lack of roads, lack of storage facilities, etc. Architects will ultimately affect everybody's rights, security and welfare, even if they never make a serious appeal to their consciences. This is simply because there is no town, village, city, human settlement, or building without architecture. The right to remake ourselves by creating a qualitatively different kind of urban society is one of the most precious benefits of empowering people's human rights. Architecture rights are human rights.

Not only can architecture acknowledge the need and help people out of hunger, it can pull a neighborhood together to help build an environment that isn't worrisome or scary.
Human rights are matters of "paramount importance" and they should also lead to a number of important design decisions.

One way to ensure human rights are honored is to ensure the effective consultation and direct participation of affected communities in the design and implementation of new spaces, particularly on matters of housing and land. When people's human rights are compromised, it makes them feel less than whole. They can feel beaten down, uncertain about the future, and unsure of their access to the conditions they need to thrive.

Obligations for architects and building professionals might be negative obligations of omission and restraint—or positive obligations of assistance, empowerment and aid.
The support for or neglect of the empowerment of human rights in space designs originate in single, simple actions. Such acts take place whenever we decide to respect or neglect considerations of people's needs in the design.

Design can increase or reduce fairness, safety, inclusion, privacy, and freedom. It can also remove barriers between communities and foster peace. It has been claimed that professionals have expertise or skill sets that may be employed to facilitate human-rights abuses (the volatile expertise claim). Similarly, professionals have expertise or skill sets that enable them to expose, report, or otherwise prevent human rights violations (the preventive expertise claim).

In essence, we like to assume that architects should be mindful of and driven by people's rights in their efforts to respect, protect and fulfill those rights; and do their best to not only fulfill those rights, but also, to make themselves accountable and responsive to the people in this regard. Architects make value judgments all time, ethical and moral judgments. And they are always making decisions that are exceedingly personal and extraordinarily subjective.

Architects, designers, and planners have an ethical responsibility to protect public health, and to ensure public safety and welfare. They also have a duty to promote social equality and find ways to ensure that our differences—be they political, social, or economic—do not infringe on the democratic, cultural, and economic rights of all. This is not only an issue of social justice. It is also one of global survival. What is our prime responsibility, at the end of the day? To treat everybody as an equal.

36) Creativity sounds better.

Hunger, violence, victimization, and injustice have long been a part of human habitats. Can we change? Or are we doomed to build as usual until the end of time?

Instead of defaulting to our traditional convergent approach we can make the best choice out of available alternatives.

An emphasis on human rights and community development is fundamental to achieving innovative and imaginative cities.

Architecture exists to create the physical environment in which people live. This is obvious a very neutral answer, but if we dig deeper into the city context we also see the power of architecture to change and disrupt: from simple design features that improve quality of life for old people and people with disabilities, to the global impact of the movement towards sustainability.

It is not surprising that cities grow: for them, the real challenge is to do so while eradicating poverty and promoting equality. The future is urban. As long as a human rights approach to architecture is established, cities will grow ever larger and will be the inevitable future of a more just and prosperous humanity. On the contrary, a lack of human rights will create crises that will cause the collapse of cities in a worst-case scenario.

So if our buildings do not respect people's rights, where should they safely live?

What is the built environment? What constitutes equality? How do architects determine whether something is fair, positive, helpful, or relevant for individuals and collectives?

And what kind of design is most likely to respect people's human rights?

If we put architects on the spot and get them to explain exactly how their design complies with the right to free speech or why violating this right is wrong, then they'll have a much harder time coming up with a solid answer.

So what for an architecture discourse? Well, because on closer inspection the architectural design matters. Divergent approach in architecture means to explore new alternatives, new solution, new ideas that have not existed before. Human rights through architecture, this is a process for the practical and creative resolution of problems or issues that seeks a better result in the future. It is an architectural thinking process based around the 'building up' of rights. Freedom of peaceful assembly is a fundamental human right that can be enjoyed and exercised by individuals and groups, unregistered associations, legal entities, and corporate bodies only if such a place exists.

Mainstreaming human rights into the practice of architecture will raise the standards of the profession in terms of meeting its obligations to the public good. Achieving the will, if not yet the ability, to promote human rights through architecture may be a small step, but it is a step in the right direction. Now, some things in cities do take time. Some things in architecture can happen much more quickly. Major structural transformations in our cities are going to happen anyway in the next two decades. But the second of the transformations, the architectural transformation, we have to decide to do now. The next two decades are decisive for what we have to do. We know little but we will learn everything along the way. Building is a powerful way to learn.

37) Small moments of attachment.

Almost a quarter of the population says they have no one to talk to. We can do something about. We can design build in-person interaction into our cities, into our workplaces.
An increasing urban population is going to have very beneficial gains.
Why is this so?
Intimacy is the opposite of loneliness and it breaks the invisible barrier of the domestic walls.

While the amount of floor space the average individual has in his or her home is increasing, the number of human interactions he or she will experience has been declining steadily. Real social interaction create biological and economical force field against disease and decline.

Making eye contact, shaking hands is enough to release oxytecin which increases our level of trust. Those asking for more rooms, more bathrooms, larger bathtubs, mega screen, triple livings, private park, private garden lower their cortisol levels.

We are one of the most loneliest societies there has ever been. Urban priorities changed because infections became the risk. However, social isolation has heralded a decline in open-mindedness and a deepening of our misunderstanding of others.

The more we add to the sum of human loneliness, the more we decrease the quality of the life within the society.

Most of the economic models are built around scarcity and growth. Exploding population, small planet, ugly architecture. Some things matter more than money. Let's image we take away land speculation and begin to lift a heavy burden on the homeless. Let's image we multiply the space available and then factor in the green spaces (including green terraces and roofs), so that we end up with more nature than we would have without the building.

It is more beneficial to build visually striking, fully efficient, real living spaces within reasonable budget and limited areas. Across the world, space, both in terms of availability and quality, is the resource that defines the capability of people to develop. Small spaces add large value to other people's life.

Our common sense suggests that big important problems need to be met with big important, and most of all, expensive solutions. So the power of reframing things cannot be overstated.

We can connect to a broader sense of the human condition rather than just design to please a few wealthy clients. We can start looking at how to prevent human rights violations where they begin; at the ground level. This is not in court houses but where we live and where we work, eat, sleep, learn, and play, where we spend our lives. Why imaging a better world matters? Because transitions are dangerous times.

38)
Building aware-
ness.

Architecture and urban design can both symbolically represent and practically promote human rights. However, representing human rights values and facilitating human rights based actions are two different things.

Ideas can be given shape in the form of space metaphors and buildings. One example is the rehabilitation of the Reichstag building in Berlin which represents a set of ideas about democracy and governance designed by Foster + Partners. As the home of the German parliament, nearly every design decision, from the major to the minutiae, took on political significance. The roof terrace and dome can be visited by members of the public, providing a visual connection to the work in the parliamentary chamber.

Architects can also design dignifying residential houses for low-income, and even no-income people. Two ways to understand the relationship between architecture and human rights: In the first case, we use space as a book; similar to language, the built environment serves as a context that frames our sense of reality and promotes certain values and omits others. In the second case, we use space as a tool, which instructs us how to enact our rights and validates our claims for recognition.

There are places of advocacy and places of empowerment. As a place of advocating for democratic values, the Reichstag, designed by architect Foster, is a fine example. Ramps lead to an observation platform allowing people to ascend symbolically above the heads of their representatives in the chamber. Advocacy architecture seeks to initiate change in society as it supports and promotes human rights. It is a strategic use of architecture as a resource to advance social and public awareness; this is a means by which architecture can plead for, support, or recommend real change.

Communication and rhetoric are inherent aspects of architecture, as it deals with thoughtful and thought-provoking concepts and topics. A building will not, alone, magically transform a government or serve some magical role in halting abuse, but it can contribute to the creation of a culture in which rights are respected. Places of advocacy can inspire people to take human-rights decisions. As buildings embody the idea of democracy and engage directly with the public, they can serve as powerful bulwarks against oppression, corruption, and autocracy: this is usually referred to as advocating or building awareness. Popular attitudes about human rights do not necessarily correspond with pressure for political change, but they may. Public opinion is a reflection of the strength and viability of human rights.

Questions of sustainability are questions about our environment choices, and therefore about an architecture that is open to examining rights and life choices. Residential segregation furthers unacceptable disparities in wealth, creating a geography of opportunity that determines who has access to the valuable resources that improve lives. Place of empowerment is another means by which we can promote human rights in a practical way.

39) Building solutions.

How could we make something architectural out of human dignity? It will come as a sudden flash of inspiration. What makes a space pleasant or even beautiful are windows placement, airflow, colors. Design allows us to translate problems and abstract ideas into specific manageable forms and to bring high value to daily life. Furthermore, architecture is the way we plan and create emissions, interactions, and actions, and all the humanely shaped processes of public and private life.

The most powerful means of effective change will occur when we can directly, tangibly, and emotionally experience some of the challenges of life today, and use these experiences to inform our future design decisions.

The task of building to ensure the protection of people's dignity necessitates architecture to consider a wide range of diverse issues. This goes hand in hand with the project of finding social sustainable approaches to building. Sustainability will follow only in a world where everyone has a decent place to live.

Describing a troubling future with the intent of helping avoid the consequences of what we do today helps us create positive actions in hostile conditions. Our initial instinct may be to run away. That instinct is wrong. These issues are manageable, not unsolvable. We can instead gain the valuable experience of having to cope with these very hard issues. Creativity is concerned with our capacity to rediscover our ability to search for design alternatives. There are not prescriptions.

Architecture is primarily space organization and space alteration. Through it, we have the opportunity to imagine new possibilities. Because other worlds are possible. We can imagine possible solutions and examine their practicality, or else play out impractical solutions until they become practical. What we imagine actually affects how we react to solutions, technically, viscerally, and morally.

Providing architectural options for the poor require us to raise our aspirations to meet those of the poor for themselves. And the ability to conceive of and implement beautiful design within reasonable budgets is a great test of architectural skill and talent.

How wonderful would it be if the progress of architecture and technological innovation would run parallel to the progress of human dignity and social inclusion?

40)
Design pooling.

There is an urgent need for a new framework of thinking to seed the creative process by promoting collaborations and sharing.

How can architects engage individuals and vulnerable groups so that the output of the people becomes something coherent and lasting, instead of just a matter of random ideas? There is an answer: factor cooperation into the architecture as a part of the project itself. Cooperative design has to be structured into places, but we still do not know how to do it efficiently. In traditional projects, sharing and collaborating with the public doesn't often occur. How do we organize these individuals into some structure that has explicit influence on the project? When we build cooperation into the project, we take the problem to the individuals rather than moving the individuals to our solution.

The challenge comes not when we present ideas in advance to an audience and receive their comments, but rather in the act of defining what form people's contribution should take. This kind of value is unreachable in our traditional, professional methods of design. As architects, we can often lose sight of how we should shape people's place, but when our design includes the views of individuals and groups, the project gains greater flexibility and value.

This is revolutionary—a profound change in the way we practice our profession.
Participative design replaces rigid and controlled planning with a cooperative system.
So, who is the architect? The answer to that question does not matter, because it is not the right question. Inclusive architecture is an answer to an even more important question which is: how does this design impact the community's well-being and their dignity?

This is a whole new way of doing things, which has downsides and upsides. Very often architecture succeeds in creating appropriate spatial and functional connections, which result in the ability of people living there to introduce required changes.

To create a space that ensures the protection of people's dignity and privacy, as well as the humanization of their conditions, the designer can strive to learn the reality of the people's situation. At the same time, the people strive to articulate their desired aims and learn the appropriate technological means to obtain them. This will not happen without architects who are open to experiencing surprise, puzzlement, and occasionally a little confusion.

When members of the community are active in designing and implementing a project, when they are invested in the work, when they are involved in all stages from planning to implementation, when they are happy with what has been done and how it was done, and when they feel they were treated respectfully and as a valued member of the building team, then we give the poor a meaningful part in initiatives designed for their benefit. A design system that coordinates the output of people or a community as a by-project is an inclusive issue. People become equal partners with a significant say in decisions concerning their lives. Every occupier is an active participant in their own social well-being and not merely a welfare consumer.

41) Power and empowerment.

Many may think that nature is finished because climate change means that every centimeter of the Earth has been altered by man. In the same way, others may say that justice is over, because architecture means that every centimeter of the city is now altered by power.

Is it really so? The way we speak, our narratives, our discourses, the images we use have huge implications on whether architects should primarily serve their clients, or accept responsibility for the easing of the stresses on our planet and its population.

Clearly private projects concentrate on monetary costs and benefits; while social ones go beyond these considerations. Because of these sort of juxtapositions, we often overlook the fact that architecture is always collective. It belongs to everybody. No matter who is paying the architect. And its purpose is all about providing a path to a future that's more sustainable, more equitable, and more desirable.

Our emphasis on solutions and on human rights should always be broad. Even when we design a private villa, not just when we design a museum or a hospital, we must look at sustainability through the lens of the public. By talking about the private project as one that lacks any public responsibility, we sometimes actually create these buildings in that way. In times of transformation, and in the changing world we live in now, luxury is a self-fulfilling, self-inflicted death sentence. While the majority of people are deprived of their basic rights, architecture cannot not just serve to consistently improve the living conditions of a small number of privileged people. If we can actually adapt to a broader theory of sustainability, the mission of architecture becomes the use of design skills to empower people to transform their cities. We are all clients of every architectural project!

The old paradigm of architecture that renders service to power and capital is now shifting to the empowerment of all human beings, allowing everyone accessibility to basic facilities. Power tends to be viewed in one of two ways, both of them extreme: command and control. Power gives us the capacity to make others do as we wish, or to reorder the environment around us.

We can imagine a scenario where collaborative practice is at the heart of shaping the built environment, capitalizing on opportunities for skills-sharing and learning, and encouraging entrepreneurial skills. That kind of engagement process—not for people but rather with people—is an opportunity to collaborate and to promote change.

If architecture is reinvented in this more strategic way, it will become a prime conduit in the creation of empowerment. Because that's what is needed for a better, more sustainable future—empower-

ment not power. So we must engage the citizens of our future cities. This way of thinking is the foundation of the future practice of architecture.

Why not? Some things are more important than power; love and freedom among them. And human rights.

42)
His and her space.

There is not now, nor has there ever been in the whole of history, a single place in the world where women have equality with men. It hasn't happened in the whole span of our evolution. This is a reality. We do this all the time even at home. Our domestic universe are designed as a sphere of significance to the construction of gender differences.

Homes has been a strategy for technical, functional, spacial and cultural reorganization.
As soon as we look into stereotype about gender it gets us into all sort of uncomfortable areas. Instead of calling us into question the typical domestic design and encouraging us to subvert societal norms and differences that grades into discrimination.

We want to have lives that are animated by terrific relationships with each other without challenging oppressive power relations. And at the same time our design rarely moves us beyond the assumed and seemingly generic six-foot tall, able-bodied male. Architecture deal with anatomy, meaning the human body or does it rather deal with the concept of body meaning the way we think about what a body is? Absence of "women" body in our design seems less an oversight than a tacit exclusion.
Living "like a man" only entrenches a masculine norm.

Every cell in the human body has a sex which means that women and men are different right down to the cellular level. From our brain to our hearts, our lungs, our joints. Too often design ignores this insight. There is so little data on our sex differences and little knowledge how we can improve the life of women with design. There is so much more to learn and architecture could make a bigger investment in understanding how to bring gender equality. Bodies can challange the norms.
There are many ways for women and men to experience self-esteem, recognition, integrity. Are we overlooking these differences? The polarization of domestic space rapidly affects our culture, our relationship, our marriage. It also affects gender and women rights. The quality and integrity of architecture can help make women rights visible.
So imagine the momentum we could achieve in advancing women rights if we consider these sex differences at the very beginning of the design. Yet difference in itself is not the issue. The differences matter, but how we consider them and how we care about the people they affect matters more. It is less about the difference and more about how we care. Class and race and gender are not about other people. They are about all of us.

43)
Poor friendly.

We rarely collect data on problems with social gradients measuring architecture and then see it in relation to the measurement of inequality. Within our societies we are looking at relative income or social position, social status—where we are in relation to each other and the size of the gaps between us. The trend is to focus on how much richer the top 20 percent are than the bottom 20 percent in each country. The average well-being of our cities may depend no longer on income, but on where we live. Poverty is not only about low incomes, but also about buildings that compound and reproduce poverty.

Place matters. And I mean that physically. There is an intuition that the more unequal architecture between the two groups may exacerbate all kind of social problems. General social dysfunction related to architecture does not just involve one or two things going wrong. Architecture affects most aspects of our lives: whether girls are safe, whether bullying occurs in schools, whether people eat lunch and dinner together, etc.

The proximity of housing to basics amenities—such as education, transportation, employment—are not only measurable, but also predictable according to the sector of the city in which we live. We speak about the toxic effect of bad housing when its design, construction, and location is dreadful, unfriendly, and alienating. But how does the experience of poverty differ when living in beautiful neighborhoods? Well-meaning but misguided ideas, popularized by mainstream thinking, suggest that pulling out of poverty is only possible when the poor are incentivized to pull themselves out of their uncomfortable zones. Hence, keeping the zone as uncomfortable as possible is seen as an incentive for improvement.

What a flawed strategy!

So, consider this an invitation to rethink this flawed strategy: a house can boost our self-esteem. We have written piles of books and columns and given lectures deploring the wealth gap that is leaving more and more people entrenched at the bottom end of the income scale. How can architecture widen the differences or compress them? Let's grasp this opportunity and look at the stories of real people.

There is a psychological effect of inequality, which produces feelings of superiority and inferiority, of being valued or devalued, respected or disrespected.

An undignified place, rather than a beautiful place, contributes strongly to these social evaluative judgments that in turn lead to insecurity, stress, and low self-esteem. Conventional thinking focuses on money, commodities, and economic growth. Architecture can contribute to a new paradigm for development centered on human well-being.

What is it about inequality that bothers us so much; the fact some people live within 400 square meters and some within 28 square meters? Or the fact that not everyone has the same shot at wealth? It is not just poverty or income that affects inequality, it is the house we live in and the pride we take in it; the school we attend and the joy we experience there; and the park where we play and the beauty we enjoy there. All these spaces encourage our involvement in community life. Marginalized communities are full of smart, talented people, hustling and working and innovating, just like our most revered and rewarded private, wealthy clients.

44)
The right footprint.

A sustainable environment is a vital necessity for every woman and man; the right of a collective group in which individuals participate (where collective rights are short-hand for the rights of each of us embodied in the rights of all). If human rights are the basic rights and freedoms that belong to everyone and, as such, are the sum total of every aspect of an individual's everyday human life, then an all-pervasive discipline such as architecture should lay the foundation for a culture of respect through its commitment, compassion, and creativity.

That's why we have to make this second transformation, the architecture transformation: and move to a human-rights approach to architecture in order to experience a more explicit vision of urban life and to understand what kind of future we may have. The first of these transformations, living in a city, is going to happen anyway. We have to decide whether we will do it well or badly, and this will determine the architecture transformation. One of the central tenets determining our success or failure will be the inclusion of human rights as a powerful guideline for future design, giving architectural objects a social and moral underpinning.

Architecture naturally thinks and acts with human rights on its core. Why? Because if so we lack the resources to shape the environment through brute force. We lack the scale to buffer change, and we constantly think about the tough odds for our survival in a new place. We all can do things to make the human-rights footprint bigger in our man-made habitat.

Although worldwide acceptance of human rights has been increasing rapidly in recent decades, the field of architecture is not in unanimous accord about the need for the universal acceptance of human rights. To say that there is a human right against torture is mainly to assert that there are strong reasons for believing that it is always wrong to engage in the design of torture chambers and that architects should refrain against this practice. Our duties in this regard always require actions involving respect, protection, facilitation, and provision. This view is attractive but has serious difficulties.

So, how do we solve a really complex problem? We cannot solve it all in one go, we can solve it step by step. People are our point of departure; universal values and the rights of our fellow human beings are the basis of which all that we do and all that we think.

Disregarding the importance of the need for human rights in a society has always been costly and dangerous. How come that we have so much trouble trying to to solve the problems that hinder the realization of human rights? Could it be that we are trying to solve the problems of human rights while not really understanding who the humans behind these problems are?

Architecture as an early warning system.

The purpose of an early warning system is to warn people that something bad is likely to happen.

Architecture is becoming the backdrop against which the drama of everyday life unavoidably plays out, constraining and shaping possible social interactions. While the narrow theories on human rights focus on civil and political liberties, the broad theories focus on a broader class of human rights and take account of poverty, hunger, and starvation. Slums work by effect if not by intention to embed the poor within the fabric of the city by providing them a place to live.

How can architecture possibly work as early warning system?

The assumption is that by monitoring architecture on progress we can trace a chain of information which can forecast and signalize lack of human rights. The aspiration is to promote architecture as a framework that integrates the norms, principles, standards, and goals of the international human-rights system into the plans and design of cities. Architecture has the power to shape how we relate to each other. The implication of grounding design in human dignity and human rights are huge.

More sustainable and inclusive architecture opens the door to a redefinition of human rights.

Whether teleological, consequentialist, deontological, or something else—we should find out the way we concretize the main features of human rights including their mandatory character, their universality, and their high priority.
People have human rights independently of whether they are found in the morality, or law of their country or culture or the place they live.
The right for all will need to be asserted and respected by every architect and every architectural project.

This claim will be unsettling for those who believe that good architecture can be designed without any particular concern for equality as well as for those who understand architecture only as the material form taken by any unit of usable—and rentable or sellable—space.
Many think that human rights sound a little impractical, a little theoretical. They seem to be saying that the key points of architecture and human rights are that it is unrealistic and complex. Not only do architecture and human rights address adhering issues but they also benefit from one another as they both target human beings.

I also know few architects that when told about architecture and human rights are searching for some place to run and hide. Well, they can run, but they really can't hide. No sustainable urbanization will be possible without pursue the effective and efficient realization of human rights for all. Indeed in a no architecture-free world as the one we inhabit, architecture is the ultimate strategy for assuring a dignified and secure existence for each inhabitant.

A right is not something that we give to people. It is what we can't take from them.

Where, after all, do universal rights begin? In small places, close to home—so close and so small that they cannot be seen on any maps of the world. Yet they are the world of the individual person; the neighborhood he lives in; the school or college he attends; the factory, farm or office where he works. Such are the places where every man, woman, and child seeks equal justice, equal opportunity, equal dignity without discrimination. Unless these rights have meaning there, they have little meaning anywhere. Without concerned citizen action to uphold them close to home, we shall look in vain for progress in the larger world.
—Eleanor Roosevelt

With such small places in mind, every architect will need to draw inspiration from human rights to explore new building approaches and to establish new architectural models with the goal of achieving the inherent dignity and the equal and inalienable rights of all members of the human family. Human rights are the crucible of our global future.

Still we know so little about how to make them a reality. So let's try, fail, try again, figure out, and resolve as architects to accomplish a better world for the future.

ECON
SOCIAL
CULT
AL R
(E S

OMIC AND

L

TUR-

RIGHTS

(C R)

International Covenant on Economic, So-cial and Cul-tural Rights (ICESCR)

THE RIGHT TO ADEQUATE HOUSING

Everyone has the right to a standard of living adequate for the health and well-being of himself and of his family, including food, clothing, housing and medical care and necessary social services, and the right to security in the event of unemployment, sickness, disability, widowhood, old age or other lack of livelihood in circumstances beyond his control.

The right to housing is one of the most widely violated human rights. The United Nations estimates that around 100 million people worldwide are without a place to live. Over one billion people are inadequately housed.Individuals as well as families are entitled to adequate housing regardless of factors such as age, economic status, groups or other affiliation or status. Thus, the enjoyment of this right may not be subject to any form of discrimination. The right to housing means more than just a roof over one's head. It should be seen instead as the right to live somewhere in security, peace, and dignity. The requirements for adequate housing have been defined in General Comment 4 of the Committee on Economic, Social and Cultural Rights to include aspects such as:

1. SECURITY OF TENURE

Security of tenure is the cornerstone of the right to adequate housing. Secure tenure protects people against arbitrary forced eviction, harassment and other threats. Most informal settlements and communities lack legal security of tenure. Hundreds of millions of people do not currently live in homes with adequate secure tenure protection. Security of tenure is a key issue for all dwellers, particularly women. This is particularly so for women experiencing domestic violence who may have to flee their homes to save their lives and for women who do not have title to their homes or lands and thus can be easily removed, especially upon marriage dissolution or death of a spouse.

2. AFFORDABILITY

The housing affordability principle stipulates simply that the amount a person or family pays for their housing must not be so high that it threatens or compromises the attainment and satisfaction of other basic needs. Affordability is an acute problem throughout the world and a major reason why so many people cannot access affordable formal housing, and are forced as a result to live in informal settlements. The lack of affordable housing is also a major problem in affluent countries where individuals and families living in poverty find it increasingly difficult to find affordable adequate housing. In many developed countries, when rental housing is unaffordable, tenants' security of tenure is threatened as they can often be legally evicted for non-payment of rent.

3. HABITABILITY

For housing to be considered adequate, it must be habitable. Inhabitants must be ensured adequate space and protection against the cold, damp, heat, rain, wind or other threats to health or structural hazards.

4. ACCESSIBILITY

Housing must be accessible to everyone. Disadvantaged groups such as the elderly, the physically and mentally disabled, HIV-positive individuals, victims of natural disasters, children and other groups should be ensured some degree of priority consideration in housing.

5. LOCATION

For housing to be adequate it must be situated so as to allow access to employment options, health care services, schools, childcare centre and other social facilities. It must not be located in polluted areas. When communities are evicted to forced eviction section from their homes they are often relocated to remote locations lacking facilities or in polluted areas, near garbage dumps or other sources of pollution.

6. CULTURAL ADEQUACY

The right to adequate housing includes a right to reside in housing that is considered culturally adequate. This means that housing program and policies must take fully into account the cultural attributes of housing which allow for the expression of cultural identity and recognize the cultural diversity of the world's population.

THE RIGHT TO AN ADEQUATE STANDARD OF LIVING AND THE RIGHT TO HEALTH

1. THE RIGHT TO AN ADEQUATE STANDARD OF LIVING

The right to an adequate standard of living requires, as a minimum, that everyone shall enjoy the necessary subsistence rights: adequate food and nutrition, clothing, housing and the necessary conditions of care when such are required. The essential point is that everyone shall be able, without shame and without un-

reasonable obstacles, to be a full participant in ordinary, everyday interaction with other people. Thus, they should be able to enjoy their basic needs under conditions of dignity. No one shall have to live under conditions whereby the only way to satisfy their needs is by degrading themselves or depriving themselves of their basic freedoms, such as through begging, prostitution or bonded labour.

In purely material terms, an adequate standard of living implies a living above the poverty line of the society concerned, which according to the World Bank includes two elements: 'The expenditure necessary to buy a minimum standard of nutrition and other basic necessities and a further amount that varies from country to country, reflecting the cost of participating in the everyday life of society.'

Even though the state obligation concerning economic, social and cultural rights, including the right to adequate standard of living, is progressive in nature, discrimination of any kind and at any stage with regard to access to adequate food, clothing and housing, on grounds of race, color, sex, language, age, religion, political or other opinion, national or social origin, property, birth or other status, with the purpose or effect of nullifying or impairing the equal enjoyment or exercise of this right, is prohibited.

2. THE RIGHT TO ADEQUATE FOOD

The right to food is accomplished when every man, woman, and child, alone or in a community with others, has physical and economic access at all times to adequate food or the means for its procurement. The right to food has to be realized progressively. However, the state has a core obligation to take the necessary action to mitigate and alleviate hunger as provided for in Article 11(2) ICESCR, even in time of natural or other disasters. The right to food and the inherent dignity of the human person are inseparable and without food it would not be possible to fulfil other rights.

The core content of the right to adequate food includes the following elements: 1) the availability of food in a quantity and quality sufficient to satisfy the dietary needs of individuals, and acceptable within a given culture, and 2) the accesibility of such food in ways that are sustainable and that do not interfere with the enjoyment of other rights.

The right to adequate food, like any other right, imposes three levels of obligations on the state: the obligations to respect, to protect and to fulfill. Under the obligation to respect the state has to refrain from depriving individuals from their access to adequate food. The obligation to protect means that the state has to take measures to ensure that individuals and enterprises are not depriving individuals of their access to adequate food. The obligation to fulfill (which also entails an obligation to facilitate and an obligation to provide) requires that the state engages pro-actively in activities to strengthen people's access to resources ensuring their livelihood, including food security.

3. THE RIGHT TO EDUCATION

Education is imperative to the promotion of human rights; it is both a human right in itself and an indispensable means of realizing other human rights. It is the precondition for the enjoyment of many economic, social and cultural rights; for instance, the right to receive a higher education on basis of capacity, the right to enjoy the benefits of scientific progress and the right to choose work can only be exercised in a meaningful way after a minimum level of education is reached. Similarly, in the ambit of civil and political rights, the freedom of information, the right to vote and the right to equal access to public service depends on a minimum level of education, i.e. literacy. As a vehicle for empowerment education can give marginalized adults and children the means to escape from poverty and participate meaningfully in their societies. Education is vital to empower women, safeguard children from sexual exploitation and hazardous labour, to the promotion of human right and democracy and to the protection of the environment.

4. THE RIGHT TO CULTURE

Cultural rights were already subject to international litigation before World War II as minorities sought protection against forced assimilation before the Permanent Court of International Justice and minorities were a major concern of the League of Nations. Cultural rights have since remained controversial and during the negotiations on the contents of the Universal Declaration of Human Rights it proved impossible to achieve consensus on the protection of cultural rights. Agreement was only reached on the right to participate in cultural life and protection of scientific literary and artistic production (Article 27 UDHR), and as such the Universal Declaration contains a very narrow definition of cultural rights. Furthermore the East-West controversies and other developments, including decolonization, made protection of minorities and of cultural rights very controversial. There were several bones of contention regarding cultural rights. One reflected the policy of many nations to assimilate minorities. National sovereignty and national identity were considered of prime importance and the recognition of cultural rights was considered a hindrance to assimilation. Another problematic aspect was the collective element of cultural rights. Should cultural practices discriminating against women be recognized, allowing collective cultural rights to prevail over an individual woman's right? Furthermore the concept of culture was considered vague. Was it to be limited to artistic expression or should the anthropological concept of culture be used? Or would a broad concept be preferable? While the field of human rights favors a broad concept of culture with all expressions of culture considered as elements in cultural rights, there is still no consensus and the rights relating to culture remain as controversial as they were in 1948. An illustration of this is Article 15 ICESC which deals with cultural rights; the ICESC Committee held general discussions concerning Article 15 ten years ago, but has still not been able to draft a general comment on it.

UNESCO has held several colloquiums on cultural rights and has even attempted to draft a declaration on cultural rights. So far, however, the best result has been a declaration on cultural diversity drafted in 2001. At the regional level, the Committee of Ministers of the Council of Europe initiated in 1993 the drafting of a protocol on cultural rights, to be added to the European Convention. The process, however, was suspended in January 1996 as the content could not be agreed on. Though the content of cultural rights is controversial, increased attention has been given to these rights in the past twenty years, especially in connection with minorities, an issue which became explosive as a result of the changes which took place in Central and Eastern Europe. Since minority rights are closely linked with cultural rights, several standards have been established both at the global and the regional level. Moreover, supervisory mechanisms have produced a wealth of material, which has gradually contributed to a better understanding of cultural rights. Cultural rights, as set out in international human rights instruments, include the following distinct rights:

1) The right to participate in cultural life.
2) The right to enjoy culture.
3) The right to choose to belong to a group.
4) Linguistic rights.
5) Protection of cultural and scientific heritage.

THE RIGHT TO EQUAL TREATMENT AND THE PROHIBITION OF DISCRIMINATION

The right to equal treatment and the prohibition of discrimination is a cross cutting issue of concern to different UN human rights instruments, such as CERD, ICCPR, CEDAW and CRC and the prohibition of discrimination has also been addressed by the Sub-Commission on the Promotion and Protection of Human Rights in its standard setting instruments. The principle of non-discrimination and equal treatment is contained in most of the human rights instruments, for example, Article 2 UDHR, Articles 2 and 26 ICCPR, Article 2(2) ICESCR, Article 24 ACHR, Article 2 African Charter. However, only a few instruments expressly provide a definition on non-discrimination. In this regard, mention can be made of Article 1(1) CERD, Article 1 CEDAW, Article 1(1) ILO Convention No. 111, and Article 1(1) Convention against Discrimination in Education.

For this purpose, it is appropriate to use the definition of non-discrimination contained in Article 1(1) of ILO 111, which provides that discrimination includes: 'Any distinction, exclusion or preference made on the basis of race, color, sex, religion, political opinion, national extraction or social origin, which has the effect of nullifying or impairing equality of opportunity or treatment in the employment or occupation [. . .].'

1. THE DEPENDENT OR INDEPENDENT NATURE OF THE PROHIBITION OF DISCRIMINATION

Sometimes the prohibition of discrimination included in human rights instruments only provide that the rights contained in the respected instruments must be enjoyed without discrimination on specific grounds. For example, Article 2 ICCPR, Article 2(2) ICESCR, Article 2 African Charter, Article 14 European Convention. Exceptionally, Article 26 ICESCR and Protocol No. 12 to the European Convention establish the prohibition of discrimination is general

and does not relate only to the rights set forth in the instruments.

2. DISTINCTIONS

Not every distinction or difference in treatment will amount to discrimination. In general international law a violation of the principle of non-discrimination arises if: (a) equal cases are treated in a different manner, (b) without an objective and reasonable justification, or (c) if there is no proportionality between the aim sought and the means employed.

These requirements have been expressly stated by international human rights supervisory bodies, including the European Court (see, e.g., Marckx v. Belgium), the Inter-American Court Human Rights (see, e.g. Advisory Opinion No. 4, para. 57) and the Human Rights Committee (see, e.g., General Comment 18, para. 13).

3. PROHIBITED GROUNDS FOR DISCRIMINATION

Article 2 UDHR refers to the following suspected grounds for discrimination: a) race; b) colour; c) sex; d) language; e) religion; f) political or other opinion; g) national origin; h) social origin; i) property; j) birth and; k) other status.

These same prohibited grounds are generally repeated in most human rights instruments. However, it seems clear that the list of grounds contained in Article 2(2) is not exhaustive but merely exemplary. The term 'others status' used in some human rights instruments also prohibits discrimination on grounds not expressly mentioned therein, such as, for example, on the grounds of (a) physical or mental disability; (b) age; (c) sexual orientation and; (d) health condition (particularly in reference to HIV positive and AIDS infected people).

4. DIRECT AND INDIRECT DISCRIMINATION

Any discrimination with the 'purpose' or the 'effect' of nullifying or impairing the equal enjoyment or exercise of the rights is prohibited under the non-discrimination provisions. In other words, the principle of non-discrimination prohibits 'direct' and 'indirect' forms of discrimination. The concept of 'indirect' discrimination refers to an apparently 'neutral' law, practice or criteria, which have been applied equally to everyone but the result of which favours one group over a more disadvantaged group. In determining the existence of indirect discrimination, it is not relevant whether or not there was intent to discriminate on any of the prohibited grounds. Rather, it is the consequences or effects of a law or action what it matters.

5. VULNERABLE GROUPS AND NON-DISCRIMINATION

The principle of non-discrimination demands that particular attention be given to vulnerable groups and individuals from such groups. In fact, the victims of discrimination tend to be the most disadvantaged groups within society.

States should identify the persons or groups of persons who are most vulnerable and disadvantaged with regard to full enjoyment of all human rights and take measures to prevent any adverse affects on them. (For an analysis on vulnerable groups see C-4)

5.1 AFFIRMATIVE ACTION OR PROTECTIVE MEASURES FOR THE MOST VULNERABLE GROUPS

In some circumstances the principle of non-discrimination requires states to take affirmative action or protective measures to prevent or compensate for structural disadvantages. These meas-ures entail special preferences which should not be considered discriminatory because they are aimed to address structural disadvantages or to protect particularly vulnerable groups, encouraging equal participation.

The affirmative actions are aimed to remove the obstacles to the advancement of vulnerable groups such as women, minorities, indigenous peoples, refugees, and disabled persons. As stated by the Human Rights Committee, '[T]he principle of equality sometimes requires States Parties to take affirmative action in order to diminish or eliminate conditions which cause or help to perpetuate discrimination prohibited by the Covenant. For example, in a state where the general conditions of a certain part of the population prevent or impair their enjoyment of human rights, the state should take specific action to correct those conditions. Such action may involve granting for a time to the part of the population concerned certain preferential treatment in specific matters as compared with the rest of the population. However, as long as such action is needed to correct discrimination in fact, it is a case of legitimate differentiation under the Covenant' (General Comment 18, para 10).

Affirmative actions are of a temporary character, meaning that they must not continue after their objectives have been achieved.

5.2 CHILDREN

Every child has the right to grow to adulthood in health, peace and dignity. Young children are vulnerable and dependent on adults for their basic needs, such as food, health care and education.

In many countries they are forced to fend for themselves, often at the cost of their full development and education. The United Nations Children's Fund (UNICEF) has estimated that twelve million children under the age of five die every year, mostly of preventable causes; 130 million children in developing countries, a majority of whom are girls, are not in primary school; 160 million children are malnourished; approximately 1.4 billion children lack access to safe water; and 2.7 billion children lack access to adequate sanitation. Furthermore, Human Rights Watch estimates that annually 250 million children between the ages of five and fourteen years engage in some form of labour often related to debt bondage, forced or compulsory labour, and child prostitution, pornography, and drug trafficking. UNICEF reports that approximately 300,000 children in more than 30 countries are currently participating in armed conflicts.

Ensuring the rights of children to health, nutrition, education, and social, emotional and cognitive development is imperative for every country and entails obligations for every government. Ensuring that children enjoy fundamental rights and freedoms not only advances a more equitable society, but fosters a healthier, more literate and, in due course, a more productive population. Clearly, children's rights are closely tied to women's rights, even before being born a child's survival and development is dependent on the mother's health and opportunities. Women are still primary care-givers for children so ensuring women's rights is positively linked to children's enjoyment of human rights.

5.2.1 CHILD LABOUR

Child labour is another issue of concern. The International Labour Organisation has estimated that 250 million children between the ages of five and fourteen work in developing countries, often supplying an essential income for the survival of their family. The CRC addresses, inter alia, child labour which is harmful to a child's development. Aware that the abolition of child labour is a long term, structural issue, organisations such as the ILO and several international NGOs have initiated programmes aimed at the abolition of child labour and at the same time improve the lives of those children that are forced to work.

Ensuring the rights of children lies largely in the hands of states and the international community. The World Summit for Children that took place in 1990 adopted concrete goals to implement children's rights: The World Declaration on the Survival, Protection and Development of Children and Plan of Action. The Plan of Action called upon nations to be guided by the principle that the essential needs of all children should be given high priority in the allocation of resources and included targets for the end of the decade such as:

- Reduction of under-five child mortality by at least one third.
- Reduction of maternal mortality rates by half of the 1990 levels.
- Universal access to safe drinking water.
- Universal access to basic education.
- Protection of children in especially difficult circumstances, particularly in situations of armed conflict.

Globally, an estimated 20-25 million persons live displaced within the borders of their home countries. These are people who have fled their homes, often during a civil war, but have not sought refuge in other nations. In general, internally displaced persons have many of the same needs as refugees, but, since they have not crossed an international border, they are not covered by the 1951 Convention or by the UNHCR's statute. International concern for the plight of internally displaced persons has acquired a degree of urgency in recent years as greater numbers of people, uprooted by internal conflict and violence, are exposed to danger and death. However, there is yet no single international agency, nor is there an international treaty, that focuses on internal displacement. As a result, the international response to internal displacement has been selective, uneven and, in may cases, inadequate. Large numbers of IDPs receive no humanitarian assistance or protection at all. The international community is now exploring ways to provide more sustained and comprehensive protection and assistance to this group of people.

5.4 INDIGENOUS PEOPLES

'Indigenous peoples' have only recently become the subject of international human rights debate. There have been numerous attempts to formulate an acceptable definition of the term 'indigenous peoples' but a generally accepted definition has not emerged. An important reason has been the fact that the term refers to a group of people who differ enormously, in their cultures, religions, and patterns of social and economic organisation, such as the Mayas in Guatemala, the Inuit in Canada, the Masai in Tanzania and the Naga in India. Some estimated 5000 indigenous peoples comprising around 300 million persons live in more than 70 countries from the Arctic to the Amazon.

In his Study of the Problem of Discrimination against Indigenous Populations, the rapporteur of the Sub-Commission, Mr Martinez Cobo, has formulated a definition, which features the most important characteristics:

Indigenous communities, peoples and nations are those which, having a historical continuity with pre-invasion and pre-colonial societies that developed on their territories, consider themselves distinct from other sectors of the societies now prevailing in those territories, or parts of them. They form at present non-dominant sectors of society and are determined to preserve, develop and transmit to future generations their ancestral territories, and their ethnic identity, as basis of their continued existence as peoples, in accordance with their own cultural patterns, social institutions and legal system.

Looking at Mr Martinez Cobo's definition and the ILO Conventions mentioned below, a number of characteristics can be distinguished:

§   Indigenous peoples have a strong affinity with the land they live on. Their environment is essential for their survival as a cultural entity; it is decisive for their social and cultural conditions.

§   They are not dominant in their present national society, usually they have little if any influence on state policy.

§ They generally speak their own language and have common cultural qualities.

§ Their political/organisational structure is generally of a decentralised nature.

Declaration on the Rights of Indigenous Populations, which was adopted by the Sub-Commission in August 1994. The draft Declaration consists of 45 articles, related to issues such as:

§ The right of indigenous populations to self-determination (Article 3),

§ The right not to be 'forcibly removed from their lands or territories' (Article 10),

§ The right 'to practice and revitalise their cultural traditions and customs' (Article 12),

§ The right 'to establish their own media in their own languages' (Article 18), and

§ The right 'to determine and develop priorities and strategies for the development or use of their lands, territories and other resources [...]' (Article 30).

5.5 DISABLED PERSONS

Discrimination against persons with disabilities has a long history and persons with disabilities are regularly excluded from participation in society and denied their human rights. Discrimination against the disabled can take many forms ranging from limited educational opportunities to more subtle forms such as segregation and isolation because of physical and social barriers. The effects of discrimination are most clearly felt in sphere of economic, social and cultur-

al rights, in the fields of, for instance, housing, employment, transport, cultural life and access to public services. The obstacles the disabled face in enjoying their human rights are often the result of exclusion, restriction or preference, and, for instance, when the disabled do not have access to reasonable accommodation on the basis of their limitations, their enjoyment or exercise of human rights may be severely restricted. In order for disabled persons to freely enjoy their fundamental human rights, numerous cultural and social barriers have to be overcome; changes in values and increased understanding at all levels of society has to be promoted, and those social and cultural norms that perpetuate myths about disability have to be put to rest. At the national level, disability legislation and policies are often based on the assumption that the disabled are not able to exercise the same rights as non-disabled persons, thus often focusing on rehabilitation and social security. It is increasingly recognised that domestic legislation must address all aspects of the human rights of the disabled, ensuring their participation in society on equal footing with people without disabilities, creating opportunities for people with disabilities and eliminating discrimination. Although domestic legislation has the prime role in generating social change and promoting the rights of disabled persons, international standards concerning disability can be very useful for setting common norms for disability legislation. Violations of the human rights of persons with disabilities have not been systematically addressed in the sphere of international legal bodies but in recent years the rights of the disabled

...have come to be discussed in various international fora. International human rights instruments protect the rights of persons with disabilities through the principles of equality and non-discrimination but several international and regional human rights instruments contain specific provisions concerning persons with disabilities. The Universal Declaration of Human Rights (UDHR) sets out in Article 25 that 'everyone has the right to security in the event of ... disability.' Article 23 of the Convention of the Rights of the Child specifically discusses the rights of handicapped and disabled children. Under the auspices of the AU, the African Charter of Human and People's Rights stipulates in Article 18(4) that the disabled shall be entitled to special measures of protection and the African Charter on the Rights and Welfare of the Child discusses the rights of handicapped children in Article 13. The European Social Charter (revised) stipulates 'the right of persons with disabilities to independence, social integration and participation in the life of the community' and sets out steps that states shall undertake to this end in Article 15. In Article 6 of the Protocol of San Salvador 'States Parties undertake to adopt measures to make the right to work fully effective [...] in particular, those directed to the disabled' and Article 9 sets out the right to social security in case of disability. Moreover, provisions in human rights instruments protecting members of vulnerable groups are applicable to disabled persons. Finally, the Committee on Economic, Social and Cultural Rights has adopted a General Comment on persons with disabilities. Two Conventions dealing directly with the rights of disabled persons are the In-ter-American Convention on the Elimination of All Forms of Discrimination Against Persons with Disabilities (1999) and ILO 159 concerning Vocational Rehabilitation and Employment (Disabled Persons) (1983).

THE RIGHT TO DEVELOPMENT

In the Declaration on the Right to Development the emphasis is both on individual and collective aspects, on basic needs of individuals as well as the need to assist peoples as a whole. The Declaration states: 'The right to development is an inalienable human right by virtue of which every human person and all peoples are entitled to participate in, contribute to, and enjoy economic, social, cultural and political development in which all human rights and all fundamental freedoms can be fully realised' (Article 1).

The right to development has been reaffirmed at the World Conference on Human Rights in Vienna in 1993 'as a universal and inalienable right and an integral part of fundamental human rights.' The UN Commission on Human Rights speaks of an important right 'for every human person and all peoples in all countries' (Resolution 1998/72). These documents show that emphasis is put on the individual as bearer of the right to development. The Commission also underlines the importance of structural measures to tackle the problems developing countries have to overcome. In a Resolution on the Right to Development, the Commission, inter alia, stated that [I]nternational cooperation is acknowledged more than ever as a neessity deriving from recognised mutual interest, and therefore that such cooperation should be strengthened in order to support efforts of developing countries to solve their social and economic problems and to fulfil their obligations to promote and protect all human rights Resolution 1998/72).

To illustrate the need for such an approach, the Commission speaks of 'the unacceptable situation of absolute poverty, hunger and disease, lack of adequate shelter, illiteracy and hopelessness, being the lot of over one billion people; the gap between developed and developing countries remaining unacceptably wide; the difficulties developing countries have to face when participating in the globalisation process, risking to be marginalized and effectively excluded from its benefits. It should, however, be noted that the states themselves are primarily responsible for development. The international community can contribute to development but cannot take over the responsibility.'

THE RIGHT TO PRIVACY AND FAMILY

. THE RIGHT TO RESPECT FOR PRIVATE AND FAMILY LIFE

The right to respect for privacy mirrors the liberal concept of the individual's freedom as an autonomous being as long as his/her actions do not interfere with the rights and freedoms of others. The right to privacy is the right to individual autonomy which is violated when states interfere with, penalize or prohibit actions which essentially only concern the individual, such as, for instance, not wearing safety equipment or committing suicide. States justify such interferences with the social costs of the actions prohibited, for

instance to the health care system. The right to privacy encompasses the right to protect a person's intimacy, identity and identity; name, gender, honour, dignity appearance, feelings and sexual orientation. The right to privacy may be limited in the interests of others, under specific conditions provided that the interference is not arbitrary or unlawful. People cannot be forced to change their appearance or name, for instance, nor can they be prohibited from changing their name o sex; however, in the interests of the rights of others they may, for example, be compelled to give biological samples for the determination of paternity. The right to privacy extends to the home, the family and correspondence. The term family relates, for example, to blood ties, economic ties, marriage, and adoption. The right to the respect for the privacy of the home has been interpreted to include place of business. A common interference with the privacy of correspondence has to do with secret surveillance and censorship of the correspondence of prisoners.

2. THE RIGHT TO PROPERTY

One of the more controversial and complex human rights is the right to property. The right is controversial because the very right which is seen by some as central to the human rights concept is considered by others to be an instrument for abuse; a right that protects the 'haves' against the 'have-nots.' It is complex, because no other human right is subject to more qualifications and limitations and, consequently, no other right has resulted in more complex case law of, for instance, the supervisory bodies of the ECHR. It is complex also because it is generally regarded as a civil right, even an integrity right. At the same time, it clearly has characteristics of social rights with significant implications for the distribution of social goods and wealth. Moreover, the right to property has major implications for several important social and economic rights such as the right to work, the right to enjoy the benefits of scientific progress, the right to education and the right to adequate housing.

THE HUMAN RIGHTS AND ENVIRONMENT

In recent years the relation between human rights and environmental issues has become an issue of vigorous debate. The link between the two is the need for a decent physical environment for all, as a condition for living a life worthy of a human being. More concretely, a decent physical environment has to do with protection against, for instance, noise nuisance, air pollution, pollution of surface waters, and the dumping of toxic substances. Principle 1 of the UN Stockholm Declaration on the Human Environment (1972), establishes a foundation for linking human rights and environmental protection, declaring that man has a 'fundamental right to freedom, equality and adequate conditions of life, in an environment of a quality that permits a life of dignity and well-being, and he bears a solemn responsibility to protect and improve the environment for present and future generations.'

Ms Fatma Zohra Ksentini, Special Rapporteur on the Adverse Effects of the Illicit Movement and Dumping of Toxic Waste on the Enjoyment of Human Rights of the UN Commission on Human Rights, has drawn attention to the fact that some 350 multilateral and 1000 bilateral conventions—to say nothing of numerous declarations, action programmes and resolutions—have already been drawn up across the world to regulate and protect areas which have a bearing on the environment. These instruments generally impose obligations on states, which means that individual citizens cannot invoke them directly. The European Convention on Human Rights does not contain provisions on the environment but instruments in the African and Inter-American systems contain provisions on the environment. The African Charters on Human and Peoples' Rights sets out in Article 24 that '[a]ll peoples shall have the right to a general satisfactory environment favourable to their development' and the Protocol of San Salvador to the American Convention on Human Rights provides in Article 11 for everyone to 'have the right to live in a healthy environment.'

1. INDIVIDUAL AND COLLECTIVE ASPECTS

The human right to a clean environment is controversial, among other things because it has individual as well as collective aspect. If, for instance, after a period of foreign domination it emerges that the physical environment of the dominated people has been severely damaged, it is generally considered logical to assign the claim to protection (i.e., restoration) of the environment not only to individuals, but in equal measure to the people as an entity which for a time suffered foreign domination. In this context, reference can be made to Article 55 of Protocol I to the 1949 Geneva Conventions. This article, which relates to the protection of the environment in time of war stipulates:

Care shall be taken in warfare to protect the natural environment against widespread, long-term and severe damage. This protection includes a prohibition of the use of methods or means of warfare which are intended or may be expected to cause such damage to the natural environment and thereby to prejudice the health or survival of the population.

The UN Special Rapporteur on Illicit Movement and Dumping of Toxic Waste has observed, as has the International Committee of the Red Cross, that the article in question is one whose significance is becoming increasingly salient with the passage of time, and that efforts should be made to establish how it can be used in a strictly legal sense.

THE RIGHTS RELATING TO LABOUR

1. THE RIGHTS RELATING TO WORK

The right to work affects the degree of enjoyment of many other rights such as the right to education, health and culture. Its realisation is not only important for the provision of income to the individual, but also for the individual's personal development and dignity, as well as for peaceful progress of society. The right to work intrinsically creates a degree of dependency of the employed on his employer. As such it is a relationship of inequality. To protect the employed and to make a more level playing field, the right to strike and the right to associate are established, as well as the right to organise and to bargain collectively.

The right to work in a broad sense implies the right to enter employment and the right not to be deprived of employment unfairly. The first component encompasses the factors that come into play regarding access to work such as education, vocational training, and unemployment levels. The latter component deals with issues regarding employment security, for instance, security from being fired unjustly.

The main elements of the right to work are the access to employment, freedom from forced labour and labour security but other important components are:

Freedom to work; freedom concerning the choice of occupation as well as the place of performance.

The right to earn a living from work of one's own choice encompasses the freedom to establish one's own independent form of employment or business.

The right to free employment services; the right to work has been interpreted as the commitment of the state to undertake continuous efforts to ensure full employment. Such efforts include the formulation and implementation of employment promotion policies and the promotion of technical and vocational education programmes aimed at increasing employment as well as free access to information and assistance for jobseekers.

The right to safe and healthy working conditions as well as rest, leisure and reasonable working hours.

The right to employment; the right not to be arbitrarily dismissed and the right to protection against unemployment.

As in all socio-economic rights, the non-discrimination principle is an important dimension of the right to work. It entails non-discrimination in recruitment, in remuneration and in promotion opportunities, and in the treatment of aliens.

IMPRINT

Writing by Tiziana Panizza Kassahun
Editing by Justin Kavanagh
Proofreading by Anna Mirfattahi
Photography by Stefano De Luigi
Design by Ralf Herms / Rosebud

The Deutsche Nationalbibliothek lists this publication in the Deutsche Nationalbibliografie; detailed bibliographic data are available on the Internet at http://dnb.dnb.de

ISBN 978-3-7212-0980-8

© 2018 Tiziana Panizza Kassahun, Stefano De Luigi and Niggli, imprint of Braun Publishing AG, Salenstein www.niggli.ch

1st edition 2018